Library of
Davidson College

THE GREAT REVIVAL

THE GREAT REVIVAL
The Russian Church Under German Occupation

by

Wassilij Alexeev

and

Theofanis G. Stavrou

University of Minnesota
Minneapolis, Minnesota

BURGESS PUBLISHING COMPANY • MINNEAPOLIS, MINNESOTA

Copyright © 1976 by Burgess Publishing Company
Printed in the United States of America
Library of Congress Card Number 76-0683
All rights reserved.
ISBN 0-8087-0131-2

No part of this book may be reproduced in any form whatsoever,
by photograph or mimeograph or by any other means,
by broadcast or transmission,
by translation into any kind of language,
nor by recording electronically or otherwise,
without permission in writing from the publisher,
except by a reviewer, who may quote brief
passages in critical articles and reviews.

All inquiries should be directed to

    Burgess Publishing Company
    7108 Ohms Lane
    Minneapolis, MN 55435

0 9 8 7 6 5 4 3 2 1

Book design by Dennis Tasa

This volume is affectionately dedicated

to

LUDMILA ALEXEEV

"More than twenty years of Soviet power and their heads are still full of incense. You hammer it into them over and over again—'There isn't any God, you're your own masters'. And still they stick to their old ideas. How long can you go on hammering?"

Vladimir Maximov

The Seven Days of Creation

Contents

List of illustrations   viii

Introduction   ix

ONE
A State of Siege: The Russian Orthodox Church and the Soviet Regime, 1917-1939   1

TWO
The Fruits of War   41

THREE
The Baltic Sector   71

FOUR
Belorussia   107

FIVE
The Ukrainian Case   147

SIX
Miscellany: Transnistria and the Front   187

Epilogue   201

Bibliography, including a brief statement on sources   213

Index   223

List of Illustrations

ORTHODOX HIERARCHS
Archimandrite 1936   31
Metropolitan 1937   32
Father Aleksei 1931   33

MONKS
Young Monks 1931/1932   34, 35
Older Monks 1933   36

NUNS
Older Nun 1933   37
Trio 1933-1935   38
Young Nun 1935   39

M. K. Kholmogorov 1935. Moscow protodeacon, famous for his bass voice   40

Metropolitan Nikolai of Kiev celebrating liturgy in the Church of the Transfiguration in Moscow, March 17, 1942   67

Metropolitan Sergii, later Patriarch of Moscow and All Russia. Died 2/15, 1944   68

Metropolitan Aleksii of Leningrad, later Patriarch of Moscow and All Russia (1945-1971)   69

Metropolitan Nikolai of Kiev and Galicia and Exarch of the Ukraine, later Metropolitan of Leningrad and in charge of the Foreign Affairs Department of the Moscow Patriarchate until his death in 1960   70

Introduction

A great number of scholarly and popular studies have been informing us rather systematically during the last decade or so on the state of religion in general and Orthodoxy in particular in the Soviet Union. In varying degrees, all these accounts attest to a religious resurgence or renaissance which has taken place despite organized persecution of religion by the regime for over half a century. To most observers of the Soviet scene, this religious resurgence goes beyond the mere survival of a few groups of believers who succeeded in preserving as well as transmitting their faith, important in itself as the latter may be.

This religious revival in its various manifestations has been interpreted as a "search for new ideals" to meet the need of a section of Soviet society disillusioned with Marxism-Leninism; as an expression of increasing concern about civil rights guaranteed by the Soviet Constitution but consistently denied to Soviet citizens; as a nostalgia for the continuity of Russian culture (a continuity which is almost incomprehensible without its religious ingredients); or, finally, as substantial evidence that religion, variously defined, is an essential part of any nation's existence. In other words, these signs of religious revival have important political, social, and cultural implications which may explain the regime's understandable concern.

No other writer in recent times has been more successful in bringing to the attention of the world the dehumanizing forces at work in Soviet society since the Bolshevik seizure of power than the Nobel prize winner Aleksandr Solzhenitsyn. His recently published *The Gulag Archipelago: 1918-1956* is undoubtedly the boldest and most comprehensive attack on the Soviet Union's degrading policy of control and repression. Solzhenitsyn has been eloquent on the subject before, of course, through his *One Day in the Life of Ivan Denisovich* and *The First Circle*. But what is astonishing about his new work is that he goes beyond the most serious censures by Soviet citizens of the abuses of the Soviet regime. Such censures as Roy Medvedev's moving chronicle of the Stalin era, *Let History Judge,* have hesitated to go beyond Stalin and Stalinism as source for the tremendous amount of suffering endured by Soviet society. In fact in his most recent study (1975) Medevedev again emerges as a champion of socialism. As he puts it ". . . perversions of socialism have done our movement and our country enormous political and moral damage. It would, however, be quite wrong on this account to jettison Marxism all together. It would also be a great mistake to imagine that Marxism-Leninism no longer offers a basis for the development of a new system of socialist ethics capable of bringing about the general moral and cultural enlightenment of our people."[1] Solzhenitsyn suggests instead that many of these unfortunate experiments with human life originated with Lenin and his legacy, implying thus that the entire Leninist revolution has been an assault on Russia's finest traditions as well as on tsarist political injustices.

He articulated his deep concern about the merciless assault on the Orthodox Church by the Soviet state in a special letter to the present Patriarch of Moscow and All Russia, Pimen. This letter, which caused a great deal of uproar both inside and out-

[1]Roy A. Medvedev, *On Socialist Democracy*, p. 75.

side the Soviet Union, is the most eloquent indictment of the Soviet regime's policy toward religion. As a historical document the letter is especially important because it illuminates probably the most controversial aspect of church-state relations in Soviet Russia—the position of the leading hierarch recognized by the Soviet government, in this case Patriarch Pimen vis-a-vis the state authorities. Ever since 1927, when the Patriarchal Deputy *Locum Tenens* Metropolitan Sergii formally accepted the role of collaborating with the regime in exchange for certain privileges, the role of the Patriarch has been under considerable suspicion. Especially unpalatable have been the periodic statements extracted from the heads of the Russian Orthodox Church from Sergii to Pimen repudiating the existence of religious persecution or the absence of religious freedom in the Soviet Union. The present Patriarch intimated as much in his first Christmas greeting in 1971, and this more than anything elicited Solzhenitsyn's now famous letter.[2]

A crucial question, of course, is whether Solzhenitsyn is an isolated phenomenon or whether he is part of a larger group of Soviet intellectuals who have redefined their attitude toward Marxism and religion, especially Orthodoxy, and have come out strongly on the side of the latter. Despite the absence of reliable statistics, fragmentary information reaching the West suggests that the Nobel Prize winner is far from being an isolated case. Assuming that this position is supportable, then one is still puzzled by this phenomenon of the survival of such individuals, and the historian looks for those interludes in the Soviet period which served as "breathing spells" and which may account for the survival and subsequent revival of religion.

The present study is an attempt to investigate in some detail precisely such a crucial interlude. Specifically, it deals with one of the most important events in the history of the Russian Orthodox Church after 1917—the three-year (1941-44) religious revival which took place on Soviet territory temporarily occupied by the German forces. This was an unusual phenomenon.

[2]There is a special edition of this letter translated by Keith Armes with a commentary by Wassilij Alexeev and edited by Theofanis G. Stavrou, published by Burgess Publishing Company, Minneapolis, Minnesota, 1972.

Both Soviet Communism and German Fascism, struggling on Russian territory during these years, were equally hostile to Christianity in general and to the Russian Orthodox Church in particular. Still, their confrontation, leading to the German occupation of a significant portion of the USSR with approximately one-third of the country's population, created peculiar conditions affecting significantly the fate of the Russian Orthodox Church. In the beginning, the National Socialist Government of Germany did not clearly formulate its religious policy on occupied territory. In general, the German forces were sympathetic toward the religious revival which greeted them as they were establishing their rule among the population of the USSR who at first, partly through misunderstanding, accepted Hitler's attack as a crusade against Communism. Even after the populace realized the objectives of this "crusade," they continued to utilize this opportunity of relative religious toleration in order to reestablish the Orthodox Church which had been persecuted by the Communists since the Bolshevik Revolution.

On the whole, in scope and intensity this religious revival on territory occupied by the Germans can be called the second baptism of Russia. It is, therefore, strange that historians writing about the Russian Orthodox Church under the Soviet regime have almost completely ignored this important chapter of twentieth-century Orthodoxy and the influence of this religious explosion on the change of Communist policy toward the Church in particular and religion in general. For example, John Shelton Curtiss, an American scholar who has studied the history of the Russian Orthodox Church for many years,[3] is silent on this most important question in his well-documented book. Only Nikita Struve touches on this theme, and then briefly.[4] A fortunate exception is the book by Friedrich Heyer,[5]

[3] John Shelton Curtiss, *The Russian Church and the Soviet State, 1917-1950.*
[4] Nikita Struve, *Les Chrétiens en U.S.S.R.* There is an English translation, *Christians in Contemporary Russia*, pp. 66-67.
[5] Friedrich Heyer, *Die orthodoxe Kirche in der Ukraine von 1917 bis 1945.* Z. Balevits's study *Pravoslavnaia tserkov' v Latvii pod sen'iu svastiki, 1941-44* [The Orthodox Church in Latvia under the shadow of the swastika, 1941-44] published by decision of the Academy of Sciences of the Latvian SSR, presents the Soviet view of some of these developments. The author utilized Latvian

which, naturally, proved exceedingly useful for this study. Unfortunately, Heyer's book deals only with the history of the Russian Orthodox Church in the Ukraine, and for this reason it fails to evaluate the influence of the period 1941-1944 on the history of the Russian Orthodox Church as a whole.

On the other hand, certain gestures by the Soviet government attest to the significance of these religious developments. The most noteworthy of these was the reception in the Kremlin by Stalin and Molotov of three surviving Metropolitans, headed by the *Locum Tenens* of the Patriarchal throne, Metropolitan Sergii, in September 1943. In fact, the religious NEP[6] in the USSR, which continued with few complications until 1960, began on 4 September 1943, and not during the first months of the war or immediately after its cessation. As is known, the patriotic announcement of the *Locum Tenens*, Sergii, at the outbreak of the war provided the Soviet leaders with an opportunity to modify their religious policy. A similar opportunity came after the war when the Kremlin leaders could have summed up their reasons for either opposing or approving the religious NEP. Yet, the religious NEP was established neither

---

archives and brings to light some interesting facts, but unfortunately suffers from poor organization and numerous contradictions. When this present study was in manuscript form ready for the press, we saw the announcement of Harvey Fireside's *Icon and Swastika: The Russian Orthodox Church under Nazi and Soviet Control.* Since the topic was closely related to our own, we waited until we had an opportunity to inspect the Fireside volume carefully. While grateful for the appearance of such a volume on this topic, it soon became clear that both the objectives and the emphasis were quite different and publication of our study should proceed as planned. That same year William C. Fletcher's *The Russian Orthodox Church Underground, 1917-1970* also made its appearance, touching on some of the aspects discussed in this study. Taking all this into consideration, we felt that this would still be the only monograph concentrating on the religious revival itself on German-occupied territories. Furthermore, it is well known that Professor Wassilij Alexeev has been a pioneer in this field and has dealt with this subject previously in his doctoral dissertation, *The Russian Orthodox Church under German Occupation, 1941-1945* (University of Minnesota, 1967) and his *Russian Orthodox Bishops in the Soviet Union, 1941-53.*

[6]NEP—The New Economic Policy, 1921-1928—a liberal economic policy instituted by Lenin to save the faltering, post-Civil War Soviet economy. It was often interpreted as a return to capitalism; consequently the acronym NEP denotes any liberalizing trend in Soviet policy and in particular a retreat from Marxist positions. As used here, it denotes a retreat from the open policies of religious persecution of the Soviet government.

at the beginning of the war nor afterward. Instead, this study maintains that the Soviet government's change of policy toward religion took place in 1943, the year which marked the beginning of the retreat of the German forces. The seizure by the Red Army of territories formerly occupied by the Germans presented the Soviet government with the serious problem of dealing with the thousands of churches and their congregations which after years of persecution had been reestablished during the German occupation. In short, the vitality of the religious revival in occupied territory forced Stalin to embark on a course of coexistence with religion as represented by the Russian Orthodox Church.

Needless to say, this reversal of Soviet policy toward religion in September 1943 was not the work of a moment. A number of less decisive and less clear actions had preceded it, such as those following the division of Poland between Hitler and Stalin in 1939, which had resulted in some relaxation of persecution of the Church in those regions. The division of Poland meant the incorporation of several million Orthodox Belorussians and Ukrainians with 1200 parishes into the Soviet Union. It also meant a temporary relaxation of religious persecution that same year. The return of occupied territory, with many thousands of reopened churches and millions of people who had returned to the Church, brought about a religious NEP in 1943. Both phenomena, the relaxation of persecution in 1939 and what appeared as a reversal of government policy in 1943, demonstrate that even a Stalin-type dictatorship must consider the mood of the population, especially in time of national crisis, a problem that merits further investigation. In addition, one must put the religious revival in its historical perspective. This requires an understanding of the nature of church-state relations from the Bolshevik Revolution until World War II when for all practical purposes the Church was in a state of siege. The first chapter aims at providing this sort of perspective. World War II broke this state of siege and opened new possibilities for the survival of the Orthodox Church. These were the fruits of war discussed in the second chapter along with an outline of Hitler's general policy toward religion in the

Soviet Union in general and the Russian Orthodox Church in particular. The heart of the subject is of course the great revival and to this are devoted the next four chapters. The epilogue is an attempt to evaluate as well as make some suggestions about the impact of this revival on the postwar religious developments in the Soviet Union.

An explanation about the use of the term "revival" may save the reader some unnecessary misunderstandings. The term is definitely not to be taken in its evangelical or charismatic meaning that an individual or group of believers may experience a renewal and enrichment of their spiritual life, usually at appointed meetings and times. For the purposes of this study it refers to the opportunity for believers to demonstrate publicly that which they had been practicing in secret for two decades because of political circumstances. A spiritual reawakening it was, attracting thousands of converts, but above all it was a testimony that the Church had not been extinguished by the Soviet government.

This study is the result of many years of research, reflection, and consultation with numerous individuals without whose advice and encouragement it could not have been completed. The following among them merit special mention: Professor Alexander Dallin was very helpful during the initial stages of this project, as was Fr. George Grabbe at the Holy Synod Archives of the Russian Orthodox Church Abroad in New York. At the University of Minnesota Professors Harold C. Deutsch, Specialist on World War II (now at the Army War College in Carlisle Barracks, Pa.) and Don Martindale at various stages made valuable contributions and suggestions. We also wish to recognize Drs. Paul Anderson and Friedrich Heyer whose pioneer work in the field made the study of the Russian Orthodox Church in the Soviet period an easier task for us and other students of this important subject. The staff members of the University of Minnesota inter-loan library service were most helpful and generous in assisting us in locating works not available at the University of Minnesota Library. Our thanks go to them as well as to the staff members of the Yiddish Scientific Institute (YIVO) in New York. Ludmila Alexeev, to whom this work is dedicated, played a major role toward its completion. She helped significantly with problems of translation, transliteration, and bibliography. Our thanks go also to Mr. Janis Cers for help in connection with the bibliography and to Freda L. Stavrou in connection with the typing of the manuscript. In conclusion we wish to express our appreciation to Burgess Publishing Company for their splendid cooperation during the preparation of this volume, especially Miss Dora Stein, an author's dream of an editor—patient, meticulous, skillful. Those of us who worked on the manuscript for many years know that it is now in print chiefly because of the strong interest in the project shown by Alexander K. Fraser, editor-in-chief of Burgess Publishing Company from 1969 to 1974. He read the manuscript carefully and in fact had it with him when he and his wife were killed in an automobile accident in New York State on June 20, 1974. We hope that this publication will serve as a small monument to the memory of a gentle man and distinguished editor.

UNIVERSITY OF MINNESOTA
SPRING 1976

WASSILIJ ALEXEEV
THEOFANIS G. STAVROU

ONE

A State of Siege
The Russian Orthodox Church and the Soviet Regime, 1917-1939

In a most perceptive and charmingly written chapter in his accounts of his travels in Russia first published in 1933, Nikos Kazantzakis offers a moving picture of the transformation of the religious scene in Soviet Russia a decade after the Bolshevik Revolution.[1] Kazantzakis belonged to the group of Western intellectuals who were fascinated by the solutions Marxism and the Soviet experiment could provide for the "hopelessly confused" world of the interwar years. Like the rest of them, he visited Russia both as the guest of the Soviet au-

[1] Nikos Kazantzakis, *Taxidevontas Rossia* [Travelling Russia], pp. 120-33. All references are from the Greek edition. An English edition translated by Michael Atonakes and Theofanis Stavrou is forthcoming. Kazantzakis' view on Soviet Russia in general can also be found in his *Toda Raba* translated by Amy Mims (New York: Simon and Schuster, 1967) and his *Report to Greco* translated by P. A. Bien (New York: Simon and Schuster, 1965), pp. 394-434.

thorities and on his own, and upon his return he shared his impressions with the Western world through his publications and speeches. Unlike most of them, Kazantzakis traveled extensively throughout the Soviet Union, and this alone adds greater validity to his generalizations about developments in the land. Also unlike most of them, upon his return to the West he did not join those who found Soviet Communism a "god that failed" and did not contribute to the "literature of political disillusionment," even though he had modified his own views toward Marxism and Soviet Communism considerably. His attitude toward Soviet Russia remained on the whole a sympathetic one and his reporting quite objective. In fact, he boasted of coming to Russia without preconceived notions, for he wanted to see exactly what was taking place there.

His commentary on the religious scene takes on special meaning when we bear in mind that he was probably the only intellectual from the West who, even though of non-Russian extraction, nevertheless shared that country's Orthodox religious heritage, having been born into an Orthodox family on the Island of Crete. And it is worth reminding ourselves that despite his conflicts with the Orthodox Church of Greece, Kazantzakis remained sensitive to the religious needs of man and above all was appreciative of the shaping influence that Orthodoxy had for the Greek and Slavic peoples. Finally, he was fascinated by the struggle between systems and ideas and the Soviet Union provided excellent testing ground for probably the greatest struggle between religious belief on the one hand and a militant materialistic philosophy on the other. He therefore spared no efforts in assessing the religious, especially the Orthodox, situation there. He visited churches, religious museums, market places, and above all talked to people from all walks of life.

The general picture he presents is grim and depressing. As he puts it in his matchless style:

> Frequently here in Soviet Russia the saints, when found in the streets, in hollow spots on walls or hanging on doors of churches, are neglected, frayed, their clothes dirty, their beards

without varnish and uncared-for. People have ceased feeding them with prayers and offerings.

I know a wooden angel in a central street of Moscow who came unscrewed from the door of the church where they had nailed him to guard the entrance and is hanging like a wounded bird. And a St. Nicholas made of tin, at a certain Moscow crossroad, has also come unscrewed and hangs above the snow-covered sidewalk ready to drop. When the wind blows he squeaks and shouts like a disjointed inscription and nobody bothers to take him by the legs, straighten and fasten him or unfasten him completely and thus end his sufferings.

The saints are starving in Russia, the angels are suffering hanging between heaven and earth and God is wandering in the streets, homeless, jobless, persecuted like a *burzhui*.

Once in the big open markets of Smolensk Boulevard, "where everybody sells whatever ugly and useless they have or whatever hunger makes people sell," he observed a crowd of old women holding icons, Madonnas and Christs, framed richly, with silver crowns, and selling them along with old iron implements and cracked cups. When he noticed that the religious objects were not selling he approached a pale old woman who was holding in her arms for sale a rosy-cheeked Madonna. Nobody had approached her. Passersby simply looked indifferently, saw that they had no use for the icons, and moved on. Then he said to the pale old lady:

"*Mamochka*, the Madonnas don't sell any more . . ."

And she, serene under her snowed scarf, answered,

"Patience, my son, they will buy it, for it has a good frame."

Then Kazantzakis mused: "They will take it and they will put in the frame the icon of Lenin. . . . . The frame remains—the heart of man—the icon only changes."

Kazantzakis viewed the whole phenomenon as a struggle for the heart of the Soviet citizens and by any measurable standards in the 1920s the atheistic regime had an advantage over any organized religion. Impressed though he was by the spirituality of the Russian Orthodox believers he met in their few cold places of worship, he likened them unto a group of people gathering for a most excruciating farewell to their religious systems to make room for the new conqueror. For he witnessed that the Bolsheviks in their speeches, newspapers, books, schools, in all their propaganda struck mercilessly not only at Christianity but at every other religion as well. Marx's phrase, "Religion is the opium of the people," was taken seriously.

He observed that in the schools not only did they abolish the teaching of religion but they also taught the child systematically and with fanaticism that God and the Devil were inventions of the priests and that man was the offspring of the earth and that in the earth he begins and in the earth does he end. The materialistic world view was taught from grade school on. Under no circumstances were books with religious bias allowed to be printed and special "materialistic" museums portrayed the Darwinian theory of evolution.

But Kazantzakis was quick to notice that the Bolsheviks while getting rid of the old religious types were creating new ones and that gradually they were setting up the new Communist liturgy. Frequently a child's appointed godfather was a workers' club and the new Red infants instead of saints' names received such names as *Ninel* (anagram of Lenin), *Trud* (Labor), *Profsoiuz* (Trade Union), etc. They gave each newborn child a diploma on which appeared, calligraphically in red ink, the following words:

> We do not bless you in the name of the cross, the sign of ignorance and slavery, rather in the name of the red banner of labor and struggle. May you love equally the workers of all places, all races, and all colors. Hate with the same passion, kings, bankers, industrialists, and the priests of the whole world. Be a faithful follower of Lenin and hold high the solid banner of science and remain always defender of the Third International.

Kazantzakis was especially impressed by the religious fanaticism of the propagandists against religion whom he observed at work when he went to see the director of the weekly journal *The Atheist*. The spacious offices were full of editors, men and women, scholars, scientists, theologians, and humorists. Bent over their tables, they were writing with religious zeal their satirical popular articles against religion. When an ugly lady with red hair, a cigarette stuck between her lips, proudly showed him the volumes of the journal, he noticed that they were full of caricatures—drunken monks, saints dancing in taverns, obscene jokes, and scandalous sayings. The walls, too, were covered with caricatures: priests with triple bellies upheld by plump little angels; a fat stupid God with sideburns; monks and nuns riding billy goats.

When he finally encountered the director, a "thin, ascetic looking, redbearded individual, his nose dripping with poison," Kazantzakis felt a strong intellectual and spiritual revulsion toward this leader of atheism and his "scientific arguments."

As a result of his Soviet exposures Kazantzakis concluded that the old religion was withering. It still had the priests, the golden sacerdotal vestments, the churches, the sweet deeppealing bells, the psalmodies, but he sensed that the sap had run out and the tree was dying. It was being replaced by atheism, a fanatical religion with its own mysticism and dogmatism.

Kazantzakis' opinions about the fate of religion in the Soviet Union were echoed by hundreds of monographs on the subject and an even greater number of memoirs and travel accounts. In fact, it is safe to argue that hardly any major study concerning Soviet society fails to inquire about the fate of religion in the Soviet Union.[2]

Two important questions force themselves to our attention,

[2]Literature on religion in the Soviet Union is enormous and especially plentiful when it comes to the Orthodox Church. Soviet literature on the subject is understandably propagandistic, but it can still shed a lot of light about religious developments if properly evaluated. By far the most ambitious study of the Orthodox Church in the Soviet period in a Western language is the three-volume work by Johannes Chrysostomus, *Kirchengeschichte Russlands der neusten Zeit*. One of the most useful general accounts in English is Walter Kolarz, *Religion in the Soviet Union*. A sympathetic and controversial early account is Julius Hecker, *Religion and Communism, State of Religion and Atheism in Soviet Russia* (London: Chapman and Hall, 1933); see also W. C. Emhardt, *Religion in Soviet Russia* (Milwaukee-London, 1929), and, of course, Paul Anderson's classic *People, Church and State in Modern Russia*. With regard to the Russian Orthodox Church John S. Curtiss's standard work *The Russian Church and the Soviet State, 1917-1950* should be usefully supplemented by much good scholarship that has appeared since, such as Matthew Spinka, *The Church in Soviet Russia*, Nikita Struve, *Christians in Contemporary Russia*, and especially R. Marshall, ed., *Aspects of Religion in the Soviet Union, 1917-1967* (Chicago: University of Chicago Press, 1971). Very valuable for the promotion of the study of religion in the USSR has been the activity of William C. Fletcher, especially his works *A Study in Survival: The Church in Russia 1927-1943* and *The Russian Orthodox Church Underground, 1917-1970*. All of the above have been useful for the preparation of this chapter. Recently a Centre for the Study of Religion and Communism was set up in London under the guidance

as they bear directly on the main part of this study, that is to say, the great Orthodox revival which took place in the Soviet Union during World War II. The first is one of almost unbelievable dimensions—the decline of religion in a society which by any yardstick was probably the most religious society in Europe at the beginning of the twentieth century. The second one is a modification, if not a contradiction, of the first. How, in an avowedly atheistic environment, did religion in general and Orthodoxy in particular survive to provide the inspiration for the great revival during World War II? The rest of this chapter is an attempt to answer these two questions.

It is conceivable that religion would have declined in twentieth-century Russia regardless of the Soviet regime as has been the case with other European states. Most likely, our scientific and technological revolution would have had its secularistic impact on the Russians as well. And there is enough evidence that the Russian Orthodox Church at the beginning of the twentieth century was beginning to reevaluate itself in relation to the industrial age. But there is no doubt that the rapid decline of religion in that country was brought about by the systematic persecution organized and executed by the regime. It was, after all, frequently stated that the political revolution of 1917 would be accompanied by other revolutions in order to effect the social and cultural transformation of Soviet society. The latter would have been impossible without first eradicating religion from the minds and hearts of Soviet citizens and without decisively breaking the authority of the organized church. As is well known, no other institution exercised as extensive social and cultural influence on Russian society as the Orthodox Church. This was certainly true of the majority of the population which officially classified itself as Orthodox and which on the eve of World War I numbered over 100 million. Despite its subordination to the state, the Russian Orthodox Church before the revolution enjoyed recognition as the official religious body and was accorded numerous privileges. Administratively, it was ruled by the Holy

---

of the Rev. Michael Bourdeaux, author of the celebrated *Patriarch and Prophets*, and began publication of a badly needed journal, *Religion in Communist Lands* (the first issue appeared in January-February 1973).

Governing Synod, established in 1721 by Peter the Great. The Synod was in turn under the control of an Overseer, *Oberprokuror,* appointed by the tsar. What the tsar's appointee oversaw was an impressive institution comprising sixty-seven dioceses with 54,174 churches, an army of 50,105 priests and deacons, and 1025 monastic institutions, accommodating 94,-629 monks, nuns, and novices. This all-pervasive institution enjoyed a generous annual state subsidy and had extensive resources of its own besides.[3]

When the Bolshevik Revolution occurred in 1917 the Russian Orthodox Church had just completed a revolution of its own. After nearly two hundred years of synodal administration the Church canonically restored the Patriarchate abolished by Peter the Great. This was a momentous act which was preceded by a series of heated debates and extensive preparation beginning at the turn of the century and culminating in the first All-Russian Sobor (Council) held in the fall of 1917.[4] The restoration of the Patriarchate demonstrated the desire of the leading hierarchs to establish the independence of the Church from the state while simultaneously holding onto the privileges it had enjoyed under the old arrangement. Be that as it may, the restoration of the Patriarchate was also a symbol of badly needed reforms in the Church which should follow. Much thought and discussion on improving the Church went on during the period of the Provisional Government from March to November of 1917.

When the Bolsheviks took over, they allowed the Sobor to

[3]For the establishment of this administrative arrangement see James Cracraft, *The Church Reform of Peter the Great* (Stanford, Calif.: Stanford University Press, 1971). For the profile of the Church at the turn of the century consult John S. Curtiss, *Church and State in Russia, 1900-1917.*

[4]For the background to the 1917 Sobor see the unpublished Ph.D. dissertation of James William Cunningham, "Reform in the Russian Church, 1900-1906: The Struggle for Autonomy and the Restoration of Byzantine 'Symphonia'" (University of Minnesota, 1973) and Nicholas Zernov, *The Russian Religious Renaissance of the Twentieth Century* (New York: Harper and Row, 1963), pp. 35-85. For the Council itself and the developments following, see A. Wuyts, "Le Patriarcat russe au concile de Moscou de 1917-1918," *Orientalia Christiana Analecta* CXXIX (Rome, 1941), which is based on the published minutes of the Council; Igor Smolitsch, "Die Russische Kirche in Russland," *Ostkirchliche Studien* XIV (1965):1-34; and G. M. Beningsen, "The Year 1917 in the History of the Russian Church," *St. Vladimir's Seminary Quarterly* VII (1963): 115-32.

continue with its deliberations concerning their newly elected Patriarch who was finally enthroned in the Kremlin Uspenskii Cathedral on 29 November 1917. But it was inevitable that Patriarch and Commissar would clash. To begin with, they represented two hostile and irreconcilable world views. Marx's statements on religion, and especially Lenin's extreme interpretation of them, ruled out any possibility of a meaningful dialogue.[5] And even though as far as the Bolsheviks were concerned all religions carried a stigma, the Orthodox Church was naturally singled out for special treatment. It had, after all, been the most influential religious group and still wielded considerable economic and political power. Above all, it was basically a conservative institution which had upheld the activities of tsarism. Another reason for the inevitability of the clash was the uncertainty about the fate of the Bolshevik seizure of power. This uncertainty forced the defenders of the Revolution to be vigilant about possible sources of opposition and at the same time urged the critics of the Revolution to be more daring in their challenge, in the beginning at least. Finally, there was total confusion during the early revolutionary months and the Civil War years (1918-1921) which forced the Bolshevik regime and the Church to take unpredicted and extreme positions which might have not been the case under less abnormal circumstances.

The first defender of Church interests against encroachments by the Soviet government was the new Patriarch Tikhon, a man of great spirituality and devotion to his flock. Before becoming Patriarch, Tikhon had served in numerous hierarchical capacities inside and outside of Russia including the administration of the Russian Church in North America. What he may have lacked in strength of character, he made up with experience in the complexity of ecclesiastical affairs. He certainly proved a successful negotiator in working not only with Russian but with other Orthodox groups of different national persuasions during his American sojourn (1898-1907). The challenge awaiting

[5]Bohdan R. Bociurkiw, "Lenin and Religion," in Leonard Schapiro and Peter Reddaway (eds.) *Lenin the Man, the Theorist, the Leader, A Reappraisal* (New York: Frederick A. Praeger, 1967), pp. 107-134 is a convenient summary.

him inside Russia, however, was infinitely more formidable. For soon after the November Revolution, the Bolsheviks began to issue a series of decrees which in effect aimed at limiting and ultimately eliminating altogether the political and social role of the Church. The first such move was part of the 4 December 1917 decree which declared the nationalization of all land. This obviously included the land which belonged to churches and monasteries. The practical result of this was to deprive the churches of material means. On 18 December of the same year, another decree started a process of undermining the social influence of religion by refusing legal recognition to Church marriages and divorces. This decree became part of the family law promulgated earlier. But by far the most significant of these decrees was the one issued on 23 January 1918, the famous Decree of Separation of Church and State and School and Church which is a landmark in the history of Soviet church-state relations. Basically the decree deprived the Church of legal status and prohibited churches and religious societies from owning property. This meant that even liturgies could hardly be performed since the Church legally could not claim the places of worship "Religious groups," as the parishes were officially called, had to negotiate for such facilities with the state but once these requests were granted they had to be considered as property of individuals and not of a religious group. This stringent requirement aimed at discouraging formal worship. To make matters worse, the Commissariat of Justice which was in charge of religious affairs until 1924 ruled that religious buildings such as churches might be used simultaneously for secular and often antireligious purposes such as lectures, concerts, cinema shows, political meetings, and popular dances. The Decree also forbade religious instruction in state and public schools and private schools where general subjects were taught. Only private religious instruction was allowed and even this was later limited by the decree of 13 June 1921 to persons below the age of 18. Adults were allowed to receive religious instruction only in seminaries where nothing but theology was taught.[6]

[6]For a general discussion of all these developments, see Matthew Spinka, *The Church and the Russian Revolution*, and Boleslaw Czczezniak, *The Rus-*

Tikhon had anticipated the Decree of Separation and he moved against the Bolsheviks by issuing on 19 January 1918 a strong condemnation, anathematizing them for their previous acts and calling them "outcasts of the human race." He furthermore urged the faithful to terminate any associations with them.[7] The fight was unmistakably on, and for eight years until his death in 1925 Tikhon struggled to preserve the autonomy and the dignity of the Church. It was a prelude to the hard road that lay ahead for Russian Orthodoxy.

Patriarch Tikhon must have felt confident in his move. He had the approval of the Church Council and he could count on the support of his huge flock, lay and ecclesiastic, a veritable force indeed. He also must have counted heavily on the unifying power the office of the Patriarchate could have for the whole country. The removal of the tsar left the Patriarch as the only symbol of national unity in the prerevolutionary sense of the word. Lenin must have appreciated Tikhon's position of strength and successfully restrained Trotsky who, as a member of the governmental committee on ecclesiastical affairs, urged a harsh punishment on the Patriarch. For the first year of the Revolution, when Tikhon was openly most polemical toward the regime, Lenin remained remarkably reserved toward him. He even ostensibly ignored the Patriarch's criticism of the separate Treaty of Brest-Litovsk which the Russians signed with the Germans in March 1918 and a scathing letter Tikhon wrote to the Soviet of People's Commissars on the occasion of the first anniversary of the Bolshevik Revolution. In the latter Tik-

---

sian Revolution and Religion (Notre Dame, Ind.: University of Notre Dame Press, 1959). All the decrees concerning the new status of religious groups can be conveniently found in P. V. Gidulianov (ed.), *Otdelenie tserkvi ot gosudarstva v S.S.S.R.; Sbornik dekretov i.t. d.* [The separation of Church and State in the U.S.S.R.: Collection of Decrees, etc.]; also the very handy *O religii i tserkvi, sbornikh dokumentov* [About religion and the Church, a collection of documents] (Moscow, 1965), part III, pp. 95-111. For the religious provisions in the Constitution see G. S. Gurvich, *Istoriia Sovetskoi Konstitutsii* [History of the Soviet Constitution] (Moscow, 1923), pp. 79-80, and the introduction in Vladimir Gsovski (ed.), *Church and State Behind the Iron Curtain.*

[7]Spinka, *The Church and the Russian Revolution,* pp. 118-22, and for more details Curtiss, *The Russian Church and the Soviet State,* chapter III, pp. 44-70.

hon recited the crimes of the Soviet government and pleaded for an end to violence and the freeing of prisoners.[8]

But the Decree of Separation was irrevocably on and its provisions were repeated in Article 13 of the first Soviet Constitution in July 1918. The Constitution further granted all citizens the liberty of religious as well as antireligious propaganda. In reality this equalization of propaganda gave the state an enormous advantage over the Church and in fact amounted to a declaration of war on religion. Tikhon's army of ecclesiastics was heavily discriminated against. Article 65 of the Soviet Constitution reduced priests and clerics to a socially inferior position. They became disenfranchized and thus could receive only ration cards of the lowest category and frequently no cards at all. They could not belong to trade unions and could not be employed by state enterprises; certain professions, especially teaching, were specifically barred to them. Worse than this, children of this "class" could not attend schools above the elementary level. Priests also had to pay higher rents for living quarters and higher rates of taxation. This was part of the Bolshevik campaign to deprive the Church of both its official and nonofficial leadership. For this proclamation was accompanied by a ruthless persecution of clerics of all ranks. Thousands of them were thrown into prison without any trial, and according to the émigré press twelve thousand others were reported as put to death.[9]

Obviously, Tikhon had underestimated the power, ruthlessness, and determination of his opposition. By the end of 1918 he had begun to advocate a moderate policy or a retreat of the faithful to the catacombs in an effort to save his flock. Despite the losses which the Church suffered as a result of the initial confrontation with the Bolsheviks, the period up to 1921 was one of calculated coexistence. In the uncertainties of the Russian Civil War and Allied intervention it was at times impossible to predict political outcomes and consequently the future of the Orthodox Church. But by 1921, despite the toll of the Civil War, the Bolsheviks were becoming confident about their

[8]Struve, *Christians in Contemporary Russia*, pp. 23-32.
[9]N. S. Timasheff, *Religion in Soviet Russia, 1917-1942*, pp. 21-28.

political victory—the elimination of opposition within Russia and the expulsion of interventionists. Consequently, they accelerated their attack on religious organizations and especially the Orthodox Church.

In this renewal of the attack on the Orthodox Church the regime was able to exploit to the utmost three incidents. The first was the controversial Karlovtsy Conference held in Yugoslavia in November 1921. The second was the Bolshevik policy of confiscating sacred objects for the alleged purpose of selling them in order to alleviate the raging famine crisis. The third, and in many respects by far the most serious, was the beginning of deviationist or schismatic groups within the Orthodox community threatening a schism of the Church organization. The most important of these "schismatic" movements was the so-called Living Church.

The Karlovtsy Conference was called by a group of Russian ecclesiastics supported by officers and former tsarist officials who had retreated with the White armies and found refuge in Yugoslavia. The driving force behind this group was the influential Metropolitan Antonii Khrapovitskii, who received the absolute majority of votes among the three candidates for the position of Patriarch in 1917. However, Patriarch Tikhon was finally selected by lot.[10] An avowed monarchist, Khrapovitskii organized the Supreme Russian Ecclesiastical Administration Abroad. Canonical issues aside, the Karlovtsy Conference proved a most unfortunate event for the Orthodox Church inside Russia. The Conference became politicized and its promonarchist faction succeeded in having a resolution adopted expressing hope for the restoration of the Orthodox Romanov dynasty. Further statements from this group made it clear that they were willing to engage in activities in the West which might precipitate the eviction of the Bolsheviks from Russia.

As could be expected, the Soviet Government exploited the Conference to its fullest, charging Tikhon with responsibility

[10] Archbishop Antonii Khrapovitskii received the largest number of votes (101 out of the 141 who voted for restoration of the Patriarchate), but the final outcome among the three contestants was determined by lot and Tikhon's name was drawn. For a discussion of the events surrounding the election of the Patriarch consult Chrysostomus, *op. cit.*, I, p. 97.

for the acts of the Karlovtsy hierarchs. Tikhon realized the consequences of this implication and, after careful investigation of the Conference and its resolutions, he speedily sought to disassociate himself from any monarchist politics abroad. He repudiated the Karlovtsy hierarchs as having no ecclesio-canonical character qualifying them to speak on behalf of the Russian Orthodox Church and liquidated the Supreme Russian Ecclesiastical Administration Abroad which was then immediately reorganized, being given a different name without further protest from the Patriarch.

Tikhon's decision had the support of his Church Council, and his move was tactically necessary if for no other reason than to prevent accusations by the regime that he was a counterrevolutionary. For the rest of the decade the Karlovtsy Conference remained an issue which was brought up by the regime whenever the time seemed politically propitious. Tikhon's reaction demonstrates the degree to which he was gradually becoming apolitical in his desperate efforts to maintain the Church's autonomy by not incurring the State's wrath unnecessarily.

In the meantime, the fate of the Orthodox Church was overtaken by the harsh economic realities of the country on the morrow of the Civil War. After eight years of war, revolutions, and a protracted confused civil war, the country was in economic ruins, and millions of Russians faced starvation. This was the horrible famine of 1921-22 which, despite various relief programs from Western Europe and the United States, continued unabated. The regime took advantage of this crisis and began to confiscate church valuables and sell them, ostensibly to alleviate the misery of the Russian people. The decision of the Soviet authorities to confiscate church valuables indiscriminately from Catholic as well as Orthodox churches deserves close attention, because among other things it attests to the speed with which they were mastering the art of psychological warfare against the Church. It is debatable whether the estimated $1,500,000 collected from the sale of church valuables offered great relief to the Russian people, especially when one compares that figure with the $13,750,000 which Bukharin admitted having spent for foreign propaganda during the famine.[11] It appears rather that this was a move to provoke the Church to open hostility against the regime for which it could be prosecuted and at the same time discredited in the eyes of a starving population. The regime was right in its prognosis, for the faithful and especially the clergy resisted courageously (and on occasion thoughtlessly) the confiscation of church valuables. This open confrontation, often resulting in bloody riots by the faithful around the churches, led to trials of leading hierarchs such as the case of Metropolitan Veniamin who was tried in Petrograd, found guilty, and executed.[12]

But the real target from now on was the Patriarch, who following the Sobor's ruling of 1918 declared confiscation of holy objects as blasphemous and the voluntary surrender of the same by priests as justifying excommunication. During the famine he instructed his clergy to surrender only unconsecrated Church objects. This of course put the Church in the position of "The Most Holy Counterrevolution." Thus Patriarch Tikhon was called to testify during the Moscow trial known as the trial of the fifty-four. He found himself in a most difficult position. According to canon law, he had to condemn the confiscation of consecrated objects, and furthermore he had to state that in the event of a conflict between civil and canon law his duty compelled him to obey the latter. This testimony further weakened the Patriarch's position vis-a-vis the state authorities.[13]

Much has been said about the courageous stand of Church leaders at this time and the embarrassment they caused the Soviet regime, especially as Western states began to register

[11]Richard Joseph Cooke, *Religion in Russia under the Soviets*, p. 149. Also see Chrysostomus, *op. cit.*, I, chapter V.

[12]Francis McCullagh, *The Bolshevik Persecution of Christianity*, 32f; 59 contains a good account of the Churchmen's trials connected with the famine incidents. There were 231 trials of nonconforming faithful. Out of the 738 accused examined, forty-four were sentenced to death. Struve, *op. cit.*, pp. 35-36, points out that such trials were common throughout Russia and that "the treatment of ordinary clergy was even more brutal; during 1922, 2691 secular priests, 1962 monks and 3447 nuns were liquidated. The total number of victims was 8100."

[13]McCullagh, *op. cit.*, p. 24; Spinka, *The Church in Soviet Russia*, p. 28.

vigorous protests against the persecution of Catholic and Orthodox hierarchs. But the fact remains that Tikhon's position was daily becoming more precarious. The Soviets in their propaganda managed to link Tikhon's opposition to the confiscation of church valuables to the Karlovtsy group (the latter continued its openly anticommunist activity abroad) and the whole crisis of 1922 precipitated the launching of an organized antireligious campaign and the beginning of the publication of the antireligious weekly *Bezbozhnik* (Atheist). Tikhon himself was under house arrest and his future uncertain.

It was during these critical days that the schism threatening the unity of the Orthodox Church began to crystallize and to undermine the position of Tikhon both as Patriarch and in his relation with the regime. The schismatic movement consisted of several independent groups bearing individual names but which ultimately came to be known collectively as the Living Church (earlier the name of a small group), with its best-known advocate Alexander Vvedenskii. A "Supreme Church Administration" was their main coordinating organ. As Walter Kolarz put it, "they all differed from the Patriarchal Church by their servile pro-Soviet attitude and a demonstratively proclaimed sympathy for Communism."[14] One of the ways by which the leaders of the Living Church, mostly progressive priests from Petrograd, demonstrated their Communist sympathy was to insist, against the Patriarch's pronouncements, that Church objects should be confiscated in order to meet a national emergency. In fact, many of them willingly came before the courts as witnesses testifying for the prosecution against their superiors, who, obeying Tikhon's declaration, resisted confiscation of Church valuables. Their evidence played a decisive role in the condemnation and execution of many church officials.

The story of the Living Church is probably the darkest page in the history of religious opportunism. Under the pretext of desiring extensive reform for the Russian Orthodox Church which would bring it in line with other reforms effected by the Revolution, they sought to usurp ecclesiastical authority by offering

[14]Kolarz, *op. cit.*, p. 39; also Curtiss, *The Russian Church and the Soviet State*, pp. 129-52.

unqualified allegiance to the regime. The latter, anxious to exploit a religious cleavage, encouraged this movement, permitted them to publish their own journal called *Zhivaia Tserkov* [The Living Church], which began publication on 12 May 1922, and through it they sought to destroy the unity of the Orthodox Church.

The resourcefulness of the Living Church was endless. While Tikhon was under arrest, they convinced him to appoint the Metropolitan of Iaroslavl, Agafangel, as his *Locum Tenens* or Keeper of the Patriarchal See. Agafangel was supposed to come to Moscow and immediately convene an All-Russian Sobor to decide on ecclesiastical policy, but he never did so. In the beginning he hesitated, and later he was prevented by the government. In the meantime, the members of the Living Church issued a major proclamation in which they accused the Patriarchal Church of attempts to overthrow the government. At the same time, they announced their recognition by the Soviet government to hold a Sobor, try the guilty hierarchs, and consider questions of ecclesiastical administration. In other words, they strove to be recognized as the official head of the Orthodox Church. By devious methods and with the help of the Soviet government they took control of the chancery and the Patriarchal office, and their control appeared quite firm, especially after 5 August 1922, when Tikhon was transferred from house arrest to the state prison. According to Stratonov, these events precipitated the beginning of the "ecclesiastical cleavage of the Russian Orthodox flock."[15]

What were the objectives of the Living Church? In the first place, since the membership of the Living Church was overwhelmingly priestly, they wanted to transfer the administration of the Russian Church from the black or monastic episcopate to the white parochial clergy. In fact, they also wanted to abolish the Patriarchate and replace it with a Synod in which the priestly element would predominate. But, more significantly, they wanted the Church to participate actively in politics and the "socialist upbuilding." In fact, the Living Church posed as a

[15]Stratonov, *Russkaia tserkovnaia smuta (1921-1931)* [The Russian church confusion (1921-1931)], p. 164.

revolutionary movement within a revolutionary state. To put it in other words, a revolutionary church group took it upon itself to do the work of the state by first dividing the faithful and ultimately destroying the effectiveness of the organized church. The confusion and the result of the activity of the Living Church were reflected in the All-Russian Sobor (according to them the second All-Russian Sobor) which they felt strong enough to call in April 1923. Of the 430 delegates 250 belonged to the Living Church. The Patriarchal party consisted of forty-five delegates selected and sent there against the Patriarch's wish.[16]

Surprisingly enough, this religious gathering could easily be interpreted as the high point of the Soviets' antireligious campaign. Aleksandr Vvedenskii and Krasnitskii, the representatives of the Living Church, denounced the Patriarchal form of ecclesiastical administration, criticizing especially Tikhon, whose trial and condemnation *in absentia,* depriving him of his clerical orders and his Patriarchal office, constituted the most sensational part of the Sobor. Thereby the Sobor abolished the Patriarchate altogether and replaced it by a Supreme Church Council.

But more significant was the political stand expressed in the various resolutions of the Sobor. In simple terms they urged the faithful to support the Communists, whom they called "warriors for humanitarian truth," and help them fulfill the lofty objectives of the October Revolution. They refuted the impression that the Soviets persecuted the Church and directed the faithful to notice that the Soviet power was attempting through state methods to realize the ideals of the Kingdom of God.[17]

Intoxicated with temporary success, the Living Church failed to realize that the Soviet government, while welcoming its services, was not anxious to recognize it as the sole official Orthodox Church by granting it special status. Other factors played a role in this decision by the government. The majority of Or-

[16]Spinka, *The Church in Soviet Russia,* p. 35.
[17]*Ibid.,* pp. 36-37, and the same author's *The Church and the Russian Revolution,* pp. 237-42. Especially informative on the "pseudo-Council" is Chrysostomus, *op. cit.,* I, pp. 271-83.

thodox people remained faithful to the arrested Patriarch Tikhon. Also a wave of protests arose abroad against the Patriarch's arrest, beginning with the Karlovtsy group (the Soviet government totally ignoring their protests) and ending with the Archbishop of Canterbury and the British government, in the person of Lord Curzon, who was at that time Foreign Secretary.

All these developments may explain the Soviet government's treatment of the incarcerated Patriarch Tikhon whom they released from jail in exchange for a controversial confession.

In this controversial confession, Tikhon repented of all his "actions directed against the government." He further declared that he was no longer an enemy of the Soviet government and that he had "severed all connections with the foreign and domestic monarchists and the counterrevolutionary activity of the White Guards."[18]

This was a strong pledge, but Tikhon honored it and for the rest of his life he struggled for the attainment of a *modus vivendi* with the government. But he was adamant in his attitude toward the Living Church whose Sobor he declared uncanonical. Still he offered members of that group a choice—repent and return to his jurisdiction or be anathematized. After the release of the Patriarch the triumph of the Living Church came to an end. There is no doubt that his confession, even if extorted under pressure from the Soviet authorities, was brought about by his realization that only thus could he prevent the schismatic movement from effecting an irreparable split in the Church.

Tikhon's confession was to be surpassed in terms of the sensation and controversy aroused only by his so-called "testament" which was published by the Soviet press under the name of the Patriarch on 25 March/7 April 1925, the day of his death.[19] The essential points of the testament are those reminding the faithful that the Soviet authority was there to stay and that they should abstain from any associations with the enemies of the Soviet state. He specifically denounced Russian

[18]Fletcher, *A Study in Survival*, p. 20, contains the entire confession. See also Curtiss, *The Russian Church and the Soviet State*, pp. 158-67.

[19]The date is here shown according to both the old and new style calendars.

émigrés, especially hierarchs of the Karlovtsy branch, who hurt both the Soviet state and the Mother Church by abusing their relationship with the latter. But the hardest point to take was that in which he refuted "rumors" that the Patriarchal office could not express itself freely.[20]

There is some evidence and indeed great room for speculation that the testament was a falsification.[21] Others explain it in terms of Tikhon's weakness of character. In retrospect, however, it illuminates Tikhon's quiet determination to attain a *modus vivendi* with the Soviet authorities without sacrificing the canonicity or purity of the Church, and, on the other hand, the Soviet government's need to secure some form of recognition by the leader of the organized Church, which, despite the acceleration of persecution, gave the appearance of a state within the state.

Tikhon's qualified success may be partly explained by the spirit of the so-called experimental twenties, when, despite persecutions, Soviet leaders concentrated on controlling the "Commanding Heights" and allowed some flexibility in the country's efforts to reach its prewar economic level which in fact they did by 1928. But the New Economic Policy was coming to an end. Stalin was gradually eliminating his "opposition" and was getting ready to embark upon a renewal of the Revolution. In this struggle to build socialism in the USSR, the government was bent on utilizing all national resources, political, economic, social, and cultural. It is in the context of this "great experiment" that one must view the fate of the Orthodox Church in the decade or so leading up to World War II.

To be sure, the legal status of the Russian Patriarchate was affected by the law of separation of 1918. In fact, individuals and special associations were recognized as representing legally the body of believers and were in charge of Church properties. The Patriarchate was further weakened by the confusion resulting from various splinter antipatriarchal groups, the most important among them being those of the Living Church. De-

[20]Spinka, *The Church in Soviet Russia*, pp. 43-45 for the Patriarch's text.
[21]Chrysostomus, *op. cit.*, I, pp. 346-47, analyses the details surrounding the signing of the confession and supports the theory that it was a falsification.

spite these limitations, symbolically the Patriarchate was the fortress of the Orthodox faith within Russia. This must have been recognized by the Soviet authorities who took advantage of Tikhon's death to allow the Patriarchal throne to remain vacant and to be occupied by a *Locum Tenens* or keeper until 1943. From the death of Tikhon to the outbreak of World War II, the fate of the Russian Church was in the hands of one of the most controversial hierarchs of the Soviet period, Metropolitan Sergii Stragorodskii (1867-1944).

A well-travelled hierarch and an able scholar, Sergii led a rather colorful life before the Revolution, moving comfortably among Church circles, the intelligentsia, and notorious individuals such as Gregorii Rasputin. His accession to the Patriarchal See as Deputy *Locum Tenens* was rather accidental in that the three others appointed by Tikhon before his death were exiled and not able to serve in that capacity. The one exception was Metropolitan Peter, who served for a short time and then was exiled on 10 December 1925 to the island of Khe on the mouth of the River Ob on forged charges of counterrevolutionary activity. Until his death there ten years later, he was the canonical *Locum Tenens*.

Sergii's dealings with the Soviet authorities have fascinated historians and puzzled and depressed the faithful. His whole policy has been described by Matthew Spinka as a necessary capitulation, however ugly, in order to save the Church and by most historians as probably the most difficult chapter in the history of the Orthodox Church's struggle for survival in the Soviet period.[22]

Sergii certainly did accomplish one thing. He managed to obtain "official recognition," however tenuous such recognitions were, of his Church administration by the government (10 June 1926). Yet the circumstances which led to this "dubious" recognition have caused the greatest misapprehension about the period of Sergii's leadership. Again, we must keep in mind the temper of the times. Tikhon's testament did not mean an end of the persecution by the state. In fact, Sergii acceded

[22]Fletcher, *A Study in Survival*, pp. 28-96; Spinka, *The Church in Soviet Russia*, pp. 51-100.

to the See as Deputy *Locum Tenens* in the midst of persecution and imprisonment of Church figures.

Sergii defined his attitude toward the regime in two major moves. The first move was a letter sent on 10 June 1926 to the bishops, priests, and faithful of the Moscow Patriarchate in which he explained to them about his dealings with the government. It was a cleverly written document which reminds us of the spirit of Tikhon's letter and confession. In other words, despite the irreconcilable differences between the Church and Communism, the Church promised civil loyalty to the regime. In no way, however, did he commit the Church to anything beyond that, that is to say to any active program to support the state in its various activities. Obviously this did not satisfy the authorities, for in December 1926 Sergii was mysteriously arrested and imprisoned for three and a half months. He was released on 30 March 1927, after having promised to issue what amounts to the most controversial document in the history of the Russian Church under Soviet rule. The document, dated 29 July 1927, was addressed to the pastors and the flock. It was an announcement of his "official loyalty" to the regime, which meant formal capitulation of the Orthodox Church to the godless government. Going beyond mere civil obedience to the authorities, the Church under Sergii became an active collaborator with the Soviet state. The document's crucial passage read:

> We wish to be Orthodox and at the same time to recognize the Soviet Union as our civil homeland, whose joys and successes are our joys and successes, and whose failures are our failures. Every blow directed at the Union, be it war, boycott, any kind of social disaster or simply murder from around the corner, . . . shall be recognized by us as a blow directed at us. Remaining Orthodox, we remember our obligation to be citizens of the Union, not only from fear but also according to our conscience.[23]

As could be expected, he then appealed to the émigré clergy

---

[23]*Patriarkh Sergii i ego dukhovnoe nasledstvo* [Patriarch Sergii and his spiritual heritage], p. 61. There are numerous English translations of this famous proclamation or parts of it. See especially Fletcher, *A Study in Survival*, pp. 28-32, and Curtiss, *The Russian Church and the Soviet State*, pp. 175-95; also Chrysostomus, *op. cit.*, II, pp. 133-35.

to redefine their attitudes toward the motherland and chided them for their past attitude which had made it impossible for his predecessor to obtain recognition from the regime. It was clear that the Soviet government demanded from the émigré clergy as well as from Sergii a written promise of loyalty.

This document of loyalty to the regime was signed not only by Sergii but by all the members of his newly set-up Synod, one of them being Aleksii Simanskii who later succeeded Sergii as Patriarch of Moscow and all Russia. In return for this endorsement of the regime, the Church was allowed to set up a proper ecclesiastical administration, officially recognized by the regime, and begin publication of an official organ, *The Journal of the Moscow Patriarchate*. Sergii himself was allowed to move from Nizhnii Novgorod to Moscow. Thus began the official "armistice" between Church and state in Soviet Russia, or the new struggle for survival.

A point of canonical explanation: Sergii knew and himself acknowledged that his action in accepting the conditions of "legalization" was not valid until it was approved by the next Sobor representatives of the whole Russian Orthodox Church. He and his Holy Synod possessed only temporary authority. As is well known, however, the announced Sobor did not convene until 1943, which means that the basic change of ecclesiastical policies effected in 1927 never received the necessary approval in accordance with canonical requirements.

The response to Sergii's declaration was on the whole hostile both inside Russia and in the diaspora. Many prominent hierarchs who expressed their disapproval by resigning their Sees were arrested by the security forces as counterrevolutionaries and were either imprisoned, exiled, or shot. Their Sees were quickly filled by individuals favorable to Sergii. Some declared their allegiance to the policy of Patriarch Tikhon and subsequently came to be known as the Tikhon Church. Others simply joined the underground or catacomb church. What this led to amounted to a schism within the old Orthodox Church itself, the extreme counterpart of the Living Church schism. If the Living Church attacked the Patriarchate for its conservative attitude toward the Soviet regime, the new dissidents, most of them conservatives, resented what appeared as the radical gesture on the part of the *Locum Tenens* of offering formal collaboration to an antireligious state. In Leningrad, for example, Metropolitan Iosif had a considerable following of conservative believers and clergy who in defiance to Sergii's practice refused to mention the Soviet government in their liturgies. From his place of exile Metropolitan Peter, the canonical *Locum Tenens* of the Patriarchate who had earlier approved Sergii as Deputy *Locum Tenens,* now rejected the latter and in essence rendered him uncanonical.[24] Probably the most moving rejection of Sergii's position came in an open letter from the bishops exiled on the island of Solovky in the White Sea (27 September 1927). They especially objected to such irresponsible phrases as "the joys and successes of the state are also the joys and successes of the Church," which could mean that they would have to rejoice while observing the destruction of the Church by the state. Also, they felt that religious persecution, especially of the Orthodox Church which was known to all of them and to Sergii, was being ignored.[25]

It is clear that Sergii's position, reflected in the declaration, lost him the support of those who approved his 1926 statements. Perhaps Sergii had no choice. For antireligious propaganda was mounting, especially after 1928 with the introduction of the first Five Year Plan. It was now clearly stated in Artcile IV of the Constitution of the RSFSR that whereas religious confession was granted to the believers, freedom of propaganda was restricted to antireligious organizations and citizens. In fact, the Fourteenth Congress of Soviets made religious propaganda a criminal offense. In schools antireligious instruction superseded nonreligious education, and the April 1929 law, in redefining the position of churches, limited their functions to the performance of services only. In other words, churches could not be used for gathering purposes for young or old people, for prayer meetings or study groups, or the teach-

[24]M. Polskii, *Kanonicheskoe polozhenie Vysshei Tserkovnoi Vlasti V SSSR i Zagranitsei* [The canonical position of the highest church authority in the USSR and abroad], p. 46.
[25]Chrysostomus, *op. cit.,* II, pp. 144-51; Spinka, *The Church in Soviet Russia,* pp. 70-73.

ing of religion. Half of the churches were closed by 1933. By contrast organized antireligious propaganda was gaining ground. Antireligious museums were opened in many cities, the most impressive ones being the ones in Moscow and Leningrad, the latter housed in the beautiful Cathedral of the Virgin of Kazan on Nevskii prospect. In charge of this vast antireligious movement was Emel'ian Iaroslavskii, notorious for his determination to cripple and ultimately eradicate the influence of religion. Beginning in 1925, he was in charge of the Union of the Militant Godless and in seven years, by 1932, he could claim over 5.5 million followers who promoted the eradication of religion with the same fanatical fervor which Kazantzakis encountered during his visit to the director of the *Bezbozhnik* (Atheist). By 1931 that journal had a circulation of nearly half a million whereas its more scientific companion, the *Antireligioznik* (Antireligious), had a circulation of 60,000 in 1938.[26] The persecution was a thorough operation. As Roy Medvedev epigrammatically puts it, "In the late twenties and early thirties the Soviet state had attacked the churches, especially the Russian Orthodox Church. . . . However, the state's punitive organs went much further than the state's interest required. Hundreds of churches and temples were simply torn down, dozens of monasteries were dissolved, and the OGPU even rounded up hermits and put them in camps. In many cities precious monuments of church architecture were destroyed —the Church of Christ the Savior and the Spasski Monastery for example. In 1937-38 this repression was continued without any necessity. Many ordinary priests and bishops were arrested."[27]

Iaroslavskii, satisfied with the results of his antireligious campaign, had, prematurely, in 1935 declared religion dead.

This brief description of antireligious activity during the decade before World War II suggests the unfortunate dilemma in

[26] For a compact compilation of statistics concerning antireligious propaganda and its effect during Sergii's administration see Robert Conquest (ed.), *Religion in the USSR*, pp. 17-30. See also Timasheff, *Religion in Soviet Russia,*, pp. 35 ff; Chrysostomus, *op. cit.*, II, pp. 267-70.

[27] Roy A. Medvedev, *Let History Judge: The Origins and Consequences of Stalinism*, p. 238. For a moving description of religious persecution see also Aleksandr I. Solzhenitsyn, *The Gulag Archipelago: 1918-1956*, pp. 36-38.

which Sergii found himself, for there is no doubt that in his dealings with the Soviets he always acted from a position of weakness. At the same time he must have been a constant embarrassment to the Orthodox faithful both inside Russia and in the diaspora when in the midst of so much overt persecution he was making declarations to the contrary. He often blamed priests for not making use of the freedom of preaching granted them and accounted for the closing of churches by saying that this was not the act of the state but of the inhabitants, often the faithful.

Hierarchically, Sergii's position improved somewhat in 1936 when with the death of Metropolitan Peter he was formally declared as the *Locum Tenens*. He continued in that capacity until he became Patriarch in 1943 during the height of the "Great Patriotic War." In 1936 the legal status of the Orthodox clergy was somewhat improved too. As mentioned earlier, servants of all religious groups were considered second class citizens. They were disenfranchised and their spheres of political or social activity strictly controlled. The Stalin Constitution of 1936 readmitted them to full citizenship even though the real status of priests did not change. Even their voting rights were restored only after they had performed "productive and socially useful work" for five years and had proven their loyalty to the regime.[28] In other words, suspicion of religious leaders, especially Orthodox ones, was fundamental in the regime's dealings with such cases. Allowing for the fact that Sergii had no choice but to capitulate in 1927 and afterwards in order to save the Church, one is still left with the impression that his policy did not make much difference as far as the persecution of the Church was concerned—or at any rate not until World War II.

Reflecting on the twenty years of Church-state relations since the Bolshevik revolution, one is struck by a twofold phenomenon: the failure of the government to exterminate the official Church even if they disfigured it, but, more importantly, the failure of the Soviet government to eradicate religion from the hearts and minds of Soviet citizens, ostensibly the main objec-

[28]Kolarz, *op. cit.*, p. 45.

tive of the Decree of Separation of 13 January 1918. That this had not been accomplished was reflected in the Soviet census of 1937 which included the religious affiliations of Soviet citizens. On Iaroslavskii's own admission, two-thirds of the urban population declared themselves unrelated to the Church, but two-thirds of the rural population above eighteen years of age were church members. After some calculation this suggests that 57 percent of the above declared themselves to be believers.[29]

But how was this survival possible? As far as the official church was concerned, Sergii's dealings with the Soviet government notwithstanding, many of the functioning hierarchs remained alive because their threat to the Soviet government was nonexistent. As a contemporary high Church official put it, not only were they not dangerous but in fact they were useful to the state. This statement corresponds with Stalin's own admission to a delegation of American workers in 1927 that despite the fact that the persecution against the Church had not been effective enough, at least they managed to suppress the reactionary clergy.

As far as the survival of Orthodoxy at large is concerned, the story is more complicated. First of all there is the obvious realization that a millenium of cultural heritage simply cannot be obliterated within a period of twenty years by a series of decrees, however ruthlessly enforced. Even many of those who conspicuously repudiated Orthodoxy and actually fought it carried many of its cultural marks for life. Secondly, it soon became clear that a large section of the population were serious about their Orthodox faith and were willing to fight for it, openly in the early years of Soviet rule. When open opposition proved useless then the believers were urged to go underground and form the so-called catacomb church. The story of the underground church is a very crucial one for the understanding of religious survival in the Soviet Union. It is also a complicated one, but basically it refers to those individuals or groups of individuals who refused to compromise with either the political or religious authorities and instead strove on their

[29]Spinka, *The Church in Soviet Russia*, p. 80; Timasheff, *op. cit.*, p. 65.

own to preserve and perpetuate their faith. The catacomb church was important not only because it sustained the community of believers but also because it exercised a subtle pressure on the Soviet government not to do away completely with the official church for fear that this might force the entire body of Orthodox adherents underground, thus destroying any means of controlling it. This view, which was usually adhered to by émigré historians, is now also shared by Western scholars.[30] But insightful observations about the significance of the underground church exist in an unusual memorandum by the Exarch of the Baltic countries, Metropolitan Sergii Voskresenskii (sometimes referred to as Sergii the Younger, in order to avoid confusion with Sergii Stragorodskii, the *Locum Tenens*) who was also a close co-worker of the *Locum Tenens*. The exarch had a very interesting career, gradually rising from the ranks after the Declaration of 1927. By 1939 he had become the second in line to succeed the aged *Locum Tenens*. Metropolitan Sergii's importance was further enhanced by the fact that he conducted the Patriarchate's relations with representatives of the Soviet government. He was, therefore, well acquainted with the affairs of the Moscow Patriarchate. In 1940 he was appointed Exarch of the Baltic Orthodox Church in Latvia, Lithuania, and Estonia, acquired by the Soviet Union as a result of the German-Soviet pact. When the German-Soviet pact ended and Hitler's army began to occupy these territories the Exarch evaded evacuation, and soon turned the above-mentioned memorandum over to the German occupation authorities. True, this memorandum was written for the Germans and undoubtedly it was prepared with certain biases. On the other hand, its historical significance is uncontestable. Despite some factual inaccuracies, it is notable that a representative of the Moscow Patriarchate officially recognized the existence of the catacomb church and its pressure on the Soviet Government.[31]

[30] Arfved Gustafson, *Die Katakomben Kirche*. See also Fletcher, *The Russian Orthodox Church Underground 1917-1970*, pp. 79-122.

[31] The authenticity of the memorandum appears unquestionable. It was discovered by W. Alexeev in the Jewish archives in New York, together with a number of other important documents which had formerly been in Nazi archives. The document is a copy with the title, *Denkschrift betreffend die*

As the Exarch put it:

> The forceful dissolution of the publicly recognized leadership of the Patriarchate would only have brought to life an underground leadership of the Patriarchate, which would have significantly complicated its surveillance by the police. In general, there did exist in Russia a very live, secret, religious life (secret priests and monks, secret places of prayer, secret services, baptismals, confessions, communions, marriages, secret theological studies, secret preservation of the Holy Writ, liturgical vessels, icons, sacred books, secret relationships between [religious] communities, the diocese and the leadership of the Patriarchate, etc.). If they had wanted also to destroy the secret leadership of the Patriarchate, then they would have had to execute all bishops, including secret ones, who were created one after another because of such need [for them]. . . . The Soviet government understood this, and, therefore, it preferred that the leadership of the Patriarchate should continue to exist.[32]

This practical consideration may explain the state's willingness to accommodate the leaders of the Church if the latter promised civil obedience and preferably collaboration. Speaking of practical considerations, it is worth keeping in mind that the liberation which the Soviet citizens were supposed to experience as a result of the removal of religious taboos and practices proved counterproductive as far as the state's designs were concerned. The state, after all, needed a disciplined population and that was hardly the case with Soviet society by the end of the 1920s. The return to strict laws regarding marriages, divorces, and sexual promiscuity during the 1930s suggests that while decidedly antireligious the state still saw the usefulness of some of the cementing and disciplining influences of religious behavior. As a matter of fact, Iaroslavskii admitted that his militant godless had failed "to offer the people moral standards for their life."[33] This, and not religious toleration, explains the gradual shift of policy toward Christianity in general

---

Lage der orthodoxen Kirche im Ostland. Ostland was the name given by the Germans to the Baltic countries during their occupation. The copy contains twenty-one large format pages of typescript. At the end of the copy there is typed: gez. Metropolit Sergius. The date given is 12 November 1941, Riga. Document Occ E (Ch) - 6.

[32]*Ibid.*, p. 7.
[33]Timasheff, *op. cit.*, p. 130.

and the Orthodox Church in particular after 1936. It was almost ironic to have a professor, A. Ranovich, allowed to address the Academy of Sciences and the Central Committee of the Union of the Militant Godless with a paper on the early Christian Church and inform them of the virtues of Christianity. According to Ranovich early Christians belonged, after all, to the underprivileged toiling masses. Some of them were slaves. And on the whole they were people of "relatively enlightened ideas and repudiated racial and national discriminations, proclaiming the equality of both slave and free, male and female, rich and poor." As for Russia, its conversion to Christianity from Byzantium introduced higher culture to that land. Much more surprising was the assertion made in a special pamphlet by the Union of the Militant Godless themselves asserting that Christianity had contributed to the improvement of family relations and social customs and had abolished many harmful practices of antiquity.[34]

Finally, one should not ignore the basic factor which accounts for the survival of religion regardless of place or time. The history of Christianity, at least, is a record of its flourishing under adverse circumstances and outright persecutions. The Orthodox believers proved themselves, as it were, and in the midst of daily threats they clung tenaciously to their faith, finding consolation therein.

On the eve of World War II the scars of two decades of merciless and ruthless persecution were readily visible on the Orthodox Church. The most elementary comparison with the situation in 1917 illustrates the general decline that had set in. In 1917 there were 46,487 Orthodox Churches, 50,960 Orthodox priests, and 130 bishops. By contrast, in 1941 there were 4225 churches, 5665 Orthodox priests, and only twenty-eight bishops.[35]

[34]Spinka, *The Church in Soviet Russia,* p. 81. For a review of Ranovich's ideas as a historian of religion see Alexander Dombrowsky, "Soviet Historians on Christianity and Its Antecedents," in *Religion in the USSR* (Munich: Institute for the Study of the USSR, 1960), pp. 219-21.

[35]Paul Anderson, *People, Church, and State in Modern Russia,* p. 192. Anderson takes this information from the official Soviet publication *Soviet War News* for 22 August 1941, and from the journal *Bezbozhnik* [The Godless] for January 1935.

According to Paul Anderson, one of the leading specialists in the field, these statistics included churches, priests, and bishops of all jurisdictions, even the so-called Living Church, which the Soviet authorities supported and exploited in varying degrees until its liquidation in 1943. Thus, the figures which apply specifically to the main branch of the Orthodox Church officially headed by the *Locum Tenens* of the Patriarchal throne, Metropolitan Sergii, would be still smaller. For example, it is well known that only four bishops who could be considered as active remained free from arrest in 1939.[36] Considering the fact that the 1941 figures include approximately twelve hundred churches located on the territory seized by the USSR from Poland in 1939, then the number of Orthodox Churches amounted to three thousand in 1939, or roughly to only 6 percent of the prerevolutionary number of churches.[37] This figure, three thousand, could be further decreased by several hundred Orthodox churches in Lithuania, Latvia, and Estonia which at the beginning of the war were subsidiary to the Moscow Patriarchate and, therefore, must have been included in the 1941 figures mentioned above. No doubt the same situation existed in 1939 with regard to the number of priests who survived persecution with the very real difference that many of them were no longer officially listed as priests but continued to conduct services in secret.

Despite this physical metamorphosis and the controversy over its canonicity, the Russian Orthodox Church survived institutionally. But, more significantly, it was unquestionable that the spirit of Orthodoxy survived and indeed flourished through the catacomb or the underground church. This latter form of survival accounts chiefly for the great revival which surfaced during World War II.

[36]Friedrich Heyer, *Die orthodoxe Kirche in der Ukraine von 1917 bis 1945*. See also Wassilij Alexeev, *Russian Orthodox Bishops in the Soviet Union, 1941-1943*, p. 5.

[37]Heyer, *op. cit.*, p. 162.

Gallery of Russian Orthodox religious figures during the inter-war years. From the collection of Pavel Korin.

ORTHODOX HIERARCHS:

Archimandrite 1936

Metropolitan 1937

Father Aleksei 1931

MONKS:

Young Monks 1931/1932

Older Monks 1933

NUNS:

Older Nun 1933

Trio 1933-1935

Young Nun 1935

M. K. Kholmogorov 1935. Moscow protodeacon, famous for his bass voice.

TWO

 The Fruits of War

For two decades the Russian Orthodox Church in the Soviet Union had been in a state of siege. Its administration was in a shambles. They could not account accurately for the number of dioceses or, more significantly, for the number of hierarchs required for such spots. Apart from the four leading ones (Metropolitan Sergii Stragorodskii, the Patriarchal *Locum Tenens,* Aleksii Simanskii, Metropolitan of Leningrad and Novgorod and future Patriarch of the Russian Church, Archbishop Nikolai Iarushevich of the Novgorod and Pskov eparchies, later Metropolitan of Kiev and Galicia, who was to achieve great fame and notoriety during and after World War II, and Archbishop Sergii Voskresenskii of Dmitrov who was to become the Exarch of the Moscow Patriarchate in the newly acquired territories as a result of the German-Soviet Pact of 1939), it is as if the rest of the hierarchy did not exist. In fact, there was an infinitely greater number of hierarchs in prison or in exile than were free.[1] Even the surviving hierarchy

[1]For biographical information on these, see especially Wasillij Alexeev, *Russian Orthodox Bishops in the Soviet Union, 1941-1953,* William C. Fletcher, *Nikolai,* and *Patriarkh Sergii i ego dukhovnoe nasledstvo* [Patriarch Sergii and his spiritual legacy].

was cut off from its flock and from any significant dialogue with religious leaders and thinkers outside the Soviet Union.

The decade of the thirties was especially harsh for the Church. Despite its efforts to accommodate itself to the regime through repeated proclamations of loyalty and cooperation, the Church continued to be in an unfavorable position and subject to continuous though modified administrative persecution. It was a "lost decade" for all practical purposes. The three five-year plans and collectivization taxed the resources of the nation and restrained to an unendurable point those of the Church and its flock.[2] The Church was further charged with complicity in the various alleged crimes committed by Soviet citizens at the time: sabotage, espionage, contacts with foreign enemies of the state, failure to perform socially useful labor, and many others.

Antireligious propaganda was gradually becoming an art. It was quite crude in the 1920s and the leader of the Union of the Militant Godless, E. Iaroslavskii, complained to that effect. In the thirties they were attempting to acquire intellectual and scholarly respectability. They even employed the services of Soviet writers and scholars to do research and write not simply refutations of Christianity but subtle and entertaining works on the limitations of religious myths and abuses of organized churches. They also imported systematically and had translated works of American writers who touched on this theme.[3] And whereas "religion is very long-lived," as was generally recognized by both its enemies and champions, this "storming of Heaven," as some call it, had done an impressive job by

[2]Fletcher, *A Study in Survival*, pp. 44-57; 70-83. John S. Curtiss, *The Russian Church and the Soviet State*, chapters 10 through 14, is a careful and thorough analysis of Church-state developments during the thirties. See especially pp. 217-27. Also see Johannes Chrysostomus, *Kirchengeschichte Russlands der neusten Zeit*, II, pp. 247-57; 270-77.

[3]For example, the Soviet poet Dem'ian Bednyi wrote many poems and a book entitled *Fables* which satirized priests, monks, and saints. Among books containing religious satire translated from the English was *Elmer Gantry* by Sinclair Lewis. On the whole, however, antireligious propaganda experienced limited success in this field. As Michael Bourdeaux puts it, it is "boring and totally without inspiration. The movement lacks great writers, and Russia's best thinkers have never shown any inclination to become embroiled in it." *Opium of the People: The Christian Religion in the USSR*, p. 125.

1939. The emergence of a society which gave the appearance of being not only secular but indeed indifferent and even hostile to religion was the result not only of a fast industrialization drive and its consequences but also of systematic propaganda. The architects of the latter felt that another twenty years of uninterrupted activity might finish the job. Such conclusions are, of course, debatable, but reports at the time and since confirm the grim reality within which Orthodoxy, institutionally and as a community of believers, struggled. When Dr. Paul B. Anderson, probably the closest Western observer of the Orthodox scene in the Soviet Union, was visiting there in the mid-thirties, he reported that a service he attended could claim "a mere handful of people," and when he asked the local priest about the future of religion in Russia, without hesitation the answer came, "There is no future for religion in Russia." The priest himself had to beg from his parishioners in order to survive.[4]

We will never know if the Soviets would have managed to extinguish religion by maintaining this "state of siege" and assault from within of the Church. For the outbreak of World War II was to provide the much-needed breathing spell and maneuverability for the survival of the Church.[5]

The war gave the Church a chance to prove its loyalty to the Soviet regime. Until now a series of proclamations or confessions by the leaders of the Church pledged loyalty and collaboration. Now the Church had the opportunity to demonstrate its usefulness in practical terms. It was a return to a traditional policy traced back to pre-Soviet times when in periods of crisis the Church rose to the occasion and rallied the faithful to a defense of the fatherland. Historical examples of this sort abound, the most readily recalled being the struggle against the Tartars and the Poles.

The Church's potential usefulness during World War II must have been appreciated by Stalin long before the German attack on Russia on 21 June 1941. As a matter of fact, the

[4]Paul Anderson, *Russia's Religious Future*, p. 21.
[5]Alexeev, *Russian Orthodox Bishops,* p. 83, makes the strongest statement on this interpretation but other scholars share this opinion as well.

Church's activities during the two years of the Soviet Pact (August 1939-June 1941) convinced Stalin of the explosiveness of the religious question. Still, it was Hitler's attack that forced both Church and State into a situation of collaborative coexistence from which they would emerge with a sense of "interdependence" and thus form a "Strange Alliance." It is an almost unbelievable story.

The partition of Poland between Germany and the Soviet Union in 1939 gave Stalin important areas of the western Ukraine and Belorussia, and before long his political domination extended to the Baltic states as well. The Soviet Union thus acquired about four million citizens with an active church consisting of approximatey twelve hundred parishes, a theological seminary in Kremenets, and four bishops. This acquisition, among other things, doubled the number of ruling bishops in the Patriarchate, increased the number of open churches by 40 percent. and again raised the problem of the Communist authorities' attitude and relationship toward clerical training institutions.

Usually the border areas of the USSR were communized with special care and almost all churches were closed. When a part of former Poland became a Soviet border area, the Soviet authorities were forced to reconsider their policies. Obviously, to begin religious persecution on a large scale immediately was too risky. They had to consider the proximity of the area to the German forces now occupying the other part of divided Poland which by then had been designated the Government-General. Just before the beginning of World War II, the Polish government had discriminated against the Orthodox Church, trying to polonize it at the same time. In particular, hundreds of churches were taken from it, usually on the excuse that in 1875 the tsarist government had transferred into Orthodoxy a large number of so-called Uniates.[6] Thus, the Poles considered the reunion of the Uniates with the Orthodox Church an act of force, and therefore they decided to restore justice after a

[6]The term refers to former Orthodox who had joined the Uniate Church beginning with the sixteenth century. The Uniate Church preserved the Orthodox rite, but was subservient to the Pope of Rome.

lapse of more than half a century. As a result of the measures taken by the Polish government (which, incidentally, brought forth protests from both Roman Catholic and Uniate clergy), of 393 Orthodox churches which had formerly been in Kholm-shchina in 1914, for example, only 227 remained in 1938, and 176 more churches were closed in 1939. Thus, at the beginning of the war, only fifty-three churches remained. Besides this, 130 church buildings, ten houses of prayer, and two monasteries were destroyed.[7] Naturally, these measures generated dissatisfaction among the Orthodox minority of Poland, and created grounds for Communist propaganda and sympathy for union with the USSR. Under such conditions, it would have been especially undesirable for the Soviet government in 1939 to begin closing the Orthodox churches which had not been closed by the Polish government. They preferred instead a more cautious policy: the subordination of former Polish parishes and bishops to the Moscow Patriarchate, which, as already pointed out, was for all practical purposes controlled by the Soviet government. In other words, this was the first opportunity for the state to make practical use of the Church in its effort to extend its influence in these territories. And since the objective was to organize the Orthodox churches in Poland on a pro-Soviet basis, Stalin realized that the destruction of what remained of the Patriarchal administration would be an unwise act.[8] In fact, two of the four remaining leading Russian hierarchs were to find themselves on the newly occupied territory with the expressed purpose of reorganizing the Orthodox Churches there. One of them was Archbishop Sergii Voskresenskii of Dmitrov, the best friend of the Patriarchal *Locum Tenens*, who in 1939 served as the Director of Patriarchal Affairs. He was immediately dispatched from Moscow to the newly annexed area of Poland and from there to Riga as the Patriarchal Exarch there. The other one was Archbishop Nikolai Iarushevich, head of the Novgorod and Pskov eparchies.

[7] Friedrich Heyer, *Die orthodoxe Kirche in der Ukraine von 1917 bis 1945*, p. 153.

[8] Stalin for some strange reason seemed to like *Locum Tenens* Sergii and often protected him from the unrestrained attacks of the Militant Godless.

who in 1940 was sent to the western Ukraine and Belorussia to replace Archbishop Sergii who at that time was transferred to the occupied Baltic republics. Here Nikolai began his meteoric rise in Church politics.[9] Thus, it is significant that the Moscow Patriarchate which could hardly spare its ecclesiastical leaders (four of them for 3000 parishes) would send two of them to occupied territory at the outbreak of the war. Poland alone already had four Orthodox bishops for its 1200 parishes.[10]

Even though extended persecution of the Church in the new territories did not begin immediately on 29 October 1939, the property of the churches had been nationalized, the clergy had

[9]Although little is known of Nikolai's activity at this time, consult Fletcher's *Nikolai*. According to the short official biography of Nikolai, however, it seems that his talents were already recognized. "Exactly he, and no one else, could successfully carry on the work of uniting the churches in the complex political conditions of the time. Bishop Nikolai, in rank Archbishop of Volyn and Lutsk, reunited the western Ukrainian and Belorussian eparchies with the Orthodox Russian Church. In March 1941, Archbishop Nikolai was raised to the rank of Metropolitan. Lutsk became his residence." V. Nikonov, "Vysokopreosviashchennyi Nikolai, Mitropolit Krutitskii i Kolomenskii" [Most Holy Nikolai, Metropolitan of Krutitsy and Koloma], *Zhurnal Moskovskoi patriarkhii* No. 4 (1952); 18.

[10]The number of bishops on former Polish territory would seem to be a simple and clear question, but in fact it turned out to be quite involved. Heyer, *op. cit.*, p. 168, mentions four bishops in the Ukrainian areas of former Poland, but there was no division between the Belorussian and the Ukrainian Autonomous churches. No ruling bishops remained in the Belorussian part of Poland. In a review, "W. Alexeev, *Russian Orthodox Bishops in the Soviet Union, 1941-1953,*" *Vestnik Instituta po izucheniiu S.S.S.R.* [Journal of the Institute for the Study of the U.S.S.R.] No. 4(21), October-December 1956, p. 98, A. Kishkovskii mentions that seven bishops lived on the territory taken by the USSR.: Archbishop Aleksii of Volyn' and Kremenets, Bishop Simon of Ostrog, Bishop Antonii of Kamenets Podol'sk, Bishop Polikarp of Lutsk, Archbishop Feodosii of Vilno and Lida, Archbishop Aleksandr of Poles'e and Pinsk, and Archbishop Panteleimon, former Bishop of Pinsk, who was under house arrest in the Zhirovetskii Monastery.

However, in comparing the number of bishops remaining in the USSR and former Poland, we must consider only bishops free from house arrest. Thus, Archbishop Panteleimon can be eliminated from the count. In addition, there is information that Archbishop Feodosii of Vilno turned out to be on Lithuanian territory, insofar as Vilno was given over to Lithuania already on 10 October 1939 before the arrival of the representative of the Moscow Patriarchate. Thus, the difference between Dr. Heyer's count and that of Kishkovskii boils down to one bishop, which in reality changes the situation little. What is important is that the Moscow Patriarchate sent a bishop to former Poland and later also to the Baltic states. It sent two of its four bishops to areas where there was a sufficient number of their own bishops. The situation in the Baltic states will be discussed later.

been assessed taxes as high as those in the USSR, and the seminary in Kremenets had been closed. According to Heyer's figures, up to 22 June 1941, in the territory of former Poland, fifty-three priests had been arrested, of whom only ten had been freed, thirty-seven had disappeared, and six had died or had been shot. The number of monks in the Pochaevsk Abbey was reduced from 300 to eighty. Religious training was discontinued in the schools, and the Union of the Militant Godless became active. Nevertheless, four new bishops were consecrated for the newly annexed territories, emphasizing again the differences between the situation in these areas and in the USSR itself. There is no information concerning any similar consecrations in the Soviet Union proper for this period. One can, therefore, safely assume that the new consecrations were connected with the replacement of former Polish bishops by an episcopate more subservient to the Moscow Patriarchate. This approximately coincided with the reorganization of the Polish eparchies followed by Archbishop Aleksandr's abandoning the staff of his own will, and the arrest of Archbishop Aleksii.[11] The Soviet ecclesiastical presence also manifested itself in occupied territory in two monks who were sent to the Pochaevsk Abbey: Archimandrite Pankratii as Vicar of the Abbey and Nektarii as its chief housekeeper.

The situation in the Baltic states during this same period is more complicated. Thanks to the memorandum of Exarch Sergii Voskresenskii of the Moscow Patriarchate referred to earlier in this study, we are able to reconstruct both the factual record and policy implications. Until the Revolution of 1917, there were no independent Orthodox churches in Estonia, Latvia, and Lithuania. With the creation of the three independent Baltic republics, as in Poland, there arose the question of the subordination of their Orthodox population to the Russian Church. The nationalistic and anti-communist governments of Latvia and Estonia put pressure on their Orthodox population, and the Orthodox churches of these countries transferred to the leadership of the Ecumenical Patriarch of Constantinople.

[11]Heyer, *op. cit.*, pp. 166-69.

Only the Lithuanian Metropolitan, Elevferii, remained under the jurisdiction of the Moscow Patriarchate. Exarch Sergii notes in his Memorandum that in contrast to the developments in former Polish regions, where by the fall of 1940 there was a complete introduction of Soviet laws pertaining to the Church, Lithuania, Latvia, and Estonia escaped this fate. The German invasion of Russia began before a commission on cults (dealing with religious affairs) had been formed in the Baltic states, and before real religious persecution was undertaken.[12]

The technique of attaching Orthodox churches of Latvia and Estonia to the Moscow Patriarchate and thus ending the schism caused by allegiance of some to Constantinople, nevertheless developed. Communities belonging to the Constantinople groups were urged to attach themselves to the jurisdiction of Metropolitan Elevferii of Lithuania. Since Elevferii never left the jurisdiction of the Moscow Patriarchate, transfer of communities to him meant a transfer to the Moscow Patriarchate. Elevferii died on 1 January 1940 and was replaced by Archbishop Serfgii Voskresenskii, who had received the title of Exarch of the Baltic states. According to the Exarch, this motivated the Metropolitans Aleksandr and Augustin, heads of the Estonian and Latvian Orthodox Churches, to request the Patriarchate in August 1940 to include them in "its canonical jurisdiction" and thus end the "schism."[13]

The Soviets and the Moscow Patriarchate displayed great sensitivity in dealing with the three Baltic republics whose total

[12]For the time being they concentrated on the nationalization of church properties. In general the attitude of the Bolsheviks toward the clergy, with the exception of individual cases, was passive. However, it was to be expected that this passivity would not hold for long. The Germans arrived exactly on time to save the Church from annihilation. See Metropolitan Sergii (Voskresenskii) "Denkschrift betreffend die Lage der orthodoxen Kirche im Ostland," 1941, p. 13.

[13]Exarch Sergii relates: "In Riga and in Revel I came into contact with both Metropolitans and with many priests, informed myself on the mood of the episcopates, and came to the conclusion that removal of the schism actually answers the wishes of the faithful. When I was still in Riga, Metropolitan Elevferii died (1 January 1941), and his chair became vacant. I participated in his funeral in Kovno, returned to Moscow and reported to the Patriarchate on my trip. Only after my report did the Patriarchate accept the solution to remove the schism and bring order . . . to church relationships in Estonia, Latvia, and Lithuania." *Ibid.*, p. 14.

Orthodox population amounted to 450,000—too small a number for the creation of several episcopates. The most logical thing would have been the creation of one episcopate headquartered in Latvia but "This would have insulted the Estonians and Latvians, since they had become accustomed to their own church institutions. Therefore, it was decided to return again to the idea of an exarchate."[14]

Besides representatives of the Soviet government and the Moscow Patriarchate, many Russians (soldiers of the Red Army, clerks, etc.) found themselves in occupied territory as well, and their conduct and relation to the relatively undisturbed church life in the areas that had just been occupied deserve attention. A very trustworthy clergyman who between 1939 and 1941 had been a Protoierei (archpriest) and a dean of a cathedral in one of the former Polish cities taken over by the USSR, in an interview related that up to 1 September 1939, the cathedral of the city served about forty-five hundred parishioners. There was an average of 125-130 baptisms a year. After

[14] As Exarch Sergii explains in detail: "Individual branches of the Exarchate were called, not vicarates, but episcopates, which also was expressed in the *tibulatura* of corresponding vicars and collegial organs which, for them, were advisory organs. This system was introduced by the Patriarchate only in Lithuania, Latvia, and Estonia. An exarchate with three vicar episcopates corresponded with the boundaries of the former full episcopates of Latvia and Estonia . . . Vicar bishops, as a rule, would be designated by the Patriarchate, and could only be removed by it. In addition, the Patriarchate, having deviated from the general rule, also stipulated in exactly which vicar-episcopates the individual vicars would dispatch their duties, so that the right to transfer any vicars from one branch to another without the permission of the Patriarchate was taken away from me. In this way the rights of the Latvian and Estonian bishops should have been satisfied. In the remainder, I have the right to evaluate the competence of individual vicars in accordance with my own judgment. Further, under my jurisdiction is the appointment and dismissal of all remaining clerical authorities of the exarchate. The Patriarchate dissolved the so-called Synod of Latvia and Estonia and episcopal administration in Lithuania. In place of these institutions I had to create the so-called exarchal administrations in the corresponding vicarial episcopates . . . which have only an advisory right in relation to me . . . by creation of three administrations of the exarchate the well-known decentralization of secretarial work was reached, which answered the custom and desires of the Orthodox Estonians and Latvians . . . Business which concerned the entire exarchate as a whole was conducted by the Synod of bishops in accordance with general canonical law. All bishops of the exarchate took part in it. It was under my chairmanship. It had only the advisory right in relation to me, and it was convened by me whenever circumstances demanded it." *Ibid.*, p. 15.

the appearance of Soviet citizens who had been sent from the USSR in the capacity of various types of specialists, the number of baptisms increased noticeably. From September 1939 to January 1940, the number of baptisms increased about 30 percent. In 1940, 400 children were baptized—more than three times the normal number. Even Communists and NKVD officials had their children baptized. The Protoierei tells of an especially interesting baptism when an old woman came to him with a child, asking that it be baptized secretly and not entered in the parish register because both the mother and the father of the child were Communists. The Protoierei answered the old woman that he could not do this, because without parental permission to christen the child he could be arrested and sent to prison. The old woman, with tears in her eyes, began to swear that she had brought the child to be baptized with the consent of the parents. Then the Protoierei agreed to the baptism without entering it in the parish register, but he nevertheless insisted on learning the names of the parents. He was amazed to learn that the father was an officer in the NKVD and head of the local prison! The parents had sent a sizable remuneration for the christening with the old woman. Knowing whose money it was, the Protoierei refused to accept it. The old woman insisted, saying that the parents gave so much money because of the "merciless" taxation from which the priests suffered.

At about the same time the Protoierei united a captain of the Red Army in marriage to a local girl. An entire Soviet division was in the city at this time, with headquarters not far from the cathedral. Many of the officers' wives brought their children to be baptized. Once the Protoierei baptized four children whose ages were seven, five, three, and one, all from one family. There is evidence that sometimes relatives of military personnel brought their children from deep within the Soviet Union especially to be baptized. In one case, the Protoierei baptized a child who had been brought all the way from the city of Voronezh.

The Easter morning service in 1940 and 1941 was not observed at twelve o'clock midnight, as was usual, because of fear of provocation on the part of the Soviet authorities. Instead it was held at 4:30 in the morning. Despite such an inconvenient and unusual time, in both instances the church was overcrowded with both regular parishioners and Red Army officers. When the Protoierei was leaving the church after one of these services, two officers approached him and said that the time change had been counterproductive, "the night-time service is more majestic; in Moscow we had the service at night." However, the caution of the Protoierei and of Soviet officers who observed the Orthodox rites secretly was reasonable.

Once a very religious young Red Army man began to appear in the church. He usually stood in front, in full view of all, and frequently went to confession and to communion. His action resulted in his arrest, which everyone could witness, as he was leaving the church. This episode indirectly reflected on the success of the antireligious propaganda in the city. At the time of the soldier's public arrest, an antireligious lecturer named Nikol'skii came to the city. In his lecture, which took place in the local theater, Nikol'skii intimated that only in the USSR was there real freedom of conscience. A din ensured and shouts of "that's not true" were heard. After the lecture Nikol'skii asked for questions. One of the parishioners of the church had the courage to stand up and ask about the soldier's arrest. Nikol'skii could not find an answer, and instead of continuing the intended series of lectures, he left the city.

The increase in the number of baptisms in formerly Polish territory and in the Baltic countries after the Soviet occupation forces and administration appeared was an introduction to the great religious revival which took place in the second half of 1941 on Soviet territory occupied by the Germans and which is sometimes referred to as the second baptism of Russia.

The Patriarchate had tasted the first fruits resulting from the changes brought about by the opening phase of World War II. True, these fruits were gathered in collaboration with the same state which had persecuted it since 1917, and some of this persecution spilled into the newly occupied territories, but on balance the Church could be thankful. It was its first opportunity to awaken from a long administrative slumber and to develop its skills in dealing not only with other religious groups but with the state itself. And regardless of its compromise with the state, the Church could not help but rejoice in the growing number of its parishes and the new converts who sought formal association with it.

In the Soviet Union proper, the fruits of war were at the beginning precarious but gradually they were increasing and were, by comparison with previous years, plentiful. This, as already suggested, in no way implies a reversal of Soviet policy toward religion. Instead, it illustrates a calculated retreat by the regime and a realistic recognition that the Church, though crippled, was a force to be reckoned with, especially in moments of national crisis. The Generalissimo had to humor the Patriarchate. And he did so by a series of minor concessions in the beginning which to the hard pressed church must have looked substantial. What some have described as the "New Religious Policy"[15] began by discouraging State agencies in their attempts to liquidate religion. They were told that the closing of churches, which had been carried out with so much atheistic enthusiasm in the thirties, should be discontinued and atheists should not offend believers. Christian children especially should not be made the object of scorn and ridicule at school. Probably the most amazing development was the instruction given to the Union of the Militant Godless to oppose the efforts of other agencies to suppress religion. Similarly, the trials against "religionists" accused of all sorts of imaginable crimes including espionage should terminate. And on the whole antireligious propaganda assumed a subdued tone.

Other little signs of the regime's mellowing attitude toward the Church included permission to artists to restore icons, availability of oil for lamps to burn before icons, making it illegal for enthusiastic antireligionists to remove icons and other objects of Orthodox worship from homes, and withdrawing objections to the practice of naming children after saints, which had been a common custom before the Revolution. After all, did not many revolutionists have Christian names? Open demonstrations of one's faith were allowed too. Easter celebration

---

[15]Nicholas S. Timasheff, *Religion in Soviet Russia, 1917-1942*, pp. 112-39, especially pp. 122-25.

could again become a festive occasion, and Sunday was declared the day of rest despite the efforts of the Militant Godless to have Monday or Wednesday designated as such.[16]

Still, one must remember, the Church did not have anything resembling a religious press, and the Bible had not been reprinted since 1927. Religious instruction was still restricted to the family, especially the parents. But at the same time, the leading antireligious periodicals suspended their publication (allegedly because of paper shortage), antireligious museums began closing down, and taxes on church buildings were considerably reduced.[17]

Remarkable as the above concessions were, the regime still held back on matters of greater significance, such as the election of a Patriarch to fill up the vacant throne and the freedom to set up a working Church administration. The Church would have to display greater feats of indispensable service to the regime before it could hope for such concessions.

Hitler's attack on the Soviet Union on 22 June 1941 provided just that. With remarkable speed the German push eastward overran the territories in Eastern Europe previously occupied by the Soviet Union and began to make gains on Soviet territory. Moving simultaneously toward Leningrad, Moscow, and Stalingrad, despite some problems of synchronization, the German advance had many observers convinced that only a miracle could save Stalin's Russia. The miracle occurred. Leningrad endured its 900-day siege, Moscow did not evacuate, and Stalingrad in its stubborn stand proved that Hitler could be defeated. What concerns us here is the contribution of the Orthodox Church to this miracle of Soviet Russia's salvation and the consequences to the Church's status and its relation to the regime. And whereas this study deals chiefly with the revival on Soviet territory occupied by the Germans, an introductory discussion of Church-state relations in the Soviet Union during the war will put the revival and its impact in proper perspective.

The Patriarchal *Locum Tenens* Sergii reacted spontaneously

[16]*Ibid.*; Curtiss, *op. cit.*, pp. 274-76.
[17]Matthew Spinka, *The Church in Soviet Russia*, pp. 81-82.

on the day of the German attack. And while Stalin was still puzzled by the whole phenomenon and offered no comments for ten days, Sergii proceeded to dispel Stalin's fear that the Orthodox Church would welcome the invaders as liberators. Promptly and patriotically Sergii urged his flock through a special message to defend the sacred frontiers of the fatherland:

> Our Orthodox Church has always shared the destiny of her people. She has suffered with them in their trials and has been consoled by their successes. And today, no less surely, she will not forsake her people. She gives her heavenly blessing to this sacrifice now to be made by the whole nation. . . . May God grant us victory.[18]

The following Sunday, 26 June 1941, in the Cathedral of the Epiphany Sergii held a solemn *Te Deum* attended by twelve thousand worshippers and declared in firm words that it was the duty of all to defend their country. He had special warnings for opportunists and for those who might consider defecting to the Germans, considering such an act shameful and sinful. Furthermore, he left no doubt in the minds of the listeners that the Church would suffer in the hands of the Germans: "Those who imagine that the enemy will not attack our sanctuaries or our beliefs are greatly mistaken." In rather prophetic words for the Church Sergii likened the war unto a storm which would bring not only "misfortune" but "alleviation" as well.[19]

This show of support was repeated by Metropolitan Aleksii of Leningrad and Nikolai of Kiev. The proclamations were warm, patriotic, but carefully worded, and Stalin must have listened carefully, especially concerning defection of any sort. As a matter of fact, six months later the *Locum Tenens* directed an appeal to those who had fallen under German rule and pleaded with them not to betray the fatherland. This was a matter of grave concern to Sergii because many ecclesiastics did

[18]This was the first of twenty-three proclamations which Sergii issued to the people urging them to support the government in the struggle against the Germans. They were all published in Moscow in 1943 under the title *Russkaia pravoslavnaia tserkov i velikaia otechestvennaia voina* [The Russian Orthodox Church and the Great Patriotic War]; p. 5.

[19]*Ibid.*, pp. 83-94; see also Nikita Struve, *Christians in Contemporary Russia*, pp. 60-61.

take advantage of the German advance and indeed did defect, among them Archbishop Polikarp of the Ukraine who proclaimed an Autocephalous Church in the Ukraine and Exarch Sergii Voskresenskii of the Baltic region who refused to evacuate. Even the celebrated Nikolai, who represented the Patriarchate in Lutsk when the Germans advanced, hesitated to evacuate immediately but did finally come to Leningrad after he was promoted to Metropolitan of Kiev and Galicia and Exarch of the Whole Ukraine.[20] Some scholars maintain that this problem of defection by leading hierarchs was probably the main reason why the Soviets insisted on evacuating the Patriarchal *Locum Tenens* to Ulianovsk in October when the Germans were approaching Moscow. Sergii, seventy-four years of age, was ill, with a temperature of 104°, and certainly could have done without a trip which lasted five days and nights and for which no preparations had been made.[21]

Sergii continued to summon the faithful to the defense of the fatherland from Ulianovsk, where he stayed until the fall of 1943, as he did from Moscow. But significantly enough, for the first year of the war the Church's proclamations made no references to either Stalin or the government. But then Sergii began to hail Stalin as "the divinely appointed leader of the nation who would save the fatherland and cleanse the Ukraine of the German filth."[22]

The Church also supported the war effort materially. The Moscow churches and clergy alone donated 1,500,000 rubles to the Red Army Fund (23 February 1942) and the Patriarchate contributed 100,000 rubles toward a fund-raising project for a tank column named after the medieval hero Dmitrii Donskoi. Sergii's major hierarchs stood behind him in this effort. This was especially true of Metropolitan Aleksii of Lenin-

[20]Curtiss, *op. cit.,* p. 291 mentions the rest of the defecting bishops.
[21]*Patriarkh Sergii i ego dukhovnoe nasledstvo,* pp. 238-39; Fletcher, *A Study in Survival,* pp. 106-7. See also the same author's biography of *Nikolai,* pp. 33-53. For a more colorful account of the evacuation of the higher clergy, including A. Vvedenskii, from Moscow, as well as the experiences of the *Locum Tenens* at Ulianovsk, the "Russian Vatican," see A. Krasnov, "Zakat obnovlenchestva" [Setting of restoration], *Grani* No. 87-88, pp. 246-49; 251 ff.
[22]Curtiss, *op. cit.,* p. 291.

grad, who during the siege of Leningrad shared the misfortunes and deprivations of the Leningraders. Yet by 15 January 1943 the Orthodox laity of Leningrad had contributed more than three million rubles to the Fund for the Defense of the Country. Metropolitan Aleksii was deservedly awarded the Defense of Leningrad medal. The third member of the ecclesiastical triumvirate was indefatigable in his speeches to rally the faithful in support of the fatherland. The total contributions of the church to the war effort amounted to the unbelievable sum of 150 million rubles.[23]

Unquestionably, the Church's contribution to the war effort was spontaneous and genuine. They simply wanted to defend the fatherland. There is no doubt, however, that the Church leaders hoped for significant concessions from the regime in return for their services. This may even explain why the Patriarchate brought out a most amazing publication in July 1942 entitled *Pravda o religii v. Rossii* (The truth about religion in Russia) under the supervision mainly of Metropolitan Nikolai (Iarushevich) who was managing the affairs of the Patriarchate from Moscow while the *Locum Tenens* Sergii was in Ulianovsk.

The book was a massive, handsome volume of 457 pages with many illustrations of hierarchs and clergy, churches throughout Russia, and pictures depicting war sufferings. The contents of the volume, many of them contributed by the ecclestiastical triumvirate, Sergii, Aleksii, and Nikolai, make it a landmark in the history of the Church during the Soviet period as well as a collector's item. Among the contents was Sergii's proclamation on the day of the German attack. The objective of this publication was to dispel any illusions about the "so-called Fascist crusade for the liberation of the Church," as well as provide an answer to those who dwelt too much on the question of religious persecution in the Soviet Union. Sergii, who set the tone of the volume in his prefatory remarks, did not

[23]*Zhurnal Moskovskoi Patriarkhii* [Journal of the Moscow Patriarchate], 1944, No. 10, quoted in Spinka, *The Church in Soviet Russia,* p. 85; Struve, *op. cit.,* pp. 61-62. For more detail and analysis of figures see Alexeev, *Russian Orthodox Bishops,* pp. 54-55.

outrightly deny the persecutions but he redefined them, calling them "simply a return to the days of the apostles," thus improving the image of the government on the subject. Other statements sought to convey the impression that the state persecuted only counterrevolutionary clergymen, and as such they were punished for their political activities against the regime and not for their convictions since the Constitution guaranteed religious freedom. But the bulk of the volume aimed at Fascist Germany and its atrocities, especially its own version of Christian persecution. The cross and the swastika were simply incompatible.[24]

The Truth About Religion in Russia contains the most patriotic proclamations and the most fervent expression of loyalty to the regime by the Church. Surely the Church hierarchy must have calculated the impact that this could have not only on the Russian people but on Stalin himself.

What then was the outcome, for the Church, of this close collaboration?

Probably the Church's first gain was that the Soviet regime was forced to recognize it *de facto* and to deal with its leaders as useful Soviet citizens. Two examples illustrate this factual recognition. The first was Stalin's permission granted to the *Locum Tenens* Sergii for the Church to open a special account in the State Bank to be used for a tank column against the Germans.[25] As has been pointed out, the decree of 8 April 1929 did not recognize religious bodies as juridical persons. As such they could not "(a) organize any sort of central booking-offices for the collection of voluntary offerings of believers; (b) establsh any compulsory collections; . . . (d) conclude any sort of agreement or bargain."[26] Thus, subtly, Sergii managed to remove a real limitation for the Church and at the same time begin a dialogue with Stalin.

[24]*Pravda o religii v Rossii* [The truth about religion in Russia], pp. 7-14; 21-28; 449-52. Struve, *op. cit.,* p. 64 suggests that the volume's condemnation of German atrocities was "an indirect hit at Communism also" and that the Russian church leaders might have had hopes "of forestalling a similar attitude on behalf of the Soviet authorities when they succeeded in regaining the occupied territories."
[25]*Russkaia pravoslavnaia tserkov' i Velikaia Otechestvennaia Voina.* p. 92.
[26]Quoted in Fletcher, *Study in Survival,* p. 111.

The second example is the case of the energetic Metropolitan Nikolai who, because of his services during the war, became the first Orthodox dignitary since the famine of 1921-22 to be entrusted with an official position with the Soviet Government. On 2 November 1942, Nikolai was made a member of the Extraordinary State Commission of Enquiry into the crimes committed in Soviet territory by the "German-fascist invaders and collaborators." Walter Kolarz describes this event as "the first formal attempt to create a Popular Front organ in the Soviet Union" consisting of the Communist Party, the Church, and various prominent non-party figures, writers, and artists. This also explains why the Church was allowed to participate in the All-Slav Committee and conferences held during the war.[27]

But the main gain for the Church occurred on 4 September 1943. On that memorable day, the ecclesiastical triumvirate—Sergii, Aleksii, and Nikolai—met Stalin and Molotov and from their private conversations an agreement, the celebrated "Concordat," ensued. Basic to this Concordat was Stalin's acquiescence for the Church to elect a Patriarch to fill the Patriarchal throne vacant since 1925.

The "second restoration" of the Patriarchate could have been as spectacular an event as the one of 1917. Instead it was a rather quiet affair with only a handful of bishops attending the Sobor held on 8 September 1943. The aged Sergii, who had been *Locum Tenens* since 1927, was unanimously declared (not elected) Patriarch and enthroned on 12 September.[28] There have been questions about the canonicity of Sergii's assuming the office of the Patriarch, and this affected a number of believers both inside Russia and in the diaspora who re-

[27]Walter Kolarz, *Religion in the Soviet Union*, p. 51. Wassilij Alexeev, *The Foreign Policy of the Moscow Patriarchate, 1939-1953*, I, discusses in great detail the Patriarchate's participation in the Slavic Committee and Conferences held during the war.

[28]Nineteen bishops attended the Sobor. It is common knowledge that even in 1943 there were more hierarchs in prisons and concentration camps than outside and allegedly the NKVD sought to produce some of these imprisoned hierarchs in the hope of making the Sobor more impressive, but without much success.

fused to offer him their allegiance. Be that as it may, the Russian Orthodox Church again had a Patriarch and a new Church Administration could be set up recognized by the regime.

In a way this recognition restored the Orthodox Church to a privileged position among religious groups in the Soviet Union. This was underscored by the setting up of a special Council for the Affairs of the Russian Orthodox Church headed by G. G. Karpov. The Council, facetiously nicknamed *Narkombog* (God's Own People Commissar) or *Narkomopium* (People's Commissar for Opium), sought to normalize relations between the Church and the state. There is no denying the policing role of the Council, but at the same time it served as an intermediary between the Patriarchate and the government.[29]

And the Church could now have a religious press. The first evidence of this was the resumption of the publication of the *Journal of the Moscow Patriarchate*. The Patriarchate also was granted permission to open a theological institute and a theological course in Moscow on 14 June 1944, where both priests and higher clergy could be trained. And, in an unexpected concession, religious instruction to children became easier, even though still not allowed in public schools. But, contrary to the law of 8 April 1929, which limited religious instruction to members of the family, priests could now take over and could use their homes to provide such training to a large number of children.[30]

Finally, as an apparent "juridical person" the Church could now own property. This worked out greatly to the advantage of the Orthodox Church which was able to take over many church buildings which until 1943 belonged to the Living Church. The latter was also sacrificed (along with the Union of the Militant Godless) as a result of the Concordat. Sergii thus had the satisfaction of seeing the schism come to an end. Most of the leaders of the Living Church returned to the mother

[29]Kolarz, *op. cit.*, pp. 53-54; Alexander Werth, *The Year of Stalingrad* (London, 1946), p. 248.
[30]Curtiss, *op. cit.*, p. 294.

church. Alexander Vvedenskii remained a "shepherd without a flock."³¹

Those witnessing the Russian religious scene in 1939, including the newly-elected Patriarch Sergii, would have found it difficult to believe the miracle of 1943. Sergii had travelled a long, hard road, but he did not live to enjoy the fruits of his labors and of the war. He passed away on 15 May 1944, and was succeeded by Metropolitan Aleksii of Leningrad, a person who had already enjoyed great visibility with the Church and the state and who would continue Sergii's policy with great skill and determination in the postwar years.

While the Church was gathering the fruits of war, important events were unfolding on occupied territory, relating directly both to the general war effort and to the future of Orthodoxy in Russia. Before directing our attention to those developments, we must acquaint ourselves with the basic philosophy and pronouncements of German policy with regard to the Orthodox Church on Soviet territory under German occupation. It is safe to assume that such policy stemmed partly from Hitler's attitude toward Christianity which he considered ". . . the heaviest blow that ever struck humanity. . . . Bolshevism is Christianity's illegitimate child. Both are inventions of the Jew."³² But the policy stemmed chiefly from the complexity of the situation on occupied territory. Even before his Russian advance, Hitler recognized that Christianity "can't be broken so simply. It must rot and die off like a gangrened limb."³³

As far as Russia and the Russian Orthodox Church were concerned, Hitler was not interested in saving the Slavic *Untermenschen* from the "gangrene of Christianity." Nonetheless, he took well into account the tremendous unifying role which the Orthodox Church had played in Russian history, and this consideration prompted his religious policy as expressed on 11 April 1942:

> We must avoid having one solitary church to satisfy the religious needs of large districts, and each village must be made into an

³¹*Patriakh Sergii i ego dukhovnoe nasledstvo*, p. 228.
³²Adolf Hitler, *Hitler's Table Talk, 1941-1944*, p. 7.
³³*Ibid.*

THE FRUITS OF WAR 61

independent sect, worshipping God in its own fashion. If some villages as a result, wish to practice black magic, after the fashion of Negroes or Indians, we should do nothing to hinder them. In short, our policy in the wide Russian spaces should be to encourage any and every form of dissension and schism.[34]

This general point of view was also gradually being developed in detail by the party philosopher Rosenberg who was designated as the head of the Ministry of Occupied Territories of the USSR. Rosenberg's appointment took place four weeks after the beginning of the war. Seized territories were to come under his jurisdiction only after the German army administration had moved farther east. He received the first territory on 20 August 1941, and two Reichskommissariats which came under Rosenberg's Eastern Ministry—Ostland and the Ukraine—were created on 1 September 1941.[35]

When on 16 April 1946, at the Nuremberg Trials, the defendant Rosenberg was asked what his attitude was toward the churches coming within the range of the Eastern Ministry, he answered:

> After the entry of German troops in the eastern territories, the *Wehrmacht* of its own accord granted the practice of religious worship; and when I was made Minister for the East, I legally sanctioned this practice by issuing a special "Church Tolerance" edict at the end of December, 1941.[36]

An important figure in the Eastern Ministry writes in a secret note of 25 October 1942:

> After talks which lasted a month, it was nevertheless decided not to proclaim religious freedom with pomp but to release the announcement quietly.[37]

Evidently discussions between Rosenberg, Hitler, and Bormann on 8 May 1942 served to determine the main line of official policy of the occupation authorities in regard to the

[34]*Ibid.*, p. 424.
[35]Alexander Dallin, *German Rule in Russia, 1941-1945*, p. 85.
[36]"Questioning of Rosenberg, Tuesday, April 16, 1946" in *TMWC*, XI (Nuremberg, 1947), p. 462. Dallin, *op. cit.*, p. 479, especially note No. 2, maintains that such an edict was not published.
[37]Otto Bräutigam, "Secret Note by Bräutigam," 25 October 1942.

Russian Orthodox Church. One must keep in mind that it was at this time that there was a powerful religious resurgence in occupied territories, frequently in the first days and sometimes even hours after the advance of the German forces. This phenomenon forced the Minister of Occupied Territories to consider seriously the religious question in Russia and to attempt to lead this spontaneous movement into a framework acceptable to National Socialism.

Hitler's attitude toward the encouragement in Russia of "every form of dissension and schism," expressed by the Führer on 11 April 1942, received its finished form during Rosenberg's visit to Hitler's headquarters on 8 May 1942. Rosenberg's own account of this conversation with Hitler and Bormann, has been preserved. It is both interesting and instructive.

When, in the course of the conversation, the question of religion in occupied territories was raised, Rosenberg informed Hitler that large religious groups had already formed there, and that one should keep them under close surveillance, and, in fact, direct them. The proposed order and the directives, he added, had as their goal the insurance of occupation authorities against any surprises in this respect.

Bormann noted that Rosenberg's name was too well known in Germany and his announcement of religious freedom in occupied territories would surely bring a flood of letters from the German clergy. He apparently implied here that these letters would demand religious freedom within the Reich itself.

Consequently, Hitler decided that the order should not originate with Rosenberg, but that it should be issued by Reichskommissars subordinate to him (in Ostland, i.e., the Baltic and Belorussia, and in the Ukraine).[38]

At first glance, and judging from this document, it would

[38] Alfred Rosenberg, "Vermerk über eine Unterredung mit dem Führer in Führer-Hauptquartier am 8.5.42," Document 1520-PS, *TMWC*, XXVII (Nuremberg, 1948), p. 286. In his discussion of this problem, Harvey Fireside, *Icon and Swastika*, p. 116, comes to the conclusion that the German authorities had forbidden the publication of information about the religious revival in Russia and in particular about the tolerant attitude toward it by the occupation authorities.

seem that Hitler repudiated his ideas expressed on 11 April 1942, but this was far from being so. Obviously the religious revival in occupied territories and mainly the protraction of the war temporarily forced the leaders of Nazi Germany to attempt to exploit the general tendency toward a revival of religion which had been violated by the Communists. That this was only a temporary measure can be seen from further reading of the document where Rosenberg notes that:

> The Führer emphasized that after the war he will undertake corresponding measures against the church. He thinks that with his authority he will be able to accomplish that which will be difficult for someone else to do at a later date.[39]

However, even at that time Rosenberg suggested to the Reichskomissariats that the necessary measures should be taken to limit the influence of the religious organizations which were being created anew. Five days after the above-cited conversation, on 13 May 1942, Rosenberg addressed the Reichskommissariats of the Ostland and the Ukraine with a letter, the gist of which is as follows: Religious groups are categorically forbidden to preoccupy themselves with politics; religious groups must be divided along national and territorial lines and the national principle must be especially strictly adhered to in the selection of leaders of religious groups (Territorially, religious unions should not go beyond the borders of Generalbezirks, i.e., in application to the Orthodox Church, approximately within the bounds of one eparchy.): religious societies should not interfere in the activity of the occupation powers; special precautions are recommended to be taken toward the Russian Orthodox Church as an institution expressing Russian national ideology.[40]

The question of the above-stated principles as applied in practice in concrete instances will be dealt with later in describing the position of the Russian Orthodox Church in individual

[39]*Ibid.*, pp. 286-87.
[40]Alfred Rosenberg, "Der Reichsminister für die besetzten Ostbebiete an a) den Herrn Reichskommissar für das Ostland Gauleiter Hinrich Lohse, Riga; b) den Herrn Reichskommissar für die Ukraine Gauleiter Erich Koch, Rowno," Document Occ E (Ch) -4, YIVO.

regions of occupation. However, it is wise to keep in mind the problem of the impossibility of completely applying them to both the Orthodox Church and the Roman Catholic Church. Rosenberg himself, in stating his wishes, understood this and even considered the possibility of selecting a Ukrainian Patriarch, which would have meant the organizational unification of many eparchies or many "Bezirks."[41] However, the antagonistic attitude toward both the Orthodox and Roman Catholic Churches can be clearly distinguished in both documents. In practice, Rosenberg succeeded only in restraining Catholic missionaries from entering the occupied territories, which indirectly contributed to the strengthening of his main enemy, the Russian Orthodox Church. As regards the latter, this Nazi theoretician's ideas remained mainly wishful thinking as far as the Baltic and Belorussia were concerned and were only partially realized in the Ukraine. Not only the religiousness of the Russian people, but also the Russian Orthodox Church as an organization, turned out to be much more powerful and vital than the occupation powers had surmised.

In executing Rosenberg's secret letter, both Reichskommissariats issued two almost identical orders dealing with the registration of religious societies without mention of religious tolerance. Religious organizations were to register in "Bezirks," and were forbidden to engage in politics.[42]

Thus, at the beginning of World War II, both sides fighting on the eastern front intended, in the event of victory, to try and destroy the Russian Orthodox Church. But during the course of the war they both realized the significance of the Church for the Russian people and modified their policy considerably. In fact, both Hitler and Stalin were forced to try and make the Church their ally in the propaganda struggle against each other. This situation made it possible for the Orthodox Church to strengthen and stabilize its position.

[41]Rosenberg mentioned the possibility of selecting a Ukrainian Patriarch in his conversation with Hitler of 8 May 1942, cited above in part.
[42]Alfred Meyer, *Das Recht der besetzten Ostgebiete: Estland, Lettland, Litauen, Weissruthenien und Ukraine*, p. 117.

As mentioned earlier, the basic objective of this study is to discuss the religious revival and the reestablishment of the Russian Orthodox Church in regions of Russia occupied by the Germans. This revival cannot be described without touching upon local church policies of the Reichskommissariats and the rivalries between the various church groupings in the occupied territories. In the preceding section we outlined briefly the basic principles of German policy toward religion in general and the Orthodox Church in particular and it is clear that they provided for a differentiation in approach to religious organizations in the various areas of Russia. Therefore, in describing the course of the religious revival in these various regions, it will be necessary to refer frequently to the peculiarities of German policy. As far as the rivalries and struggles of the various church jurisdictions are concerned, they certainly provided an element of intrigue that often interfered with the revival, and for this reason they form part of this study as well. In fact, at times these rivalries assumed such complicated and substantial proportions that they could easily become the subject of a separate and lengthy study. For our purposes, the description of these struggles will be limited to outlining these inter-church disputes, and explaining the circumstances in which believers and clergy found themselves in areas occupied by the German army.

Although unable to limit church organizations to the boundaries of "Bezirks," the Germans were able to divide the Orthodox Church on occupied territory into four parts according to territorial characteristics alone:

1. The northern occupied areas, approximately from the station of Porokhovo in the north to the northern border of Belorussia in the south, with their natural center in the city of Pskov were under the direction of Exarch Sergii (Voskresenskii). United under his administration were also the Russian congregations of Lithuania, Latvia, and Estonia. For purposes of this study we shall call this region the Baltic Sector.

2. Farther to the south, the territory of Belorussia, the Belorussian Orthodox Church was organized. It extended its jurisdiction to the Smolensk and Briansk oblasts, but did not include Poles'e which had gone to the Ukraine.

3. Still farther south, in the Ukraine, two churches were organized which struggled for influence on one and the same territory: the Autonomous Church which sought to preserve ties with the Russian Orthodox Church and the Autocephalous (Separatist) Church which had broken away from it.

4. Finally, the so-called Transnistria, i.e., Bessarabia and other regions of southern Russia, including Odessa, were transferred to Rumania. Consequently Russian Orthodox congregations were transferred to the Rumanian Orthodox Church.

In addition to these clear divisions, it is important to keep in mind the frontal and rear regions of German occupied territory. In the rear the process of religious revival and the organization of the Church had a clearly developed form; this was less so in the areas near the front.[43]

[43]Dallin, *op. cit.*, p. 92 and also Chapter 5.

Russian hierarchs during the Second World War

Metropolitan Nikolai of Kiev celebrating liturgy in the Church of the Transfiguration in Moscow, March 17, 1942.

Metropolitan Sergii, later Patriarch of Moscow and All Russia. Died 2/15, 1944.

Metropolitan Aleksii of Leningrad, later Patriarch of Moscow and All Russia (1945-1971).

Metropolitan Nikolai of Kiev and Galicia and Exarch of the Ukraine, later Metropolitan of Leningrad and in charge of the Foreign Affairs Department of the Moscow Patriarchate until his death in 1960.

THREE

The Baltic Sector

The Orthodox religious experience in the Baltic region, including the region of Pskov, during World War II is intimately linked with the life and activity of the colorful and enigmatic Exarch Sergii (Voskresenskii). As stated in the preceding chapter, when the Baltic states were seized by the Germans, the Exarch of the Moscow Patriarchate, instead of fleeing with the Soviet troops and administration, evaded compulsory evacuation by hiding in the cellar of the cathedral in Riga. Metropolitan Aleksandr, the former head of the Estonian Orthodox Church, and Metropolitan Avgustin, the head of the Latvian Orthodox Church, both of whom had been subordinated to the Moscow Exarch during the Soviet occupation, seized the opportunity during the German invasion to break away, taking with them congregations consisting mainly of Estonians and Latvians. Only parishes dominated by Russian parishioners remained with the Exarch. Thus the Russian Orthodox Church in the Baltic region began to divide according to territorial and national lines, approximating the church policy outlined by Rosenberg. Special German plans for the Baltic states led to a significant softening of German policy toward the Church in this region, however. As early as 18 June 1942 (two days before the publication of the official *Verordnung* of 20 June 1942) there was a meeting at the office of Ministerialdirektor Leibbrandt on the question of *Religionserlass* (Toleration Edict).[1] Leibbrandt also announced that a complete division of the devout along strictly national lines was not being undertaken, since the main political aims made this unnecessary. The Orthodox Churches in Estonia, Latvia, and Lithuania, being Russian cultural institutions, were alien to the concept of *Lebensraum* and therefore were to be removed to the Reichskommissariat Moscow (which was never organized since the Germans never occupied that capital). Leibbrandt thus even considered it desirable for the Orthodox churches in the three Baltic republics to remain Russian without becoming Estonian, Latvian, or Lithuanian. On the other hand, in Belorussia he reversed his policy; here he proposed to protect both the Orthodox and the Catholic churches from Russian and Polish influences, respectively. Here Leibbrandt makes a direct reference to the Bishop of Vilno, apparently to Exarch Sergii, in terms of his possibly undesirable Russian influence on the Belorussian Orthodox Church. The Orthodox Church in the Baltic was, however, allowed to carry on its work in the area of operations of the Army North, i.e., in the Pskov region.[2]

Jurisdictionally the Exarchate of the Russian Orthodox Church in the Baltic area maintained a geographic unity. That is to say, thanks to the policy of the occupation powers Russian Orthodox congregations in Estonia, Latvia, and Lithuania were not divided into three separate and autonomous parts. In the event of victory the Germans had planned to resettle all Russians from the area into the Reichskommissariat Moscow. (It is interesting to

[1] Alexander Dallin, *German Rule in Russia*, p. 87. Leibbrandt was the head of the main department I: Political Eastern Ministry.

[2] Der Reichskommissar für das Ostland. Abt. II Politik RRTr./Ko.-Tgb. No. 2239/428. Riga, 19 June 1942. Document Occ E (Ch)-4, YIVO, pp. 1-2. The same statements are found in an earlier document: Moscow, Sachbearbeiter, Abt. II Politik 2230/42. Riga, 20 May 1942. Document Occ E (Ch)-7-8E, YIVO. See also the interesting but rather propagandistic account by Z. Balevits, *Pravoslavnaia tserkov' v Latvii pod sen'iu svastiki, 1941-1944* [The Orthodox Church in Latvia under the shadow of the swastika, 1941-1944].

note that the Germans identified Orthodox Latvians and Estonians as Russians.) Exarch Sergii was also permitted to be in charge of the Pskov region, a purely Russian territory, although he was forbidden to become involved in affairs of the reestablished Belorussian Church.

The personality of Exarch Sergii (in secular life Dimitrii Voskresenskii), who had already had a great deal of experience in negotiating with the NKVD as a representative of the Church, had a significant influence on the position and attitudes taken by the Germans in the Baltic regions toward the Russian Orthodox Church. This training stood him in good stead in his negotiations with the German occupation authorities. The fact that an ecclesiastical mission (which will be discussed in more detail later) was sent from the Baltic to Pskov, a territory which had been completely devastated by the Soviets, was largely the Exarch's doing and attests to his diplomatic skills.

An understanding of the Exarch's personality is pertinent to this study. In 1939 he was, at about forty years of age, the youngest of the four surviving Orthodox bishops in the USSR. He had matured under the Communist regime and was the only Soviet bishop of the new type to find himself in occupied territory as the head of several hundred congregations and several bishops who had received their ranks under democratic regimes. His complex personality would justify a biography which would illuminate significantly not only his success in dealing with the Germans but also the relationship of Russian Orthodox hierarchs with the Soviet regime.[3]

Exarch Sergii was born in Moscow in 1898 or 1899 into the family of a Moscow archpriest. Until the Communist revolution he studied at a seminary but did not graduate. Despite his lack of formal education, Sergii impressed acquaintances as being a well-read person. At the beginning of the Revolution, he was a novice under the last rector of the Petrograd Theological Academy, Bishop Fedor, who at that time lived in the Dani-

[3] For more details on the personality of Exarch Sergii see Wassilij Alexeev, *Russian Orthodox Bishops in the Soviet Union,* pp. 85-97, and the same author's "Le drame de l'exarque Serge Voskresenskij et l'élection du patriarche de Moscou," *Irénikon* 30 (2e trimestre, 1957), pp. 189-202.

lov Monastery in Moscow. He became a monk in 1923, assuming the name Sergii. The Danilov Monastery was known for its stringent discipline, which proved a hardship for the young monk who, although truly religious and brought up strictly, nevertheless enjoyed worldly pleasures, especially drinking and the company of young people. On several occasions he was disciplined by his superiors, but they recognized his brilliance and many skills and more often than not he was let off with a mere reprimand.

In 1926, the young Sergii, evidently against the wishes of Bishop Fedor, began to work in the chancellery of the Moscow Patriarchate. This was a critical period for the Russian Orthodox Church. Patriarch Tikhon had just died. The Patriarch's substitute, Metropolitan Petr of Krutitsy, refused to make the concessions demanded by the authorities and was exiled. The Deputy of the *Locum Tenens,* Metropolitan Sergii (Stragorodskii), the future Patriarch, was an intelligent, erudite man but of weak character. In 1927 there appeared the Declaration which divided the Russian Orthodox Church into those who accepted the compromise with the atheistic government and those who went underground (into the catacombs). Under these conditions, and because of his compromise with the Soviet authorities, monk Sergii's church career began to change rapidly. In 1929 he was elevated to Bishop of Dimitrov with the Moscow eparchy also under his control. Thus by the time he reached the age of thirty Bishop Sergii had become one of the governing figures of the Patriarchate. And it is important to keep in mind that the year of Sergii's appointment to the episcopacy coincided with the last days of what came to be known as ecclesiastical NEP. The First Five-Year Plan and the beginning of collectivization were all part of the "renewal of the Revolution" which involved a new and systematic attack on the Orthodox Church. Although most of the surviving Russian hierarchs chose to go into the catacombs, many chose the path of compromise. Among the latter was Sergii. His ambitions and abilities were now directed toward defending whatever still seemed salvagable, employing methods and techniques suitable to the new political realities. The Deputy *Locum Tenens* was already advanced in years, a venerable hierarch, sufficiently compliant but too accustomed to good form to be able to cope with this task, and young Bishop Sergii therefore assumed this dangerous and unpleasant role. The deep attachment of the older Sergii for the younger, noted by all who knew them, may have stemmed from the old hierarch's gratitude toward his colleague for undertaking this unpleasant role.

The course which Bishop Sergii had adopted was hardly calculated to inspire the trust of those around him. Indeed, many believed him to be simply an agent placed in the Moscow Patriarchate by the NKVD, though many of the specific accusations levied against him have yet to be documented. On the other hand, the fact that his father was arrested in 1935 does not clear the son of any suspected connection with the NKVD. It is common knowledge that devotion and service to the regime in the Soviet Union in the thirties was no guarantee against the arrest and execution of one's parents. Frequently parents would be held as hostages when their children were assigned special missions, a fate soon to be experienced by Sergii's mother. We cannot know what impressions are left in the minds of people who are subjected to such contradictory treatment—recognition and intimidation. For it did amount to a special sort of recognition by the state when, after the occupation of the Baltic states and the eastern regions of Poland by the Soviet Union, Sergii of Dimitrov, now an Archbishop, was the first high-ranking clergyman from the USSR to visit those areas. For most Soviet citizens such a trip would have been impossible, since only persons sent on official missions by various Soviet agencies could obtain the necessary travel documents, and then only after a special check by the NKVD. Thus these circumstances only strengthened the belief of many Moscovites that Sergii was an especially trusted representative of the Soviet authorities in the Moscow Patriarchate.

According to Heyer, the Moscow emissary made an unfavorable impression in the regions which had formerly belonged to Poland—an impression not of a bishop but of a "typical" Moscow merchant.[4] In the Baltic states, however, he made a much

[4] Friedrich Heyer, *Die orthodoxe Kirche in der Ukraine*, p. 166.

more positive impression[5] This was probably due at least partly to the general attitude of the Orthodox in the Baltic states. As we have already noted, the Orthodox congregations in all three Baltic countries consisted of both Russians and non-Russians. According to Exarch Sergii's own data, in 1939 there were approximately the same number (100,000) of Orthodox Russians and Orthodox Estonians in Estonia, about 150,000 Orthodox Russians and 50,000 Orthodox Latvians in Latvia, while in Lithuania the total number of Orthodox was about 40,000, almost exclusively Russian.[6]

After Estonia and Latvia achieved independence in 1918, the government of both republics exerted pressure on the Orthodox believers to break their canonical ties with the Russian Orthodox Church. In both cases bishops of non-Russian origin were brought forward to head the churches—the Estonian, Metropolitan Aleksandr, in Estonia and the Lithuanian, Metropolitan Avgustin, in Latvia. The separation of the Estonian Church from the Russian Orthodox Church took place in 1924, three years before Metropolitan Sergii's (Stragorodskii) 1927 Declaration which brought about the schism in the Tikhon Church in the USSR. The separation of the Latvian Church from the Russian Orthodox Church occurred in 1936, a considerable time after the Declaration, and was connected with the mysterious and tragic death of Archbishop Ioann of Latvia (1934), himself a Latvian by nationality, and a proponent of the continuation of canonical ties with the Russian Orthodox Church. The Lithuanian Church, headed by Metropolitan Elevferii, who had been exiled from Poland for resistance to a similar separation of the Polish Orthodox Church from that of Russia, remained loyal to the Moscow Patriarchate to the end. Thus it was possible for many Russians living in the Baltic states and remaining anti-Communist to oppose canonical separation of their churches if not from the Moscow Patriarchate, at any rate from the Russian Orthodox Church in general.

[5]Based on extensive interviews with individuals who watched Sergii's activities closely during his stay in the Baltic area.
[6]Metropolitan Sergii (Voskresenskii)," Denkschrift betreffend die Lage der orthodoxen Kirche in Ostland," pp. 9-10.

Moreover, this separation signified estonianization and latvianization, which in turn suggested the strengthening of Protestant influence on Orthodoxy. The Moscow Exarch's arrival therefore elicited a mixed response—on the one hand apprehension since they knew that Sergii was there with the knowledge and permission of the Communist authorities, on the other hand joy at seeing their own Russian bishop. Metropolitans Avgustin of Latvia and Aleksandr of Estonia probably did not share any of this joy. Nevertheless they quickly expressed repentance for their separation from the Russian Orthodox Church, recognized the Moscow Patriarchate, and visited Moscow. Metropolitan Elevferii of Lithuania, a true supporter of the Moscow Patriarchate, who at first had been designated its Exarch in the three Baltic states, died on 1 January 1941. His place was occupied by Archbishop Sergii, who was then elevated to Metropolitan.

Soon after Exarch Sergii's arrival in Riga he was invited to tea by an intelligent, educated, and observant archpriest. The Exarch accepted with alacrity. "One felt," in the words of the archpriest, "a great thirst in him to see everything and know everything." The archpriest also invited several friends, young priests, to make the acquaintance of the bishop from the Soviet Union. Sergii was relaxed, quite down-to-earth, but at the same time maintained his dignity. His mental alertness and tact impressed everyone. But, as the archpriest observed, one sensed that to the grandeur of a prince of the church was added the power of an individual who had a "solid position to back him up." Having greeted the guests, the Exarch noticed a radio, turned it on, and immediately displayed a good knowledge of music and Soviet musicians. Later, after becoming better acquainted with the archpriest, the Exarch remarked that in his youth he had considered singing as a career, but had given up the idea partly because his extreme nervousness would not permit him to conduct himself well on the stage. This nervousness did not, however, prevent him from serving brilliantly in church and showing an enviable deportment in difficult situations. However, he undoubtedly was neurasthenic and, although he possessed a gift for words, sometimes delivered poor sermons. From the very first, the archpriest could not help noticing that the

Exarch did not belong to the category of ascetic bishops; rather one felt that he was the embodiment of religious opulence.

Having succeeded to the direction of the Exarchate, Metropolitan Sergii began by tightening up purely regulatory matters and restoring the line of the Moscow Patriarchate. For example, he forbade the abridgement of services and the burial of Protestants with Orthodox rites (which had previously been happening in the Baltic countries) and so on. He himself performed his religious offices with beauty and fervor although, according to the archpriest, at the altar he permitted himself some liberties which did not conform with the general tone assumed by him.

The Exarch chose Father Vasilii Evstaf'ev, a modest and very devout prior of the Riga cathedral, as his confessor. The Exarch displayed a strong interest in émigré religious literature. The archpriest once found him reading a book by a well-known émigré theologian. "Why does your professor make such a hash of Athanasius the Great?" asked the Exarch in a dissatisfied tone. It was obvious that the Exarch had studied the Holy Fathers thoroughly and was not indifferent to the émigré interpretation of their works.

In an attempt to void suspicion the Exarch refrained from interrogating the clergy under him, but there were members of his entourage who took upon themselves this unpleasant mission. Gradually, from such questioning, the activities of various representatives of the clergy in the pre-Soviet period came to light. At times it was felt that the Exarch himself did not trust those who surrounded him.

The NKVD, having given permission for Metropolitan Sergii's stay in the Baltic, nevertheless surrounded him with men *they* could trust. Furthermore, one must remember that his mother, whom he loved dearly, remained in Moscow as a hostage.

Then came 22 June 1941, and the Exarch was faced with the question of evacuation There is every indication that the authorities had received the order to evacuate him. Instead, he hid in the basement of the Riga cathedral. It was rumored that his secretary was shot. One wonders why the personal friend of the *Locum Tenens,* Metropolitan Sergii (Stragorodskii), an advocate of the compromise of the Church with the antireligious rulers, acted so decisively and definitely in spite of the danger that threatened his mother (on whose fate there is no information whatsoever).

In June 1941 many Soviet citizens thought that the Communist regime would not live through a serious war. The rapid advance of the German forces and the panic in the Soviet rear could only reinforce such assurance. For one accustomed to all sorts of compromise and nimble tactics it was natural to try to find a compromise with the new power, the German *Wehrmacht,* which was in the process of supplanting the Communists. The fact that the *Locum Tenens* Sergii had come forth with patriotic exhortations on the first day of the war meant nothing. On the contrary, to Exarch Sergii it was more important to try to effect a compromise with the Germans. All his later actions point to the fact that his behavior was not dictated solely by efforts to save his own life. To hide in the cathedral was twice as dangerous as to be evacuated. If the Soviets had discovered him, he would have been shot. Immediately upon taking Riga, the Germans in their turn arrested the Exarch and for four days it seemed that he would not be given his freedom.

An important question, however, is whether the *Locum Tenens* knew in advance that his Exarch would avoid evacuation. There can be no documented answer to this question. In the second message, released on the Feast of the Holy Virgin, 14 October 1941, by the *Locum Tenens,* entitled "To the Orthodox and God-Loving Christians of Moscow," there is the following revealing statement:

> There are rumors going about which I would not want to believe that among our Orthodox pastors there are those who are prepared to go into the service of the enemies of our Homeland and our Church.

The *Locum Tenens* threatened such pastors with church trial, but he did not name them.[7]

By 30 June Riga had fallen and by 14 October the Anti-Communist position of the Moscow Exarch in the Baltic was

[7] Archbishop Dimitrii (Gradusov), "Poslaniia Sviateishego Patriarkha Sergiia" [Message of His Holiness Patriarch Sergii] in *Patriarkh Sergii i ego dukhovnoe nasledstvo* [Patriarch Sergii and his spiritual heritage], p. 81.

common knowledge. The *Locum Tenens* may have been alluding to the Exarch when in his second message he threatened only "traitors to the Socialist Motherland" with a church court trial but in reality took no concrete measures to that effect. Such moderation on the part of the *Locum Tenens* could be fully explained; aside from the close personal relationship of the two religious leaders, the Soviets would gain little for such open attacks on the Exarch. Furthermore, the conditions under which this second message was published were quite unique. Protoierei Smirnov testifies that:

> In regard to the Patriarchate, the Executive Committee of the Moscow City Council on October 7, 1941, in decision N. 3/331, proposed that it temporarily leave Moscow, especially since a great number of the faithful, orally and in writing, begged Metropolitan Sergii to take care of himself and other workers of the Patriarchate.[8]

The evacuees left on 14 October, that is, on the very day on which the exhortation was issued. In addition, writes Smirnov, "The second night of our journey, October 15-16, we spent in alarm because of the aggravated illness of the Metropolitan. His temperature rose to 40° (104° Fahrenheit). At times he was delirious."[9]

In all probability the *Locum Tenens* was forced to evacuate so as to prevent a repetition of the Riga episode of Exarch Sergii who avoided evacuation. On the day after the evacuation of the *Locum Tenens,* the notorious panic of 15-16 October occurred in the capital; the majority of the Communist upper echelons fled the city and the population littered streets, yards, and sewers with portraits and works of the leaders of world communism. Thus this was a time when any extra heightening of the volatile situation, any possible increase in the panic, was dangerous for the Soviet government. Publicizing the political defection of the Exarch of the Moscow Patriarchate in the Baltic would have been most undesirable at this time. On the other hand, the vague criticism of some traitors emphasized the loyalty of the *Locum*

[8] A. P. Smirnov, Protoierei, "Moskva v Ulianovske" [Moscow in Ulianovsk] in *ibid.,* p. 237.
[9] *Ibid.,* pp. 238-39.

Tenens. It is highly probable that the second message was not written by the *Locum Tenens* since, as we know, on that day he was already on board a train bound for Ulianovsk, and on the next night he became ill.

In September 1942, however, the Moscow Patriarchate undertook more decisive steps in regard to the Exarch. The latter's anti-Communist stand had by then become so obvious that it could no longer be ignored. The *Locum Tenens* of the patriarchal throne published a "position paper" (*Opredelenie*) which denounced the actions of Exarch Sergii and his vicar. The document was signed by twelve "representatives from the episcopates" (apparently by all bishops who at that time happened to be available to the Moscow Patriarchate).

Yet even the term "position paper" suggests a cautious, soft policy of the Patriarchate. The document itself also suggests caution. It begins by proclaiming that, "until all of the details of this question are clarified, the decision shall be postponed." An "explanation" is demanded from the Exarch and if this substantiates the facts which reached the Moscow Patriarchate, the accused will be required

> . . . immediately to undertake all measures to correct the allowed deviation from the line of behavior which is mandatory for bishops who are members of the jurisdiction of the Moscow Patriarchate, with a report of the following measures sent to the Patriarchate—in order that the future church court, during the final decision on the case, would have in front of it not only the misdeed, but also its rectification.[10]

Apparently the technical aspects of delivering the "explanation" from German-occupied Latvia to the Patriarchate did not particularly interest the latter. The document gives the impression of a formal execution of an obligation. Furthermore, the term "treasonous activity" was not used in the judicial position paper. It was employed, however, in a message on the same subject directed by the *Locum Tenens* to all Orthodox and "es-

[10] "Opredelnie No. 27 ot 22 sentiabria 1942 goda . . . po delu metropolita Sergiia Voskresenskogo s drugimi" [Position paper No. 27, of 22 September 1942 . . . in regard to Metropolitan Sergii Voskresenskii and others]. See this document in *Russkaia pravoslavnaia tserkov' i velikaia otechestvennaia voina* [Russian Orthodox Church and the Great Patriotic War], pp. 35-36.

pecially those living in Latvia and Estonia," a propagandist document, published under the same date as the position paper. But even this document seems moderate by Soviet propaganda standards.[11]

The above still does not give a direct answer to the important question: Was there any sort of advance agreement between *Locum Tenens* Sergii, who had been evacuated to Ulianovsk, and Exarch Sergii, who had remained in Riga and who came out directly against Soviet rule? The conditions of the evacuation of the *Locum Tenens*, however, would permit one to feel that Exarch Sergii, counting on the victory of the Germans, thought not only of himself but also of the Moscow Patriarchate, which his deed might have saved from much unpleasantness if the military and political events of 1941-1945 had taken another path. It is quite probable that such consideration led the Exarch to risk staying in Riga.

In a memorandum given by Exarch Sergii to the German occupation authorities on 12 November 1941 he touches on the question of the loyalty of the Moscow Patriarchate to the Soviet Government and points out that, in the first place, inwardly the Moscow Patriarchate had never been reconciled to the Godless authorities. Secondly, the Patriarchate submitted to the Soviet power only *de facto* and only after the latter's victory in the Civil War. For this reason the obligation to cooperate with the Soviet power ceased with the beginning of the present war; therefore, states Exarch Sergii, he has the moral right to publish his message which calls on the people of Russia to revolt.[12]

No answer can be found to the question of how the Exarch appraised the possible consequences of his anti-Soviet stand for the *Locum Tenens* of the Moscow Patriarchate, to whom the Exarch continued to be loyal. But Metropolitan Sergii Stragorodskii, in the name of the Moscow Patriarchate, had, in 1927, proclaimed his loyalty to the Soviet authorities, "not because of fear but because of conscience." Evidently in this part of his memorandum the Exarch assumed that the Germans were ignor-

[11]*Ibid.*, see "Poslanie ot 22 sentiabria," pp. 32-34.
[12]Metropolitan Sergii (Voskresenskii), "Denkschrift betreffend die Lage der Orthodoxen Kirche im Ostland," p. 8.

ant of the exact conditions under which the Moscow Patriarchate reconciled itself to the state authorities. After the arrival of the Germans in Riga, Exarch Sergii immediately commenced a very bold and dangerous policy in relation to occupation authorities by taking a sharply anti-Communist position and at the very same time maintaining his loyalty to the Moscow Patriarchate. From a purely personal standpoint, such a course was unusually difficult, for his mother was being held as a hostage in Moscow.

As mentioned before, after the Germans occupied Riga, they arrested the Exarch but he was soon released. Apparently he was imprisoned for four days. Upon his release, the Exarch called the clergy of Riga to the Trinity-Sergiev Monastery and announced: "Fathers and brothers, the political situation has changed. What next?" Those assembled remained silent. "I must inform you," continued the Exarch, "that I was and remain obedient to Metropolitan Sergii Stragorodskii. And you?" All were again silent. The Exarch was also silent. Finally, one of the priests rose and added his voice to that of the Exarch, and the meeting closed. The *Locum Tenens* of the Patriarchate continued to be mentioned in the prayers of the Baltic churches.

There is evidence that the Exarch was able to convince the Germans that for them it would be politically more advantageous to accept his subordination to the Moscow Patriarchate than to push for the return of the Estonian and Latvian Orthodox churches to the jurisdiction of the Patriarch of Constantinople, whose Exarch was in London at the time. At the beginning of the war it could be that the Germans feared the influence of London in the Baltic countries more than the influence of Moscow. This information agrees with the following quotation from Metropolitan Sergii's *Denkschrift* which he wrote for the occupation powers:

> The Orthodox Episcopates of Finland, Estonia, and Latvia transferred into the jurisdiction of the Constantinople Patriarch which occurred with the aid of his Exarch, Archbishop Germanos who resides in London; the latter maintains some unclear relations with the British government.[13]

[13]*Ibid.*, p. 9.

Not long after his release, Exarch Sergii obtained permission from the Germans to send a mission of clergymen to those areas near the city of Pskov, recently taken by the German armies, where all religious life had been destroyed. The sending of this mission to Pskov can probably be considered the most laudable deed performed by the Exarch during the course of his short life.[14]

The Exarch gave specific instructions to the departing missionaries to mention the name of Metropolitan Aleksii of Leningrad (the future Patriarch of Moscow) in church services, since the Pskov area was in Aleksii's diocese. However, after Soviet leaflets signed by Metropolitan Aleksii appeared in the German held territories, the local German authorities forbade the mention of his name in services.

Despite the fact that he did not know the German language, the Exarch was able to impress the Germans. He held receptions for the representatives of the occupation forces in his home and gained their affection by serving good food, obtaining in return a good carriage and horses in addition to an automobile. Once the archpriest who supplied the basic material for this description of the Exarch was present during a typical conversation between the Exarch and one of the Eparchy staff, an old émigré who was Metropolitan Sergii's intermediary between himself and the German authorities because of his knoweldge of the German language.

"The Germans will never agree to this," said the émigré in regard to one of the missions entrusted to him by the Exarch.

"We've fooled cleverer ones than the Germans!" quietly answered the Exarch. "We've gotten around the NKVD and it's not difficult to fool these sausage-eaters."

And the business proposed by the Exarch was accepted by the Germans.

The strong expressions of speech used by the Exarch were sometimes felt to be not quite suitable for an Orthodox Metro-

[14]The activity of this mission forms one of the main chapters of the history of the Russian religious renaissance of 1941-1943 and will be touched upon at the end of this chapter. According to Balevits, *Pravoslavnaia tserkov' v Latvii*, p. 28, the mission left for Pskov on 18 August 1941.

politan. Later, when his position was uncertain, when he had begun to have forebodings of the tragic end of his career, at a dinner which included many of the foreign clergy, the Exarch irritably exclaimed: "If you fathers had lived through my Moscow life, and if they had roasted you on the skillet as they did me, you would have also jumped!"

The roasting on the skillet did not end for the Exarch even after the Germans arrived. He was able to fool the "sausage-eaters" regarding his loyalty to the Moscow Patriarchate only for a time. Nonetheless, the Exarch's tactics with the occupation authorities were always aggressive.

The Exarch concluded his *Denkschrift* to the German occupation authorities by stating that under the present conditions, in his opinion, in order to understand the situation of the Orthodox Church in Reichskommissariat Ostland one should keep in mind certain principles:

1. The principle of unity. It would be strange to organize four separate churches in Ostland: the Belorussian, Lithuanian, Latvian, and Estonian churches. The last three were already united under the Exarchate; however, he recommended that the Belorussian church be included in the Exarchate also. For this purpose he asked to be given the opportunity to meet the Belorussian bishops; this meeting could lead to the formation of an Autonomous Church of Ostland.

2. The principle of canon law. In order to avoid a schism, the Ostland Church should remain within the framework of the Russian Patriarchate; the future separation of the Ostland Church should be accomplished with the consent of the Russian Church at a later date.

3. The principle of autonomy. Until the final normalization of relations with the Mother Church (an autocephalous church, be it Russian or some other) or until the Ostland Church acquired an autocephalous status (which is less desirable), the Ostland Church would have to remain autonomous.

4. The principle of church validity. One should not reinstate democratic church charters (apparently in Estonia and Latvia). The whole Ostland Church should have a uniform charter: (a) elective officers should be replaced by appointive;

(b) all collective organs should remain only in a consultative capacity; (c) the priest should have the deciding voice in the parish, a vicar bishop in the vicariate, the ruling bishop in the bishopric, and the Exarch in the Ostland Church; and (d) the whole Church administration should be centralized.

Exarch Sergii proposed to create an episcopate with a number of vicariates in Belorussia. The churches of Latvia and Estonia would be united into one episcopate with three vicariates, divided according to either territorial or national principles. In the latter case in Lithuania there would be only a Russian vicariate; in Latvia there would be a Russian and a Latvian vicariate; while in Estonia there would be a Russian and an Estonian vicariate. All of the bishops should be appointed by the Exarch and their appointment ratified by the German authorities.[15]

The argument of the *Denkschrift* was designed according to the totalitarian views of the occupation forces, but the idea of a centralized church power in the hands of the clergy was peculiar also to the position of the Moscow patriarchate at that time. Of special interest is the obvious wish of the Exarch to subordinate to himself the neighboring Belorussian Orthodox Church; this was partly based on the fact that Belorussia was under Reichskommissariat Ostland together with Latvia, Lithuania and Estonia, whose center was in Riga. Later events showed that this effort of the Exarch bore no fruit.

There is no information to indicate that the Belorussian Orthodox Church was in official touch with the Exarch, nor was there any hint of unification. In this respect the policy of division of the Orthodox Church, formulated by Rosenberg, was in no degree corrected by actual events. The Exarch, whose efforts were to the contrary, was able to deceive the Germans only when they had some personal reason for agreeing to such deceit, as in the case of the Orthodox Latvians and Estonians and their Metropolitan who had revolted against the power of the Moscow Exarch after the Soviet troops had left and the Germans had appeared.

From this point of view one must consider the question of the possible creation of an Autocephalous Orthodox Church

[15]*Ibid.*, pp. 20-21.

which would unite Latvia, Lithuania, Estonia, and Belorussia. It was completely impossible, canonically, to set up such autocephality during the war. As will be noted below, it was on this point that the German divisive policy in Belorussia foundered. If the occupation powers could not understand the impossibility of establishing a legal autocephality under wartime conditions, then, as far as the Exarch was concerned, who in all other instances upheld the preservation of a single Russian Orthodox Church, such a proposal on the part of the Exarch must be considered as an effort simply to deceive the German forces.

In the same memorandum, along with religious-canonical arguments the Exarch also used political reasoning. In Latvia and Estonia, writes the Exarch, there still remains a small but active group of Orthodox politicians. Formerly they played a leading role as members of the so-called synods. Now, they aspire to restore their former importance. Both Metropolitans, Avgustin of Riga and Aleksandr of Revel, belong to this group. However, the other bishops, priests, and the faithful in an overwhelming majority are far from agreement with this group and, in fact, are often hostile to it. On the other hand, this group is supported by certain non-Orthodox Estonian and Latvian circles. Such a sad state of affairs is turning the Orthodox Church in Estonia and Latvia into a plaything of separatist-nationalists. These non-Orthodox nationalists are attempting to: (1) renew the schism, (2) reinstate old Church statutes (which existed in the free Latvia and Estonia), and (3) bring about a renaissance of an anti-Russian policy in the Orthodox Church.[16]

It is strange that an experienced politician like the Exarch Sergii would appeal to the occupation authorities with an argument such as point three—a misunderstanding characteristic of the majority of Russians who were not able to imagine the scope of the German plans in regard to the division and subjugation of Russia in the event of victory.

The Germans met the Exarch's last demand with the idea of transplanting the Orthodox people into a Reichskommissariat of Moscow after victory. The "sympathy" of the occupation authorities for the Russian Orthodox in the Baltic became evident

[16]*Ibid.*, pp. 17-18.

in 1942, when dioceses were being registered. At the end of 1942 a complete break occurred between Exarch Sergii and the former head of the Estonian Church, Metropolitan Aleksandr, in the course of which the second Orthodox Bishop in Estonia, Pavel Narvskii, remained in the Exarch's jurisdiction.

Among the German documents in the Jewish archives in New York there is the following *Erlass* explaining how to conduct registration of Orthodox people in Estonia. In summary, the occupation authorities give each Orthodox the freedom to register in a parish under the jurisdiction of Exarch Sergii or the Estonian Metropolitan Aleksandr. Furthermore, the *Erlass* specifies that despite the occupation authorities' nonintervention in the registration practices, their aim is to register the majority of Orthodox in the Russian and not the Estonian parishes.[17]

On November 19 the same Section I Politik again wrote to the Generalkommissar in Revel, referring to the *Erlass* summarized above. The main theme of the document is as follows: since Metropolitan Aleksandr (of Estonia) failed to come to an agreement with the Exarch at the conference of 2 November 1942, and was forbidden to conduct services by the latter, the German policy was restated. Firstly, the policy of freedom to join one of the two factions by the faithful, parishes, or priests remained in effect. And secondly, since Exarch Sergii was recognized as the Exarch of Latvia and Estonia, Metropolitan Aleksandr was recognized only as the Metropolitan of Revel and not as Metropolitan of Estonia.[18]

Thus, Metropolitan Aleksandr of Estonia openly broke with the Moscow Exarch after the arrival of the Germans. Some of the parishes, Estonian in national composition, followed his example. The Russian parishes in Estonia remained true to the Russian Orthodox Church. There was no open rupture in Latvia, but Metropolitan Avgustin, who theoretically remained in the

[17] See II Politik Tgb.-Nr. 2456/42g Bu./Ko. 26 Oktober 1942. An den Herrn Generalkommissar in Revel. Betrifft: Anmeldung der Religionsgesellschaften. Bezug: Mein Erlass vom 25. August 1942. Document Occ E (Ch)-1, YIVO.

[18] See II Politik Nr. 2456/42 . . . 19. November 1942. An den Herrn Generalkommissar in Revel. Betrifft: Anmeldung der Religionsgesellschaften. Bezug: Mein Erlass vom 26.10.1942. Document Occ E (Ch)-1, YIVO.

structure of the Russian Orthodox Church, personally broke with Exarch Sergii, for he wanted independent administration for the Latvian episcopate. In Lithuania, where the few Orthodox were all Russians, there was no split.[19]

The occupation authorities remained neutral in general but favored the Exarch somewhat. The danger to the energetic head of the Orthodox Church in the Baltic states now came from another source. This crisis of relations between the Orthodox Church and the Germans occurred on 4 September 1943, when Stalin and Molotov received the three remaining Metropolitans in the USSR at the Kremlin, and four days after *Locum Tenens* Sergii, who had returned to Moscow from Ulianovsk, became Patriarch of Moscow. This meant that the Communist government had drawn the correct political conclusions from the spontaneous revival of religious feeling which had erupted on territory taken by the Germans and by taking prompt action had broken Hitler's propaganda initiative on yet another point. It is characteristic that one of the four documents published by the Council of Bishops which had selected the Patriarch was "Condemnation of Betrayers of the Faith and the Fatherland."

> Along with the comforting phenomena of the patriotic activity of the Orthodox clergy and laity, it is that much sadder to see phenomena of the opposite character. Among the clergy and laity there are also those who, having forgotten fear of God, by using the general misfortune, build their own well-being: they meet the Germans as desirable guests, set themselves up in their services, and sometimes even go so far as direct treason, giving up their fellow-neighbors to the Germans, as for example, partisans. . . . Everyone who is guilty of treachery in general church affairs and who has gone over to the side of Fascism, as an enemy of the Holy Cross, may he consider himself excommunicated and (bishop or clergy) deprived of his rank.[20]

[19]Balevits maintains that on 23 February 1942 Reichskommissar Lohse gave instructions according to which Metropolitan Avgustin was to hand over all church affairs to Bishop Aleksandr. In his turn, Exarch Sergii relieved him of his duties on 24 February 1942, and on 15 June 1942 he "placed on him a prohibition"—apparently a prohibition against conducting church services (Balevits, *op. cit.*, p. 25).

[20]"Osuzhdenie izmennikov vere i otechestvu" [Condemnation of betrayers of the faith and fatherland], *Zhurnal Moskovskoi patriarkhii* 1(1943):16.

If he read it, it is certain that the Exarch of the Baltic was not greatly impressed with this "Condemnation." Beginning with the Declaration of 1927, people like him must have stopped taking such documents very seriously. The German command, however, reacted quite differently. The year 1943 was, in general, extremely critical for them. Mention of the partisans who literally swarmed over the rear of the German Army could only increase their nervousness. The Kremlin's open bid for the help of the Moscow Patriarchate and finally the prestige of the Patriarch's title among the population who expressed, as will be seen below, an extremely strong desire to reestablish the Church—all this forced the Germans to take decisive countermeasures.

The Nazis remembered that a Russian Church existed abroad among the émigrés which, beginning with the Declaration of 1927, did not recognize *Locum Tenens* Sergii as the legal head of the Russian Orthodox Church. The Synod of this Church, headed by Metropolitan Anastasii, was located in Belgrade at the beginning of the war. The Church had a number of parishes in Germany, which were headed by Metropolitan Serafim, of German extraction.[21]

Up to September 1943, the attitude of National-Socialist Germany toward the Russian Church abroad was extremely cautious. The authorities did not permit its representatives to set foot on occupied territory and, in general, its activity was limited. A political communiqué drawn up by the SD in February 1942 informs us that the Orthodox Metropolitan Sergii (the Exarch of the Baltic) undertook an action for removal of the Karlovtsy Bishop of Berlin, Seraphim (Lade). It was clear that after the solution of the Bolshevik question (apparently the defeat of the USSR) the Karlovtsy question also had to be solved.[22]

Thus the election of a Patriarch in Moscow forced the Nazis to remember the Russian Church Abroad. From 8 to 13 October 1943 there was a meeting of Orthodox émigré clergy in Vienna.

[21] Here the Russian Church Abroad is understood. U.S. National Archives and Records Service, Reich Chief Security Office, *Ereignismeldungen. UdSSR*, No. 163 (2 February 1942), Roll 234.
[22] *Ibid.*

Three metropolitans, one archbishop, three bishops, six archimandrites, protopresviters, and protoiereis, and the Secretary of the Synod of the Russian Orthodox Church Abroad, attended the meeting. The conference confirmed the old position of the Russian Church Abroad: the nonacceptance of the way of compromise with the atheistic government, a course on which Metropolitan Sergii (Stragorodskii), who had just been chosen Patriarch, had already embarked in 1927.

The first point of the resolution of the conference read:

> The election of Metropolitan Sergii to the Throne of the Patriarch of Moscow and all Russia is an act that is not only uncanonical, not even religious, but rather political, elicited by the interests of the Soviet Communist Party authorities and their leader-dictator Stalin, who were undergoing a difficult crisis during the war, required the help of the Orthodox Church which was hateful to them and which, not long ago, had been obviously persecuted.[23]

Further, it is noted that:

> The election of a Patriarch and convocation of the Synod is necessary to Stalin and his party as a means of political propaganda. The Patriarch is only a toy in his [Stalin's] hands. So long as there was no war, the election of a Patriarch and the organization of a Synod was impossible in Russia. But when the threat of death hung over the communities, then it turned out to be completely possible to do this in the fastest and simplest manner.[24]

Then the council posed a purely canonical argument against the manner in which the Patriarchal elections were conducted. The resolution pointed out that the council which elected Patriarch Sergii was not convened in accordance with a decree issued by the All-Russian Council of 1917-18. The council was not a full one: bishops who were exiled and in the catacomb church were absent. Only bishops who subordinated themselves to the

[23]See Soobshcheniia i rasporiazheniia Vysokopreosviashennieishago Serafima, Mitropolita Berlinskago i Germanskago i Sredne-Evropeiskago Mitropolich'iago Okruga. Mitteilungen und Verfügungen des orthodoxen Metropoliten des Mitteleuropäischen Metropolitankreises und othodoxen Bischofs von Berlin und Deutschland Seraphim; Rundschreiben. Berlin - Chbg., den 27 [Oktober] 1943, p. 5.
[24]Ibid.

Godless government, an insignificant number, purported to express the will of the entire Russian Church. Finally, "they elected as Patriarch a hierarch who has . . . for a long time bowed before the satanic authority." To prove this statement Metropolitan Sergii's 1927 announcement of Church support of the government as well as his 1930 denial of religious persecutions in the USSR (to the foreign press) were cited in the resolution.[25]

The Vienna Conference of the Karlovtsy jurisdiction further elaborated on the absence of a full All-Russian council in the election of the Patriarch in its "Appeal to all Faithful of the Russian Orthodox Church in the Homeland and Dispersed Throughout the Earth." During the war such a council could not possibly take place: nine Russian bishops were in North and South America, eight in the Far East, eleven in Europe, and no less than twenty-four bishops were on German-occupied territories.[26]

It is interesting to note that Archbishop Venedikt from Belorussia took part in the Vienna Conference, thus symbolizing the tie between the Russian Church Abroad with churches organized on territory occupied by the Germans.[27]

The Soviet propaganda maneuver of electing a Patriarch so alarmed the Nazis that they violated their principle of separation of the Orthodox Church into parts, and allowed the Russian Orthodox Church Abroad to express its negative attitude toward the Moscow Patriarchate.

Exarch Sergii was not in Vienna, which corresponded fully not only with the German policy of division, but also with his own personal position in regard to the Russian Church Abroad. However, the question of his attitude toward the transformation of the *Locum Tenens* of the Patriarchal See into the Patriarch of Moscow was immediately set before him.

[25]*Ibid.*

[26]*Ibid.*, p. 7. The reader should bear in mind that the Moscow Council of 8 September 1943 was a purely episcopal council, without the participation of other clergy or laity, and that nineteen bishops were gathered for it. (After the beginning of the war, the official number of bishops was increased. See Alexeev, *Russian Orthodox Bishops*.)

[27]For a characterization of Archbishop Venedikt, see below in the section on the Belorussian Orthodox Church.

In the Jewish Scientific Institute (YIVO) in New York[28] there is a small folder of documents devoted to the Exarch of the Baltic states, Metropolitan Sergii Voskresenskii. The second document of eleven in the folder is a copy of an "SD Ostland" report to the "Politik" section of the German Ministry of Propaganda. Accompanying the report is a note signed by Kurtz of the East Section of the Ministry of Propaganda to Mehne in the Propaganda Section of the same ministry. In the report the SD gives detailed information on the position of Exarch Sergii regarding the Vienna Declaration. On 3 November 1943 the *Deutsche Zeitung in Ostland* published an article under the heading, "Answer to Stalin," devoted to the speeches of all the bishops gathered in Vienna.

It is more than probable that Exarch Sergii was simply interrogated, but it is possible that a representative of the SD acted as interviewer. In either case, the Exarch, quite experienced in similar types of conversations, knew with whom he was dealing and that unsuccessful answers would be a threat to him. The document written by the SD and distributed to all German establishments is of great historical and psychological interest. The impression remains that the personality of the Exarch, this man who was formed psychologically exactly as a result of similar talks with representatives of the NKVD and SD, is very clearly reflected in the detailed and evidently accurate account of the "talk" with him by an unidentified member of the German secret police.

Sergii began with the affirmation, usual for him, that he was in complete agreement with the political part of the Vienna Declaration, but he could not accept its verdict on canonical grounds. Further, quite logically he stated that since he did not have the documents on the Moscow Council, he could not judge it from the canonical point of view, but here he added, not altogether cautiously, that he did not believe that the Patriarchal *Locum Tenens* who had been made Patriarch could perform an uncanonical act. Further, he made a thrust against the émigré bishops, calling them schismatics for their opposition to the Moscow Patriarchate. The break with the Moscow juris-

[28]Under the Code Occ E (Ch)-3.

diction, in his opinion, deprived these bishops of the right to judge Moscow affairs from the canonical point of view. The Exarch's argument was aimed at convincing the Germans of the correctness of his position by attacking Communism concurrently with a silent defense of the Moscow Patriarchate. One cannot deny his resourcefulness and understanding of the psychology of totalitarian propagandists, both German and Communist.

According to this SD report, the Exarch attempted to show the uselessness of the Vienna Conference's canonical stand from the standpoint of German propaganda. Therefore he first outlined what he believed to be German propaganda reasoning: Because the Patriarch, in his political capacity, issued anti-Fascist appeals, the Germans would have liked to "strike at him from the ecclesiastical side and set him up as a scoundrel." In other words, by demonstrating that the *Locum Tenens* was elected Patriarch with the aid of Stalin's destruction of canonical rules, the German propaganda hoped to blacken not only the Patriarch, but also Stalin. Exarch Sergii agreed that if one could prove this it would be to the German advantage, but he expressed doubt that one could achieve that.

Then the Exarch explained the reasons why he did not believe that the German authorities should meddle in canonical law. For one thing, a possible propaganda value of the canonical irregularities would be definitely useless in Germany. In England, because of the Archbishop of York's close ties with foreign churches, the entire canonical question would appear groundless. In Russia they would only laugh at it and thus it would only serve Bolshevik propaganda since the Bolsheviks would present the émigré bishops as completely will-less tools in the hands of German politics. If the eastern patriarchs could be convinced to declare the elections uncanonical, then, certainly, some propaganda value could be derived from this. But the Exarch felt that the patriarchs would recognize them and therefore this propaganda action would be employed to the detriment of the Germans.

The Exarch furthermore pointed out to his interviewer that *it would be ludicrous if the state were to assume the role of an advocate of canonical law,* an unfortunate position that Germany apparently had already taken up under the influence of the Karlovtsy bishops. To underscore this point he hinted that the Vienna conference resolution could have been motivated by an attempt to demonstrate the political reliability of the bishops. In addition, if the German authorities were so concerned with canonical regularity, why did they foster uncanonical movements in Belorussia and the Ukraine?

At this point Exarch Sergii assumed another line of reasoning. *The Bolshevik deception,* he said, *would be more significant for German propaganda purposes if everything took place canonically in Moscow.* He built his argument on the premise that *it could not be true that Bolshevism was so powerful that even the Church was under its control.* If the Germans adopted the propaganda line of Bolshevik control of the Orthodox Church, then they would not win any friends in Russia: the Russians would conclude that the Germans were enemies of Russia because they were enemies of the Russian Church. At any rate, the Exarch emphasized, this propaganda line would not counteract Bolshevik leaflets signed by the Patriarch. Consequently, he suggested, an effective propaganda line would be to point out the canonical Moscow patriarchal election as a symptom of Bolshevik weakness and as a temporary deception forced on them by circumstances. He pointed out another forced change in Bolshevik policy not sufficiently utilized by German propaganda, namely, the dissolution of the Comintern!

Finally, Exarch Sergii summarized his suggested propaganda policy:

> *One should play the Moscow Patriarch against Stalin.* In propaganda against Bolshevism, according to his view, it should have been emphasized *that the Soviets today are even forced to recognize the supreme head of the Church as a representative and symbol of anti-Sovietism.* It is obvious that this recognition could not be sincere. *It would be a bankruptcy of Bolshevism if, in its retreat, it was forced to go so far as recognition of God and "the Church."*[29]

[29]Der Befehlshaber der Sicherheitspolizei und des SD Ostland. Abt. IV Bc

In the above argument, two points stand out. In the first place, the trick of the Soviet Government with the elections consisted, at least in theory, in strictest adherence to church canons, and, secondly, the Patriarch's election attested to the failure of atheistic ideology by the government, which was forced to mobilize the help of Orthodoxy, exactly as before the war it had to exchange Russian patriotism for Marxist internationalism. But the Exarch was not able to disprove the simple fact that for Stalin canons were only a cover for a new deceit, and the Patriarchal *Locum Tenens* with all his erudition could hardly be considered the true guarantor for faithful fulfillment of canons under the conditions of continued pressure from the authorities.

The canons of the Russian Orthodox Church did not represent any greater value to the Nazis than they did to Stalin, but both of them were forced, paradoxically, to attempt to decipher the question also on its canonical merits. In the *addendum* to the above-quoted position by Exarch Sergii there is the following request by Kurtz, who apparently handled this problem for the Ministry of Propaganda:

> Enclosed I am forwarding you the attitude of Exarch Sergii in Riga to the Vienna Bishops' Council with the request to forward it to the Ministry of Church Affairs, which was in charge of this matter at the Council[30] and to inquire about its position in regard

Tgb. Nr. 524/43g. An den Reichskomissar f.d. Ostland, Abt. I. Politik, z. Hd. von Herrn Ministerialrat Burmeister, in Riga. Instead of a signature. i.A. gez. Unterschrift SS-Sturmbannführer. A copy. Document Occ E (Ch)-3, YIVO. Italics in original.

Balevits's explanation of the controversy between Exarch Sergii and the German occupation authorities over the election of the Patriarch in the USSR is not convincing. If we were to accept the view that the Exarch completely subjugated himself to German policy it would be impossible to explain his constant refusal to proclaim his denunciation of Patriarch Sergii and the Council of Bishops which elected him, particularly in view of the fact that according to Balevits this refusal led to the tragic death of Exarch Sergii. See Balevits, *op. cit.*, pp. 78-87.

[30] See also W. Alexeev's article, "The Death of Exarch Sergii Voskresenskii and the election of the Patriarch of Moscow," published in the Journal of the Archierical Synod of the Russian Orthodox Church Abroad, *Tserkovnaia Zhizn'* Nr.7-12 for 1958, pp. 108-19, and the following note by the publisher in regard to the above statement (p. 116):

This announcement is incorrect. The Church Ministry only executed the to the questions of the canonical legality which had been touched upon. The Reichskommissar for Ostland, in whose Bezirk Exarch Sergii belongs, asked for the corresponding position in order to forward it again to the Exarch, since his point of view could be changed by this. If the arguments of the Exarch turn out to be of substance, then the propaganda which we conduct in connection with the Vienna Council ought to be changed to a different track.[31]

On that same day, the same Dr. Kurtz sent a similar request to the Anticomintern. On 18 January 1944 Dr. Mehne from the Propaganda Section of the Propaganda Ministry, in his turn, sent a request on the same question to the Ministry of Church Affairs. On 7 February of the same year, Dr. Kurtz sent the Anticomintern a reminder prodding it for an answer. On 11 February the Anticomintern answered that its conclusions would soon be forwarded. On 14 February Dr. Kurtz forwarded the Anticomintern's conclusions to the "Landspropagandaamt Riga," informing them in an addendum that the author of the corresponding document was himself an Orthodox priest who knew everything related to the Church and its development in the Soviet Union, and that his point of view reflected that of the Orthodox Church in Germany. The name of this priest was not given, unfortunately,[32] and his conclusions are not in the archives, but the point of view of the head of the Orthodox Church in Germany, Metropolitan Serafim, is known. He was among those signing the Vienna Declaration. That means that this point of view was directly opposed to that of Exarch Sergii.

insistent requests of the Synod for permission for a meeting of the Russian Orthodox bishops. Such permission was granted only when the council declaration based on the negative attitude of the Synod to the activity of Metropolitan Sergii Stragorodskii, known to the Ministry, was recognized as entirely desirable also from the German standpoint. All the work of the Episcopal Council was conducted without any influence of the Ministry of Church Affairs, which could hardly have tolerated the writing of such a memorandum to the German Government, which contained criticism of its policies in regard to the Russians.

[31]Abteilung Ost [das Reichsministerium für Volksaufklärung und Propaganda] Ref. Dr. Kurtz. Herrn Dr. Mehne, Abt. Pro. Berlin, den 13. Januar 1944. 26/44g (1). Signed by Doctor Kurtz. Document Occ E (Ch)-3, YIVO.

[32]In connection with this see the speculative reference to an Orthodox priest who worked in the foreign branch of the Antikomintern, a certain Paul Gekke, in Balevits, *op. cit.,* p. 78.

The last document in the folder contains a new inquiry of the Reichskommissariat Ostland, addressed to Kurtz in the Ministry of Propaganda, on the occasion of the publication in Moscow of the book *Pravda o Religii v SSSR* [The truth about religion in the USSR].[33] The inquiry sets forth Exarch Sergii's opinion on this question (the latter, in particular, advised a comparison of the texts of both English and Russian publications of the given book).

Almost exactly two months after this last document,[34] on 28 April 1944, Exarch Sergii was killed. This took place on the road from Vilno to Riga. The Metropolitan was hurrying to the funeral of the famous émigré tenor, Smirnov, his personal friend. In the automobile, in addition to the chauffeur and the Metropolitan, were a former artist of the Bolshoi Theater in Moscow, the bass Redikul'tsev, and his wife. According to a priest who had seen the Exarch's body on the scene where the tragedy occurred, he had been riddled with burp-gun bullets. It was rumored that the Exarch's car had passed a car with people dressed in German military uniforms who opened burp-gun fire.[35]

The occupation authorities cooperated to arrange a pompous funeral for the Metropolitan, and in every way emphasized that the murder was the work of Soviet agents. This seems possible. While refusing to speak out against the Moscow Patriarch, the Exarch had continued to criticize the Soviet Communist government. His last public statement contained the sharp reminder: "Stalin is not Saul, and will not be Paul," which meant that from the standpoint of the Soviet authorities, the softening of the religious policy was simply a forced play. Nonetheless, the documents cited above point to the conclusion that the murder was more likely to have been the work of the Germans, especially since other terrorist acts were perpetrated against Russian leaders who had come forward during the occupation at approximately the same time and in similar fashion to the Exarch's murder. For example, General Kaminskii, the organ-

[33]The Russian version was published in 1942 by the Moscow Patriarchate.
[34]In the possession of W. Alexeev.
[35]Compare also Balevits, *op. cit.*, pp. 78-87.

izer of the so-called Russian Liberation People's Army (RONA), was killed under very strange circumstances and also on a deserted road.

It is interesting that, according to witnesses who knew the Exarch, he himself felt that his position was becoming dangerous. This realization depressed him, but it did not make him change the line of church policy he had taken, and this speaks in his favor. Thus, even this hierarch, who was suspected of every sort of improper action during his stay in Moscow, under new conditions of relatively greater, although still restricted, freedom, displayed the positive side of his character with great strength. The undisputed fact remains that when Metropolitan Sergii died, he was sincerely mourned by a very significant part of his new flock.

The Exarch's personality and a description of his interrelations with the occupation authorities have led us far afield from a description of the religious revival in the northern part of the German zone of occupation—the most important theme dealt with in the present work. Now we must return to 1941, to the moment when the Exarch received his freedom, having been freed by the Germans after an arrest of short duration.

As stated before, after his liberation he received permission to send a church mission into the Pskov region occupied by the Germans. Many émigrés who took part in this mission are still alive, and three of them have been interviewed in connection with this project.

In the small church journal, *Po stopam Khrista* [In Christ's footsteps], published in Berkeley, California, there appeared in 1954 "Zapiski missionera" [Notes of a Missionary], written by Protoierei Aleksei Ionov, a participant in this mission. From "Notes of a Missionary" and from an interview with Father Aleksei, it is established that the mission left for Pskov in August 1941. Originally it consisted of fifteen priests. "A huge territory from the old Siverskaia railway station near Petrograd to Opochka had been turned into an ecclesiastical desert by the Soviet authorities."[36]

[36] See No. 50 (September-October 1954), p. 11.

Throughout the entire area in which the mission was active, it did not find one open church, although in Pskov alone there had been forty-four churches before the Revolution. According to another member of the mission, Father X, one open church in the city of Gdov survived. In Pskov the missionaries discovered only two surviving priests, exhausted morally and physically by the persecutions. The first church to reopen in Pskov was the historically famous Trinity Cathedral, which could hold several thousand worshippers, and which even at the first service was filled to capacity. On the streets people approached the priests of the mission and asked for their blessing. Immediately the population began to repair churches in the environs of Pskov and asked that priests be sent to them. Hundreds came for confession, and mass confessions had to be organized.

This same story was repeated in the city of Ostrov, where Father Aleksei Ionov went. The cathedral in Ostrov was used for the storage of grain. It was desecrated and dilapidated, and services had to be held in the less ruined cemetery church. Because of the small size of this church, hundreds of people were unable to attend services. When the cathedral had been repaired by the efforts of the parishioners, from five to eight hundred persons took Holy Communion at every Liturgy during the course of the first months after the cathedral was opened. As many as eighty children were baptized at one time. Services usually began at seven in the morning. Afterward there were the offices which extended until four in the afternoon. People filled the church long before services began.

Gradually fifteen churches were opened in the Ostrov area. Similar observations were made in the entire region where the Pskov mission operated. By an approximate calculation for the first months of the mission's work, about fifty thousand children of all ages were baptized. According to Father X,

> When in August of 1941 we arrived in Pskov, parishioners with tears in their eyes approached us on the streets for our blessing. At the first service in the Cathedral, all worshippers confessed. It seemed to us that it was not the priests who had come to strengthen the people, but the people were there to strengthen

the priests. Middle-aged people were in the majority among the worshippers, but there were also young people.[37]

Shortly afterwards Father X was sent to Gdov, about a hundred kilometers north of Pskov. It took him two weeks to get there in a carriage. He visited about forty former churches. All the churches were closed, and the majority of them were destroyed. In places where it was still possible to reestablish churches, the people immediately restored them. The morale of the population was so high that often the thought came to mind: "Were there persecutions here?" And it seemed that the air itself was permeated with religious fervor. The young people quickly returned to the faith. Usually Communion lasted longer than the service itself—as many as five or six hundred persons took Communion. In Pskov, at the Feast of the Baptism in January 1942, ten thousand worshippers took part in the religious procession (of approximately twenty-five thousand inhabitants remaining in the city). From the entire area of the mission's activity, it was only in Gdov that churches remained open by the beginning of the war.

Services usually had to be held from six in the morning until ten at night. Children up to sixteen years of age were baptized. From twenty-five to thirty children, and as many as a hundred, were brought in at one time. From August through November 1941, Father X personally baptized thirty-five hundred children.

Young women who sang in the choir went to other parishes which did not have choirs, sometimes covering twenty-five to thirty *versts* (fifteen to twenty miles) on foot. This same zeal was observed in the repair and restoration of churches. During sermons the people sighed and wept, and at the end of the sermon they thanked the preacher aloud.

The work of the mission encompassed the cities of Pskov, Ostrov, Porkhov, Opochka, Gdov, and Luga. No less than three hundred parishes were opened throughout the area. A description of the first religious services in the Pskov Cathedral is given in a book by the Russian émigré journalist, N. Fevr,

[37]From W. Alexeev's notes of conversation with Father X.

who was in Pskov in 1941. According to his observations, elderly people were in the majority in the Cathedral. There were few young people and children.[38]

Protoierei Aleksei Ionov, both in oral testimony and in his memoirs, notes that the young people did not immediately return to the church, but when they did they did so very strongly and sincerely. Especially interesting testimony of two participants in the mission, questioned for this project, refers to the fact that almost all former Soviet high school teachers in this area who were required to conduct antireligious propaganda in Soviet times returned to the church. In many schools in the Pskov area, the teaching of religion was introduced.

The conclusion of the clergymen was that before the return of Soviet troops the "religious desert" of the Pskov region had experienced a rechristianization. Some maintain that if the mission could have prolonged its work a few more years, the Pskov region would have recaptured its ancient splendor as a bastion of Russian Orthodox culture.

The reports of Orthodox clergymen, members of the Pskov Mission, for obvious reasons might present a favorable picture of developments in this region at the time. But they stand the test of objective criticism remarkably well when compared with what might be described as hostile German sources.

Among captured German documents, there exist informative communiqués of the "Sicherheitspolizei und SD" which gave the leadership of Nazi Germany systematic information on all countries occupied by Germany, and especially on the occupied part of the USSR. Considerable attention is devoted to the position of the Church in the occupied areas of Russia. Unfortunately, these reports give less material on the Pskov area, though what was found fully confirms the picture painted by the Orthodox priests. In the communiqué of 26 July 1941, after an indication that in the city of Ostrov there are many exiled

[38]Nikolai Fevr, *Solntse voskhodit na Zapade* [The sun rises in the West], pp. 71-78. Balevits, usually reticent on the results of the mission's work, nevertheless mentions that by August 1942 the mission had seventy-seven priests and 200 parishes (*op. cit.*, p. 28) and later on acknowledges 175 priests participating in the work of the mission (pp. 40-41).

people unhappy with Soviet rule, which is not the case in the city of Porkhov, the report states that the older generation at the town of Ostrov is sympathetic to the coming of the Germans, because the occupation permitted them to worship openly. From this data the author of the report makes a characteristic conclusion that for other segments of the population and their attitude to the Germans the religious question will play a leading role. Intelligent propaganda may find a base for a breaking of ties between the populace and the Soviet government in the religious question.[39]

The author of the report obviously considers that the religiousness of the population is so strong that it is possible to tear the Russian people away from the Soviet government by simply relying on it. We find analogous conclusions in other SD reports. For instance, the communiqué of 15 August relates that in the cities of Pskov and Ostrov almost the entire population without exception gathers for church services in churches and on the squares and that one can influence the people through the clergy.[40]

In another report dated 6 February 1942 it is mentioned that the German authorities gave to the Orthodox Church the miraculous icon of the Mother of God of Tikhvin, and that two thousand worshippers were present at the transfer.[41]

In the report dated 6 November 1942 we find the information that after the occupation of Pskov by the German troops in three open churches about two thousand children under the age of sixteen were baptized and six hundred burials were performed (probably including burials of persons who had died earlier and had not received a religious burial during the Soviet rule), as well as twenty marriages. Church services were performed in the Cathedral of the Holy Trinity (*Troitskii Sobor*)

[39] U.S. National Archives and Records Service, Reich Chief Security Office, *Ereignismeldungen. UdSSR*, No. 34 (26 July 1941), Roll 233.
[40] *Ibid.*, No. 53 (15 August 1941), Roll 233. Communiqué No. 156 of 16 January 1942 (p. 34), referring to the increase of popular interest in the Orthodox Church "im russischen Gebiet" states that this relates principally to the older generation. Similar information can be found in Communiqué No. 162 of 30 January 1942 (p. 9). For both communiqués see Roll 234.
[41] *Ibid.*, No. 165 (6 February, 1942), Roll 234.

daily, in the morning as well as in the evening and in the remaining two churches two to three times a week, serving the ten thousand believers.

In the same communiqué data are given about the juridical and financial situation of the mission. The most important part of this information follows: the leaders of the mission were appointed by Exarch Sergii and were recognized by the occupation authorities, who had to give support to the mission's activities. The mission was responsible for the checking of clergy from the canonical viewpoint and also had to assume responsibility for the political activities of the missionaries. The mission was recognized as a part of the Russian Orthodox Church. The mission had the right to send candidates to be ordained as priests as well as to send students to Riga and Vilno for the purpose of acquiring a theological education. The parishes and all church enterprises were exempt from all taxes. The clergy of the mission received no salary, living only on voluntary contributions made by the believers. Ten percent of the parishes' income was transferred to the mission in the city of Pskov. Half of this sum the mission sent to the Exarchate in Riga.

After special petitions from the mission permission was given to begin religious education in schools, to hold public prayers at the beginning of school classes, and to put up icons in school buildings.

The most important fact is that all this gigantic work was possible due only to the voluntary contributions of the believers, who had been ruined by the war, and despite over twenty years of systematic antireligious upbringing of the entire population.[42]

In a dispatch to the Minister of Occupied Regions, compiled by Leibbrandt in November 1941, there is a reference to a region (most likely Pskov) where the Great Russians are exceptionally receptive to church questions and attend church services willingly (*spontan besucht*). He speaks of the small number of old clergy and the new clergy which calls itself "missionaries" and who had arrived there from Ostland.

[42]U.S. National Archives and Records Service, *Meldungen aus den besetzten Ostgebieten*, No. 34 (18 December 1942), Roll. 236.

THE BALTIC SECTOR

In that same document, Leibbrandt, who had studied the region carefully for medical reasons, writes of the strength of the Russian family and the high morals of the Russian women who had placed the German soldiers and officers in a "very difficult" position by their inaccessibility.[43]

Thus, in the former border region of the USSR, the Pskov region, in which communization of the population had been conducted very thoroughly (which was reflected in the closing of a great number of churches), in a little over thirty months of work the mission had almost completely restored Orthodoxy.

The head of the Russian Orthodox Church in the Baltic states, Metropolitan Sergii (Voskresenskii) graphically proved that even a bishop formed by the Soviets, under certain conditions, will display not only the capacity of taking risks but even a readiness toward martyrdom for the Orthodox faith and Russia. Also, the congregations consisting of those with a Russian background in the Baltic states remained true to the Exarch who had come from the USSR, even after the arrival of the Germans.

All these phenomena, taken together, speak of the fact that even under adverse conditions of World War II and with differences in the understanding of their Orthodox faith and patriotic duty, the Russian people, as was traditional with them during a time of crisis, sought for union around the Russian Orthodox Church, whose strength had been weakened but which was far from being destroyed by decades of rule of militant atheism in the USSR.

---

[43]See Lieutenant Leibbrandt an den Reichsminister für die besetzte Ostgebiete, November 1941, Königsberg. Bericht No. 8, p. 4, Document Ng-4435.

FOUR

Belorussia

From the very beginning of the war a different picture emerged in Belorussia from that which developed in the Baltic and Pksov regions. This may have been partly the result of the fact that when German troops seized Belorussia, the Exarch of the Moscow Patriarchate in western Belorussia and the Ukraine, Metropolitan Nikolai Iarushevich, was in Moscow, and he stayed there on the Soviet side of the front. But the main factor determining developments in the region was German policy toward the Orthodox Church in Belorussia which had been formulated by Rosenberg in May 1942. According to this policy, the Russian Orthodox Church was not allowed to extend its influence on the Orthodox Belorussians and its activity was to be restricted to areas populated by Great Russians.[1] This policy enabled the so-called Belorussian Autonomous Orthodox Church to separate completely from the Exarchate in the Baltic states, despite the well-known claims of Exarch Sergii and despite the fact that the Baltic states and

[1] See Rosenberg, "Der Reichsminister für die besetzten Ostgebiete an a) den Herrn Reichskommissar für das Ostland Gauleiter Hinrich Lohse, Riga; b) den Herrn Reichskommissar für die Ukraine Gauleiter Erich Koch, Rowno," 13 May 1942, p. 2, Document Occ E (Ch)-4, YIVO.

Belorussia belonged to the same Reichskommissariat Ostland. That this separation had not taken place accidentally can be seen, for example, from secret notes on the conference with Ministerialdirektor Leibbrandt on 18 June 1942 in Riga, the administrative center of the Reichskommissariat Ostland. At the conference it was emphasized that the Belorussian Orthodox Church should be protected from Russian influence, and the Catholic Church (on Belorussian territory) from Polish influence.[2]

Encouraging total Belorussian separation, including that of the Church, was not an easy matter for the German authorities. The latter soon discovered that the townspeople of Belorussia used the Russian and not the Belorussian language, evidence perhaps of the tsarist and Soviet policy of extinguishing Belorussian separatist tendencies. A Belorussian national consciousness did persist, needless to say. It had reached its highest point in 1918, when the Belorussian independence was announced, but, according to the German report, these separatist aspirations were completely repressed by the sovietization policies in Soviet Belorussia.[3] It is interesting to note that the "high point" of Belorussian separatism attained in 1918 was also reached during German occupation. Perhaps the Germans were hoping to recapture this "high point" of the 1918 separatism and that is why the German command had brought with it a group of Belorussian nationalist émigrés.

This group consisted of approximately thirty Belorussian separatist members of the intelligentsia from Poland and Austria brought into the city of Minsk with the purpose of establishing ties with the few remaining members of the Belorussian movement who had managed to survive in the USSR and thus rekindle the Belorussian national consciousness which at that time was manifesting itself only in the form of language spoken by the Belorussian masses.[4] In order to revive Belorus-

[2]See Reichskommissar für das Ostland, Abt. II Politik RR TR/ko - Tgb. no. 2239/428. Riga, 19 June 1942, Document Occ E (Ch)-4, YIVO.

[3]See Wehrmachtsbefehlshaber Ostland Ic. 14222, den 22.VIII.1942. Betr.: Stimmungsbericht aus Weissruthenien, p. 6. Document Occ E 3a-14, YIVO.

[4]U.S. National Archives and Records Service, Reich Chief Security Office, *Ereignismeldungen. UdSSR*, No. 11 (13 July 1941); No. 23 (15 July 1941), Roll 233.

sian national consciousness which had suffered seriously as a result of russification and communization,[5] the Germans also imported Belorussian emigrants from Warsaw, Litzmanstadt, Berlin, and Prague to organize a civil administration. Lithuanians, Latvians, and Ukrainians (entire subdivisions) served in the police. Poles were appointed as burgomasters. But all this had a negative effect on the local population; especially the treatment of the population by the Ukrainians provided grounds for deserved criticism.[6]

Still, neither the low moral quality of the workers who had been brought in nor the dissatisfaction of the local population troubled the occupying forces. It was the Polish underground and the Roman Catholic Church which disturbed them most of all, even more than the pro-Russian sympathies of the majority of the population. According to German communiqués issued on 28 July and 28 September 1941, the Catholic Church in the Belorussian area, headed primarily by Poles, was conducting an increasingly noticeable amount of missionary work, with political repercussions, as this could lead to polonization of Belorussian Catholics. Furthermore, the Catholics were attempting to utilize for their own interests some of the Belorussian nationalists who were brought in by the German forces. In connection with this the author of the communiqué proposed the following measures: (1) prevention of entrance of Catholic clergy into Belorussia; (2) expulsion to the place of origin of clergy who had already entered; (3) limiting travel for the local clergy; (4) a thorough check of the religious background of émigrés brought in by the German forces; and (5) support and activation of the Orthodox Church. The communiqué also explained that the Orthodox clergy in Minsk who had arrived from Volkovyisk were conducting services in the cemetery church. About two thousand faithful attended and forty-five children were baptized. The sermon included thanks to Hitler.[7]

A second communiqué issued one month later expounded

[5]*Ibid.*, No. 17 (9 July 1941), Roll 233.
[6]*Ibid.*, No. 154 (12 January 1942), Roll 234.
[7]*Ibid.*, No. 36 (28 July 1941); No. 97 (28 September 1941), Roll 233.

on the provisions of the first. The new communiqué listed police measures against Polish activites in the former northeastern area of Poland. The Polish activity, according to this source, was directed at the removal of Belorussians from important posts of administration and their replacement with Polish intelligentsia who, because of their knowledge of the German language and because of their diligence, acquired all of the command posts in local administration and even in the local police. They accused the Belorussian intelligentsia of being Communists and in this way removed them from office. A great number of Belorussians in that area belonged to the Catholic Church and were being polonized by the Catholic clergy. The number of the Polish intelligentsia was increasing as Polish landowners were returning to their estates (apparently after their escape from the Red Army in 1939),[8] and, furthermore, anti-German propaganda kept emphasizing that the Germans neither brought Belorussia its independence nor did they grant self-government.

This communiqué considered the organization of surveillance of the Poles as being extremely necessary. It also insisted on the equalization of Belorussians to Poles in administrative affairs and the removal of Polish activists from the administration. The Germans could take advantage of an alleged request by the Belorussians to help them in their struggles against the Poles.[9] Judging from German comments, "the Polish advance" had already moved to old Soviet boundaries in Belorussia. The Roman Catholic clergy had played a major role in this offensive. Information received from the Belorussian clergy indicated that the Poles planned an uprising after the German troops had advanced. As an example of the Polish advance, the communiqué cites the case in the village of Mir, where the burgomaster's post was seized by the former head of the government. In addition, many Poles came from Warsaw illegally.

What especially alarmed the Germans was that on the former Polish territory the larger part of the local police was now composed of local citizens in contrast to the time when the Soviets occupied the territory. The author of the communiqué

[8]*Ibid.*, No. 97, Roll 233.
[9]*Ibid.*

concluded that this police force could be utilized by Polish nationalists in case of rebellion against the Germans.[10]

The Roman Catholic Bishop in Vilno was regarded with the greatest suspicion by the occupation authorities. They even claimed that he was sending disguised missionaries to Belorussia illegally under direct orders from the Pope.[11]

Thus, the increasing German fear of the Polish-Catholic influence prepared the ground for a liberalization of the German attitude toward the reestablishment of Orthodoxy, which they viewed as the lesser of the two evils.

To understand the organization of the Orthodox Church in Belorussia, one must take into account the fact that Belorussia was reduced in the west by the addition of Grodno to East Prussia and Pinsk to the Reichskommissariat of the Ukraine.[12] The Germans had enlarged Belorussia in the east by the addition of Smolensk and the Briansk oblast.[13]

Three forces were at work against each other in the creation of the Orthodox Church hierarchy in Belorussia: (1) the divisive policies of the occupation authorities described above; (2) the centralizing national Russian policies of the great majority of bishops and clergy; and (3) the separatist Belorussian policy of a small group of Belorussian chauvinist émigrés who carried on a narrow Belorussian line which, in many instances, corresponded with the divisive interests of the Eastern Ministry. Bishops termed this group "Aktiv," and it consisted of approximately thirty persons.[14] At the outbreak of official hostilities

[10]*Ibid.*

[11]*Ibid.*, No. 154 (January 12 1942), Roll 234. See also the previously mentioned *Ereignismeldungen* No. 32 (21 July 1941), No. 35 (27 July 1941), and No. 36 (28 July 1941). For all these *Ereignismeldungen*, Roll 233.

[12]This change in borders evidently was made at the request of Reichskommissar of the Ukraine Erich Koch. Koch ensured for himself the post of Gauleiter of East Prussia, and wanted the Reichskommissariat and the Gau administered by him to have common borders. See Jurgen Thorvald, *Wen sie verderben wollen,* p. 38.

[13]This is true, in any case, from the standpoint of the organization of the Belorussian Orthodox Church, to which were added the Smolensk and Briansk dioceses. The division into regions administered by the Ostministerium and the so-called military regions under administration of the army changed, depending on the movement of the front. In the case of Polotsk, for example, it was under the administration of the army, but not of the Belorussian Reichskommissariat.

[14]Sources for these developments include a report of the struggle between

between the Germans and the Soviets there were no active bishops or clergy serving in the Soviet part of Belorussia. When the Germans occupied Belorussia, only the Orthodox Metropolitan Panteleimon and his vicar, Bishop Venedikt, found themselves there. Since the Eastern Ministry transferred the Poles'e bishopric with Archbishop Aleksandr (Inozemtsev) to the Ukraine, Western Belorussia remained without a bishop and clergy.

Therefore, Metropolitan Panteleimon through Bishop Venedikt obtained permission from the German military authorities for the organization of an Orthodox Church of Belorussia under his leadership. During the course of the negotiations, reports Archbishop Venedikt, the German authorities presented Metropolitan Panteleimon with a list of conditions: (1) the newly organized Orthodox Church was to be completely independent of Moscow, Warsaw, Berlin, or others; (2) it was to be named "The Belorussian Autocephalous Orthodox National Church"; (3) the church was to be free of German interference in its internal life; (4) church administration, religious instruction, and sermons were to be conducted in Belorussian; (5) bishops were to be appointed with knowledge of the German authorities; (6) a legal statute of the "Belorussian Orthodox Autocephalous National Church was to be drawn up and presented to the Germans; and (6) the church was to conduct its services in church-Slavonic.

Metropolitan Panteleimon accepted these conditions with a reservation which actually had the effect of refuting them. This reservation was that separation from the Russian Orthodox Church could occur only after the Belorussian Orthodox Church

the head of the Belorussian Orthodox Church, Metropolitan Panteleimon, and the "Aktiv," by the Metropolitan's closest assistant and supporter, Bishop Venedikt, which was presented to the Synod of the Russian Orthodox Church Abroad. The official representative of Metropolitan Panteleimon, Archbishop Filofei, who had been mediator between the Metropolitan and the "Aktiv," was interviewed for this project. A representative of the "Aktiv," I. Kasiak, devotes considerable space to this problem in his book on the Belorussian Orthodox Church, *Z historyi pravoslaunai tsarkvy belaruskago narodu* [From the history of the Orthodox Church of the Belorussian people]. Finally, there is information from the German Sicherheitsdienst which greatly supplements the above sources. Interestingly enough, these sources do not contradict but rather supplement each other.

was organized, matured for autocephalism, and formed its own separate canonicals, i.e., with the permission of the Russian Orthodox Church.

Archbishop Venedikt reports further that Metropolitan Panteleimon and the newly consecrated Bishop Filofei came to Minsk in November 1941 to take over the administration of the Metropolis. Metropolitan Panteleimon acquired the title of Metropolitan of all Belorussia while Archbishop Venedikt received the appointment to the Bialyastok-Grodno diocese attached to Prussia and "was set up as a sort of separate autonomous exarchate of the Belorussian Church."[15]

The second-in-command of the Belorussian Orthodox Church from 1942 to 1944 was Archimandrite (later Archbishop) Filofei. He was sent to German-occupied Minsk in Belorussia by Metropolitan Dionisii, head of the Autocephalous Polish Orthodox Church, who had plans of his own for the subordination of Orthodox churches in Russian territories now occupied by the German forces.[16]

Metropolitan Dionisii's intentions are revealed in other sources too, notably in A. Svitich's account. Svitich, a Russian journalist from Poland, states in his history of the Orthodox Church in Poland that Metropolitan of Warsaw Dionisii along with the Belorussian National Committee maintained that the Orthodox Church of Belorussia was separated from Dionisii's jurisdiction in 1939 " . . . only temporarily, by virtue of military conditions." Thus, on 9 September 1941, the "so-called 'Belorussian Church Rada' " was organized under the chairmanship of Metropolitan Dionisii. A special memorandum was sent to the German authorities which contained proposals for the Belorussian Church. In particular, Archimandrites Feofan (Protasevich), Filofei (Narko), and Afanasii (Martos), all Polish residents, were named as candidates to episcopal chairs. Filofei and Afanasii were consecrated as bishops, the former

[15]Archbishop Venedikt, " 'B.A.P.T.s.'—novaia sektanskaia gruppirovka v Belorusskoi tserkvi v emigratsii," [" 'B.A.O.C.'—a new sectarian grouping in the Belorussian Church in emigration"] *Tskerkovnaia Zhizn'* No. 3-4 (March-April, 1952): 53. "B.A.P.Ts" stands for Belorussian Autocephalous Orthodox Church.

[16]Interview with Archbishop Filofei in New York City on 24 March 1964.

on 23 November 1941 in the Zhirovetskii monastery and the latter on 8 March 1942 in Minsk.[17]

Engineer I. Kasiak, mentioned above, supplements the testimony of both Archbishop Filofei and Svitich. Kasiak confirms that Metropolitan Dionisii, for the purpose of subordinating Belorussia to his jurisdiction, created a special Belorussian committee in Warsaw, with himself as chairman. The committee consisted of Archimandrite Filofei (Narko), Ivan Ermachenko, and three other persons. The committee nominated candidates to fill the Belorussian episcopate: two archimandrites, Filofei (Narko) and Afanasii (Martos) both of Belorussian origin.[18] Despite the failure of Metropolitan Dionisii's general project, both candidates became bishops of the Belorussian Orthodox Church.

Further, according to Kasiak's information, Metropolitan Dionisii sent a corresponding memorandum to Berlin with Ermachenko, and to the monastery of Zhirovitsy; to Metropolitan Panteleimon he sent Archimandrite Filofei, who arrived there when Metropolitan Panteleimon had already been designated the head of the Belorussian Orthodox Church by local occupation authorities.[19]

Evidently when Kasiak wrote his book in 1956 he was not familiar with the secret German documents. The nonrecognition of Metropolitan Dionisii, who was in former Poland which had been established under a general-governorship, can be attributed to the German policy set forth at the beginning of this chapter and not to the fact that Metropolitan Panteleimon had, by chance, been designated at the moment of Archimandrite Filofei's arrival. Raevskii writes that the claims of Metropolitan Dionisii were upheld by Frank, the Governor-General of occupied Poland. According to Raevskii, Frank even wanted to make Metropolitan Dionisii the head of the entire Russian Orthodox Church after the USSR was crushed by the German forces. There were even supposed to have been printed blanks with the title "His Holiness Dionisii, Patriarch of Moscow and

[17] Aleksandr Svitich, *Pravoslavnaia tserkov' v Pol'she i ee avtokefaliia* [The Orthodox Church in Poland and its autocephality], p. 199
[18] Kasiak, *op. cit.*, p. 85.
[19] *Ibid.*, p. 86.

of all Russia." This information again supplements other sources and in no way contradicts them. At the beginning of the war, the subjugation of the USSR seemed assured, and every Hitlerite satrap in occupied territory dreamed of the extension of his own personal influence.[20]

According to the words of Archbishop Filofei, having come to Metropolitan Panteleimon he quickly understood that Metropolitan Dionisii's plans were inopportune. Therefore, at the suggestion of Metropolitan Panteleimon and Archbishop Venedikt, he took an active part in the organization of the Orthodox Church in Belorussia.

Since Metropolitan Panteleimon is a central figure in the entire course of the organization of the Orthodox Church in Belorussia during the German occupation, as Exarch Sergii was in the Baltic region, a general introduction to this hierarch at this point is appropriate.[21]

The Metropolitan's father was a Pole named Rozhnovskii; his mother was a Russian named Korovina. The family lived in Russia, where the father was in charge of state lands in the Kostroma, Chernigov, and Novgorod guberniias. The future Metropolitan first graduated from the Nikolaev Engineering School and then from the Kazan Theological Academy, which was known for its missionary spirit. In 1913 Father Panteleimon (then an Archimandrite) was in charge of transferring the relics of St. Evfrosiniia of Polotsk from the city of Kiev to Polotsk (Belorussian). In 1915 he became Bishop of Dvinsk, and lived in Polotsk. After the Revolution he turned up in Polish territory, where he was an avid opponent to the declaration of the autocephality of the Polish Orthodox Church, which had been until then part of the Russian Church. For his failure to cooperate with this undertaking, he was "retired" by the Polish Government. Panteleimon was living in the monastery of Zhirovitsy when the Red Army came in 1939. His loyalty to the Russian Orthodox Church made him the natural candidate to head the Orthodox Church in the territory of former Poland

[20]S. Raevski, *Ukrainskaia avtokefal'naia tserkov'* [The Ukrainian Autocephalous Church], p. 1.
[21]Much of this information comes from an extensive interview with Archbishop Filofei, held in New York City on 23 and 24 March 1964.

now controlled by the Soviet Union. By order of the Moscow Patriarchate, he was designated Exarch of Western Belorussia and the Ukraine on 17 October 1939.[22]

Naturally the Metropolitan could not play an important role within the confines of the Moscow Patriarchate, which was subject to Communist rule. In July 1940 Metropolitan Panteleimon was replaced by Metropolitan Nikolai (Iarushevich) who had been sent from Moscow. The arrival of the Germans found Metropolitan Panteleimon again "retired" in the monastery at Zhirovitsy, and again he was the natural candidate to head the Orthodox Church in Belorussia.

Thus the basis on which the German occupation powers gave permission for the organization of the Orthodox Church in Belorussia had been established by the time Archimandrite Filofei arrived. The newly consecrated Bishop Filofei became Metropolitan Panteleimon's vicar of Minsk. Panteleimon's relations with the German authorities soon deteriorated to pretty much what they had been with the Polish and Soviet authorities, not to mention the Belorussian "Aktiv," that is to say, the Belorussian émigré-separatists brought in by the Germans. This moved Vicar Filofei up to a key position, determined both by his Belorussian ancestry and his activity in the Belorussian committee created by Metropolitan Dionisi. The importance which the Germans attached to the representatives of the Orthodox Church at this time can be ascertained by the fact that when Filofei and Panteleimon arrived in Minsk they were received by the Generalkommissar of Belorussia, Kube, himself.

In Minsk, Metropolitan Panteleimon began a struggle with the Belorussians who had been brought from former Poland by the Germans, as cited from Archbishop Venedikt's report.

> In its struggle with Metropolitan Panteleimon, the Aktiv set the German commissars against him, and on 1, June 1942 he was removed from the administration of the Church. The administration of the Metropolis and the Eparchy was transferred to Archbishop Filofei (Narko). As the German authorities had demanded, the Metropolitan was sent to the abolished and half-demolished monastery in the village of Liady, forty kilometers

[22] Svitich, *op. cit.*, p. 196.

from Minsk, where he remained until December 1942, when he was taken to the town of Vileika and placed under the SD [German political police]. where he had to register daily. On 16, May 1943 he was freed, and permitted to return to Minsk.[23]

Archbishop Filofei relates the following regarding the same events: The pressure toward the creation of a Belorussian Autocephalous Church was exerted in February 1942, when Bishop Filofei was summoned to the head of the political sector of the Reichskommissariat of Belorussia, who spoke of his dissatisfaction with Metropolitan Panteleimon because the latter continued to mention the head of the Russian Orthodox Church, Metropolitan Sergii (Stragorodskii), in church services. Such independent behavior caused the head of the Political Section to send to Kube the order to exile him back to the monastery of Zhirovitsy. Bishop Filofei noted that the question of the canonical position of the Orthodox Church in Belorussia could be decided through Warsaw, i.e., through the Metropolitan of the Polish Orthodox Church, but this was unacceptable to the Generalkommissariat of Belorussia, as was Bishop Filofei's proposal to contact the Synod of the Russian Orthodox Church in exile in Belgrade.

Thus the Generalkommissariat continued to insist on a demand for the declaration of an Autocephalous Belorussian Orthodox Church without receiving permission from the Mother Church—necessary according to canon law—not to mention the immediate recognition of this autocephality by other Orthodox Churches, including the Eastern Patriarchates which were entirely outside the sphere of German influence. In other words, the demands of the Germans were practically impossible in a wartime situation and under conditions required by the canons of the Orthodox Church. Bishop Filofei could not agree to such demands, and stated he would prefer to return to Warsaw. The head of the political sector now relented, and permitted Metropolitan Panteleimon to remain in Minsk, evidently understanding the canonical absurdity of the German demands and hoping to gain his goals later with the help of the Council of the Orthodox Church in Belorussia. This supposition can be considered as

[23] Archbishop Venedikt, *op. cit.*, p. 54.

probable, since all later actions of the Generalkommissariat reveal such a plan.

After Bishop Filofei, Metropolitan Panteleimon was summoned to meet with the Generalkommissariat.

At the beginning of March 1942 a Council of Orthodox Bishops in Belorussia was held. Bishop Venedikt of Grodno attended. The Council regularized the division of Belorussia into eparchies. Filofei enumerates six eparchies: (1) Minsk-Vilno (without the city of Vilno), headed by Metropolitan Panteleimon; (2) Grodno-Bialystok (beyond the boundaries of the Belorussian General-Governorship and therefore receiving the status of an exarchate), headed by Bishop Venedikt who received the title of Bishop of Bialystok and Grodno; (3) Mogilev, under the direction of Bishop Filofei, who received the title of Bishop of Mogilev and Mstislavl; (4) Vitebsk, headed by Bishop Afanasii Martos, who was made a candidate for the rank of Bishop with the title of Bishop of Vitebsk and Polotsk; (5) Smolensk, to be headed by Bishop Stefan (Sevbo), who at the time was still Protoierei Simeon;[24] and (6) Baranovichi-Novogrudok, which they wished to be headed by Bishop Veniamin (Novitskii), a Belorussian by extraction, at the time of the decision a Bishop of the Autonomous Ukrainian Church, occupying the chair of Poltava.

Bishop Afanasii was consecrated on 9 March 1942. However, he was not sent to Vitebsk, as proposed, but to Baranovichi-Novogrudok temporarily, until the arrival of Bishop Veniamin from the Ukraine.

At the same council, Bishop Filofei was officially elected second in charge to Metropolitan Panteleimon with his place of residence in Minsk. The council raised Bishop Venedikt to the rank of Archbishop for his work in organizing the church. Bishop Filofei also received the rank of Archbishop. The consecration of Protoierei Simeon to bishop was delayed by Metropolitan Panteleimon, who feared too great an increase in the influence of Belorussians. This consecration took place (in June 1942) under German pressure.

[24] According to Kasiak, Bishop Stefan was to receive the title of Bishop of Smolensk and Briansk (*op. cit.*, p. 94).

Several weeks after the consecration of Bishop Stefan, Metropolitan Panteleimon and Archbishop Filofei were again summoned to the Generalkommissariat, where the Metropolitan, "in view of his advanced age," was given orders to go to the monastery at Liady situated some thirty kilometers from Minsk. When Panteleimon asked why he was being sent away, the representative of the Kommissariat repeated the same phrase about the "advanced age" of the Metropolitan. Panteleimon then said that he would prefer to go to the monastery of Zhirovitsy, but the representative of the Kommissariat repeated his phrase a third time, and on this the very characteristic conversation ended. The next day Panteleimon was sent to Liady, where he remained under the supervision of the occupation authorities.

Kasiak describes these same events from the standpoint of the "Aktiv," i.e., the Belorussian separatists. He writes that Panteleimon was of interest to the "Aktiv" only from the point of view of the formal observance of canons, as the Bishop who was the most respected and oldest in rank. The "Aktiv" hoped to conduct, through the Belorussian Archbishop Filofei, its separatist policy. With this goal in mind, there was a meeting of the "Aktiv" with Archbishop Filofei in Kasiak's home. Filofei verbally agreed with the "Aktiv," but Metropolitan Panteleimon continued to use the Russian language in his sermons and not the Belorussian language, as the "Aktiv" wished. The other clergy did the same. Panteleimon also continued to mention Metropolitan Sergii, as head of the Russian Orthodox Church, in the services. He justified his use of the Russian language in his sermons by the fact that the population in the towns and cities spoke only Russian. He proposed the introduction of the Belorussian language after the end of the war.[25]

Insofar as during the meeting with the "Aktiv" Archbishop Filofei always pointed out that he was only Metropolitan Panteleimon's vicar and that he himself could not decide anything, the "Aktiv" presented the Metropolitan with a memorandum outlining the following demands: (1) inform the people that the Belorussian Church considered itself autocephalous; (2) designate Archbishop Filofei as head of the metropolitan

[25] Kasiak, *op. cit.*, p. 91.

administration in Minsk; (3) assign members of the "Aktiv" to the metropolitan administration (that is, the priests N. Lapitskii and Kushnir); and (4) give a series of recommendations on appointing clergy, mainly based on their Belorussian nationality.

Metropolitan Panteleimon and Archbishop Filofei did not introduce the measures of this memorandum, which had been based on the closeness of the "Aktiv" to the occupying powers.[26] The "Aktiv" gave the memorandum to the occupation authorities, requiring the removal of Metropolitan Panteleimon, the promotion of Archbishop Filofei, and the announcement of autocephality. This memorandum was evidently the reason for calling these two bishops to the Generalkommissariat and for the exile of the aged Metropolitan.

Kasiak makes an interesting addition to Archbishop Filofei's narrative. Before exiling Panteleimon, the Generalkommissariat made him issue a decree on conducting services in the Belorussian language, announce a prohibition against baptizing Jews (who in this way could hide more easily), and transfer authority to Archbishop Filofei.[27]

Our third source of information on the position of the Church in Belorussia is the SD communiqués. From them it is evident that the German secret police attentively followed the progress of the organization of the Orthodox Church in Belorussia and, no less than the Belorussian activists, were concerned with the failure to create an independent Belorussian church. Despite all the pressures, and the arrest of the Metropolitan, it is evident that a general Russian and not a Belorussian ideology had been created there.

The communiqué of March 1942 notes that on 8 March 1942 (and not on 9 March, as Archbishop Filofei related from memory), Metropolitan Panteleimon consecrated a new bishop, Afansaii Martos, in Minsk. The consecration took place in the presence of "all officials and with a great participation of the populace."[28]

[26] *Ibid.*, pp. 91-92.
[27] *Ibid.*, pp. 93-94.
[28] U.S. National Archives and Records Service, Reich Chief Security Office, *Ereignismeldungen. UdSSR*, No. 180 (13 March 1942), Roll 235.

In addition, the communiqué notes that the question of the autocephality of the Belorussian Church was discussed at the Council of Bishops in Minsk. An interesting and detailed analysis of this period from the German point of view can be found in an SD communiqué dated 5 June 1942. According to this source, the Great Russian question, as far as church affairs go, was quite simple. The Generalkommissar of Belorussia "brought to life" the Belorussian Autocephalous Church in order to separate Belorussia from Russia ecclestiastically as well as politically. However, Belorussian Orthodoxy became the center of the Great Russian clergy. The Belorussian clergy (or, to put it plainly, Belorussian separatist priests) were nonexistent in Belorussia. The pronouncements of the head of the Belorussian Orthodox Church, Metropolitan Panteleimon, and his entourage indicated their unwillingness to undertake the Belorussification of the Orthodox Church there. The Russophilism was especially noticeable in the Bishop of Grodno, Venedikt.

The Russophile clergy by utilizing the Belorussian Orthodox Church in their own interests had "outplayed" the civil administration (let us remember that the "civil administration" consisted of the thirty German-imported Belorussian émigré separatists mentioned above). Further, a number of accusations were at the head of the Belorussian Orthodox Church in relation to his alleged connections with the *Locum Tenens* Metropolitan Sergii in Moscow and with Exarch Sergii in Vilno.[29]

This communiqué further tells of the dissatisfaction in Belorussian circles with the fact that Metropolitan Panteleimon refused to consecrate their candidates for bishops. The communiqué returns to the question, trying for the occupation forces, of the separation of Belorussia from Russia and of the Belorussian Orthodox Church from the Russian Orthodox Church. To illustrate the difficulties of separatism, the author of this document relates how one Russian in the German civil administra-

[29]U.S. National Archives and Record Service, *Meldungen aus den besetzten Ostgebieten*, No. 6 (5 June 1942), Roll 235. Very similar information including a detailed analysis of the political situation in Belorussia is given in No. 11 (10 June 1942), Roll 235. Artificial Belorussification suffered a defeat among the population and even among members of the civil administration organized by the occupation authorities.

tion of Belorussia expressed an opinion that "there exists only one inseparable Russian people" which should "unite all of the Slavs"; he said that Belorussian language was only a dialect of Russian and was the result of the German "divide and rule" policy.[30]

Military intelligence held a somewhat different point of view than that of the SD. One army report on the reasons for the removal and arrest of Metropolitan Panteleimon attributed it to the machinations of Belorussians outside the Church who misinformed the German authorities..[31]

After Metropolitan Panteleimon's exile and the transfer of church administration to Archbishop Filofei (Narko) under pressure from the "Aktiv" group and the insistence of the German authorities, Archbishop Filofei on 30 August 1942 summoned a meeting of elected representatives from the clergy and laity; this was loudly proclaimed by the "Aktiv" as an All-Belorussian Council. Actually, only three of the younger bishops took part in it—Archbishop Filofei, Bishop Afanasii (Martos), and Bishop Stefan (Sevbo). Archbishop Venedikt, who was on his way to Minsk, was removed from the train by German soldiers and ordered to return home. Moreover, the notice of the meeting sent him had been delayed deliberately in Minsk. The German authorities had forbidden Panteleimon to take part in the council. Participants in the council, primarily designated (and not elected) were from only two bishoprics—Minsk and Novogrudok. There were no representatives from the Vitebsk, Smolensk, and Mogilev eparchies, and the Grodno eparchy was not informed of the meeting and therefore sent no one. In consequence only two of the six eparchies and three of the five bishops took part in this council.[32]

Metropolitan Panteleimon had, however, given written permission to Archbishop Filofei for convocation of the council. Archbishop Venedikt believes that this permission was given, first of all, under pressure from the German authorities, and,

[30] *Ibid.*
[31] Wehrmachtsbefehlshaber Ostland Ic. 14222, den 22.VIII.1942. Betr.: Stimmungsbericht aus Weissruthenien. Document Occ E 3a-14, YIVO .
[32] Archbishop Venedikt, *op. cit.,* p. 54.

second, with the idea that the council would consist of representatives elected from all the eparchies of the metropolis.

This convocation worked out a statute of the "Belorussian Orthodox Autocephalous Church," but announcement of the autocephality was not made. Paragraph 113 of this statute states: "Canonical announcement of the autocephality shall be made after recognition of it by all autocephalous churches."[33]

The council decided to ask the Council of Bishops of the Belorussian Church to concern itself with the affirmation and formulation of autocephality. Meanwhile, the political activists, unfamiliar with the canons of the Holy Orthodox Church in the matter of setting up autocephality, considered the wishes expressed at the council as final establishment of autocephality, and the council as an All-Belorussian Council, and hurried to announce this in the newspapers. Unfortunately, no refutation of these announcements was made by church authorities—because of conditions independent of the church. "To anyone familiar with the canons and rules of the Holy Orthodox Church, the absurdity of these announcements is evident."[34] Further, Archbishop Venedikt enumerates three reasons why the meeting could not be recognized as a council: (1) the absence of the two eldest bishops from the meeting, (2) the absence of four elective representatives from four of the six dioceses, and (3) the lack of affirmation of the decisions made at the meeting by the Council of Bishops and all further necessary measures, such as correspondence with the heads of local churches, announcement of autocephality to the people, etc.

In his exposition, Filofei views these same events as follows: After the removal of Metropolitan Panteleimon, no longer the Germans but instead their Belorussian protégés came to Archbishop Filofei, demanding from him the Belorussification of the Orthodox Church in Belorussia. Archbishop Filofei promised to do everything possible in this regard. The Belorussians also demanded a convocation of the council and the announcement of autocephality. Filofei called Bishops Afanasii and Stefan to

[33]The full text of the statute was published in an appendix to Kasiak, *op. cit.,* pp. 173-88.

[34]Archbishop Venedikt, *op. cit.,* p. 55.

Minsk, and the three bishops decided that it was impossible to convene the council without Metropolitan Panteleimon. Filofei went to see the Metropolitan in Liady, and the latter gave his blessing for the convocation of the council. Besides the bishops, there were representatives of the clergy and laity at the council. They succeeded in assembling representatives of only the Minsk and Baranovichi eparchies. Archbishop Filofei refused to open the council in the absence of Metropolitan Panteleimon, and he and Bishop Stefan went to the Generalkommissariat to request permission for Metropolitan Panteleimon to attend the meeting. The representative of the Kommissariat called the Metropolitan a saboteur. "You, yourselves, spoil everything by your politics," Archbishop Filofei answered him.

Returning home, Filofei locked himself in his room, and did not open the council. Then a special delegation from the council went to the Metropolitan, and received his blessing to begin the work in his absence. The number of participants in the council was approximately 150, of whom 50 percent were from the laity.[35]

Regarding the first question considered by the Council, the restoration of the dissolved bishops' councils and of the metropolitan council, on the recommendation of Archbishop Filofei, they acted positively. Action was postponed indefinitely on the second question, which dealt with the problems of autocephality. The decision led to the council's asking the bishops to turn to the Mother Church and to the other autocephalous churches for their intercession for establishment of autocephality for the Belorussian Orthodox Church. This was a completely unrealistic action under wartime conditions. Further, such a wish freed the clergy from the continual importunities of both the German Occupation authorities and the Belorussian Nationalists.

[35] According to Kasiak's data, the composition of the council was as follows: (1) three bishops—Archbishop Filofei, Bishop Stefan, and Bishop Afanasii: (2) from the Novogrudok-Baranovichi diocese—seventeen representatives of the clergy and twenty-two of the laity; (3) from the Minsk diocese—twenty-six representatives of the clergy and forty-two of the laity; (4) from the Smolensk diocese—one representative of the laity; and (5) several members of the pre-council commission (Kasiak, *op. cit.*, p. 110).

Some newspapers published in occupied territory announced autocephality as an accomplished fact. After waiting two months, the Germans asked the Belorussians why autocephality was not mentioned in the official name of the Church. Logically, the answer given to this question was that the consent of the Orthodox Churches had not been given and that Metropolitan Panteleimon was the only one who could approach them. At the council the text of a letter to be sent by Metropolitan Panteleimon to the heads of the autocephalous churches was prepared, and Panteleimon was brought to Minsk for three days for this purpose, after which he was sent to Vileika under stricter supervision.[36]

Still later the Metropolitan was again returned to Minsk, where he signed the letters to the heads of the autocephalous churches. Each copy of the letter was written in three languages: Belorussian, German, and the language of the church to which the letter was to be sent. Only the occupation powers themselves could distribute the letter under wartime conditions. Because of the many delays, the letter was not given to the occupying forces for delivery until 1943.

Although in the interpretation given by the two bishops the Council of 1942 could not be called a Council, from the standpoint of Kasiak it was the main event in Belorussian church life during the entire German occupation. He is correct in that the Council of 1942 was the main effort of the "Aktiv" to force its policies on the Orthodox Church in Belorussia. Disregarding his interpretation of the events, the general picture given by Kasiak in his book mentioned above agrees with the facts given by Archbishops Venedikt and Filofei. According to his account, the Generalkommissar of Belorussia established "trusted persons" attached to the Departments of Culture and Politics in the Generalkommissariat. Ivan Ermachenko was assigned to the Generalkommissariat in such a capacity. He evidently was a

[36]According to Archbishop Filofei, this measure was taken not as an indication of the failing health of the aged Metropolitan or of his attitude, but because of the German command's fear that he might fall into the hands of Soviet partisans whose numbers were growing continually.

former member of the Belorussian Committee organized under Metropolitan Dionisii. The "trusted person" attached to the cultural and political section of the Generalkommissariat was I. Kasiak himself.[37]

Kasiak wrote a report to the head of the political section of the Kommissariat on the establishment of autocephality through the All-Belorussian Council. In addition, he emphasized that the Germans were in favor of a meeting of the clergy and that he had insisted on the inclusion of the laity, evidently relying little on the separatist mood of the clergy.

According to Kasiak's information, Bishops Stefan and Afanasii insisted on the return of Metropolitan Panteleimon to Minsk, but Archbishop Filofei was supposedly against such a return. At the beginning of June the three bishops interceded with the occupation authorities for the return of the Metropolitan to Minsk.[38] The Generalkommissariat refused their request, for it felt that Archbishop Filofei could do everything himself. The bishops once more appealed, and were again refused.[39]

In the middle of July 1942, the Belorussian "Aktiv" intercepted letters of the priests Ivashkevich and Balai about the unofficial meetings of the pro-Russian oriented clergy and their relations with Cracow and Vilno, that is with former Poland and the Baltic states. Copies of the letters were forwarded to Archbishop Filofei, and also became known to the Generalkommissariat of Belorussia.[40]

News of all these measures evidently reached Metropolitan Panteleimon, and Kasiak, with a somewhat naive and rather inexplicable pride, notes that the Metropolitan once said he had survived the Poles and the Bolsheviks, and he would survive the Kasiaks.[41] The Metropolitan lost patience and, not limiting himself to this comment, wrote a memorandum on 30 July 1942 to the Generalkommissariat in which he stated that the activists brought from Poland did not represent the Belorussian people, and besides were absolutely incompetent in church affairs.[42]

[37]Kasiak, *op. cit.*, p. 101.
[38]*Ibid.*
[39]*Ibid.*, p. 102.
[40]*Ibid.*, pp. 102-3.
[41]*Ibid.*, p. 103.
[42]*Ibid.*, pp. 103-4.

In the middle of July the head of the Political Section of the Generalkommissariat of Belorussia summoned Archbishop Filofei and Bishops Afanasii and Stefan before him, and, in the presence of I. Kasiak, demanded the immediate announcement of autocephality without calling together the council. The bishops agreed to call the council, and were informed that the Belorussian Self-Help organization which was controlled by the separatist "Aktiv" would provide technical help during the council gathering.[43] A precouncil commission was created, during the organization of which the "Aktiv" was circumvented. The "Aktivist" Ermachenko protested, and the membership of the commission was changed.

Already in the commission, arguments were generated concerning the Church Slavonic language, in which services continued to be conducted, concerning the transcription of saints' names according to Belorussian custom, and in regard to the projected letter to the heads of the autocephalous churches.[44] The argument spread to embrace the principle on which the delegates would be selected. The "Aktiv" demanded that all members of the Council be Belorussian nationals, and opposed the requirement that delegates be pious and members of congregations for at least three years.[45] (Evidently the "Aktiv" candidates were new people and active in political matters rather than in church affairs.) It is typical that, according to Kasiak's information, the Germans forbade the convention of eparchial meetings to elect delegates to the council.[46]

The Germans demanded that the statute proposed for approval of the council should be first presented to the Generalkommissariat for approval.

On 19 August 1942 the occupation authorities forbade Metropolitan Panteleimon to participate in the Council, and ordered that Archbishop Filofei be the chairman. The council opened on 30 August 1942.[47]

[43]*Ibid.*, p. 104.
[44]*Ibid.*, p. 105.
[45]*Ibid.*, p. 106.
[46]*Ibid.*, p. 107.
[47]As pointed out Archbishop Venedikt's report concerning the incompleteness of the council's composition is confirmed by Kasiak. *Ibid.*, pp. 110-12.

Actually, the council considered mainly the question of autocephality, which was accepted by all except for three abstentions, with the aforementioned limitation on the observance of canonical rules, which required the agreement of the remaining autocephalous Orthodox churches. The statute on the Belorussian Orthodox Church was affirmed. The formation of autocephality was delegated to the bishops. Thus the requirement of the occupying authorities was formally met, but in reality everything remained exactly the same as it had been before the council.

The formal observance of the occupation authorities' requirements evidently satisfied them but did not satisfy the "Aktiv," who again began to complain to the Germans about the bishops' lack of action on the question of putting autocephality into official form.[48] Again the Germans put pressure on the bishops, and the bishops once more began to demand the return of Metropolitan Panteleimon. He was allowed to return on 16 April 1943. A letter to the heads of autocephalous churches was signed, given to the occupation authorities, and was sent nowhere. Also, the text of the letter accepted by the council was changed.[49]

On 11 July 1943, a new bishop of Briansk, the vicar to Bishop Afanasii, was consecrated at the request of Afanasii. Bishop Pavel was a Russian, and this evoked new protests from the "Aktiv."[50] In its memorandum the "Aktiv" alleged that the Orthodox Church in Belorussia had assumed the character of a Russian church and even an anti-Belorussian church. That statement was true only if one considers the thirty-odd Belorussian émigrés working in German establishments, and brought in by the German army as being "the Belorussian people."

At that time the "Aktiv" began to lose its position. Ivan Ermachenko was dismissed. The occupation authorities were in the process of creating the so-called Rada, using Belorussian Catholics for this purpose.[51] According to Kasiak's data, up to 90 percent of the clergy of the pro-Russian and anti-

[48]*Ibid.*, p. 124 .
[49]*Ibid.*, pp. 124-26.
[50]*Ibid.*, p. 127.
[51]*Ibid.*, p. 128.

chauvinistic Belorussian Church reconstructed during the occupation consisted of priests of Belorussian nationality.[52]

On 19 September 1943 still another bishop, Grigorii, was consecrated as Bishop of Gomel and Mozyr. Bishop Grigorii was a Ukrainian who considered the Ukrainians were also Russian. His consecration coincided with the reestablishment of the Moscow Patriarchate. The Germans were at a loss. Their single propaganda trump, the greater freedom of religion in the occupied territories than in the USSR itself, was seized from them by Stalin.

As mentioned before, bishops of the Russian Church Abroad who were distrusted by the Germans were allowed to assemble in Vienna. Members of this church had not been permitted to go to occupied territories, and the reorganized churches had been guarded from them in every way. Now they were necessary as the most authoritative representatives of the Russian Orthodox Church in order to counterbalance Stalin's efforts to draw the Orthodox Church in Russia to his side.

The Bishop of the Orthodox Church in Belorussia, the Ukrainian Bishop Grigorii, went to Vienna for consecration, and in this way demonstrated his adherence to the Russian Orthodox Church Abroad. Metropolitan Anastasii, the head of the Russian Orthodox Church Abroad, and other bishops of this church took part in the consecration of Bishop Grigorii.

One of the most noteworthy events in Belorussian church history under the German occupation was the Council of Bishops which gathered on 12 May 1944, about two months before the Soviet troops advanced into Belorussia. Again, we have to rely on Archbishop Venedikt's account.

According to the Archbishop, the full council included: Metropolitan Panteleimon, Archbishops Venedikt and Filofei, Bishops Afanasii, Stefan, Pavel, and Grigorii. In addition, Archbishop Ioann (Lavrinenko) of Brest, Ukraine, took part in the council. After an examination of the statute enacted in the Council of 1942, the Council of Bishops rejected it, but utilized it in compiling a statement "on the subject of a systematic,

[52]*Ibid.*

gradual development of the church-national life of the country." Further, Archbishop Venedikt stresses that "the council completely ignored the question of autocephality, did not affirm and did not announce it," but only clarified certain points in the proposals for autocephality. Furthermore, the council clarified church relations to the civil authorities in its reply to the "Central Rada" (the newly-created highest civil authority in Belorussia) in connection with the correspondence between Metropolitan Panteleimon and the "Central Rada" President Ostrovskii.

Archbishop Venedikt explains the relative freedom of the council by the proximity of the Soviet advance, by the difficulties of the German forces, and by the resulting confusion of local administration. All of these factors allowed the council to even "ignore the demand to introduce 'autocephality' of the church by non-canonical means."

The Archbishop also notes that "for the entire period of German occupation . . . [the Orthodox hierarchy] did not use the word 'autocephalous' in the church seal, despite the repeated demands and threats of the German powers." What is striking, however, is that two months after the Council of Bishops took place, the Orthodox hierarchy of Belorussia in its entirety turned up in Germany as refugees.[53]

Additional light is obtained from an interview with Archbishop Filofei, who stated that in January 1944 the Belorussian protégés of the German command, disillusioned with him, wanted to replace him with Bishop Stefan. A corresponding request was sent to Metropolitan Panteleimon. The Metropolitan conferred with the clergy of Minsk, and Archbishop Filofei remained. This refusal was officially based on the fact that he could not replace bishops without a corresponding decision by the Council. In May 1944, at the insistence of occupation authorities, a council of Belorussian bishops was called. The council officially attached two eparchies to the Belorussian Church, those of Poles'e and Brest. Metropolitan Aleksandr (Inozemtsev) was already the head of the Polish eparchy, and Archbishop Ioann (Lavrinenko) was in charge of the Brest eparchy. Two new bishops took part in the affairs of the council.

[53] Archbishop Venedikt, *op. cit.*, p. 56.

The Belorussian civil authorities again used the council in an attempt to get rid of Metropolitan Panteleimon, and turned to Archbishop Filofei with the wish that Panteleimon be replaced by Metropolitan Aleksandr whom they considered more flexible even though he was not of Belorussian extraction but a native of Siberia. Archbishop Filofei answered that in order to avoid a schism among the bishops of the Belorussian Church he could not take this course; it would be more sensible to wait since the aged Metropolitan might die in a few years.

At the council Archbishop Filofei presented the question of substituting someone else in his place, but at the request of the other bishops he remained at his post.

As stated above regarding the two Archbishops, President Ostrovskii, again promoted by the Germans, wanted to exchange Bishop Stefan for Archbishop Filofei as the real leader of the Orthodox Church in Belorussia. Later, his candidate became Metropolitan Aleksandr of Poles'e, who had been attached to Belorussia along with the Poles'e Eparchy. Metropolitan Aleksandr, a Russian about whom more will be said later, was more submissive.

Kasiak confirms that the Council of Bishops of 12 May 1944 was convened at the insistence of the Germans who had become alarmed by the election of a Patriarch in Moscow. The council did not raise objections to Belorussification, but it stated that the lay powers, in the person of President Ostrovskii, should not interfere in church affairs.[54] A series of decisions were reached, on opening a seminary, etc., which were of no consequence, in connection with the retreat of the German forces. After the council there were nine eparchies in the Belorussian Church, but this also was of no significance because of the general evacuation of the entire administration of the Orthodox Church in Belorussia. Once emigrated, the Belorussian episcopacy immediately began to seek a rapprochement with the Russian Orthodox Church Abroad.[55]

[54]Kasiak, *op. cit.*, p. 132.
[55]On 7 January 1945, General Vlasov, the head of the all-Russian movement of the peoples of Russia, published in his newspaper *Volia Noroda* the blessing of the movement signed by Metropolitan Panteleimon, Archbishop Venedikt, and Bishops Stefan and Grigorii.

After the end of the war, the episcopacy of the Belorussian Orthodox Church was united to the Synod of the Russian Orthodox Church Abroad, on 23 February 1946. This was preceded by a struggle with a group of separatists who had convened a council in occupied Germany. This struggle took such a sharp form that the Belorussian bishops forbade Father Lapitskii, the chairman of the council, to perform his priestly duties, and Kasiak was not allowed to take communion for three years.[56] The following bishops joined the Synod: Metropolitan Panteleimon, Archbishops Venedikt and Filofei, Bishops Stefan, Afanasii, and Grigorii.

※❦❦❦※

Such mishaps as those described above connected with the organization of the church hierarchy in Belorussia retarded a spontaneous religious rise among the population. Nonetheless, despite such handicaps all sources agree that in Belorussia there was a definite religious renaissance with the coming of German troops.

In particular, Archbishop Filofei in his interview gives some extremely interesting details on Minsk, Belorussia. He was familiar with the city from the beginning of the Revolution. Until the persecution began, two theological seminaries, two eparchial schools for girls, two cathedrals, fifteen churches, a convent, and a monastery were in use in Minsk. There were about four hundred churches and six hundred and fifty priests and deacons in the eparchy. After the retreat of the Red Army in 1941, none of these institutions remained. After a search of two months, two former priests were found, and later on several other priests turned up. The two cathedrals in Minsk had been destroyed. The convent's chapel had been divided into two floors and equipped as a gymasium. Archives were housed in the church of the monastery; the cemetery church had become a garage. The last church service held in the city was in 1937 at the new cemetery. In the course of the first three or four months after the Communists left, seven churches were opened and

[56]Kasiak, *op. cit.*, pp. 144-45.

22,000 children were baptized.[57] Priests married twenty or thirty couples at one time. Many post-burials were performed. In the eparchy about 120 parishes (approximately 30 percent of the pre-Revolution number) were opened. Naturally, the number of clergymen was insufficient, and priests traveled about the eparchy visiting and ministering the various congregations. Pastoral courses were inaugurated. Even though the Germans did not permit the opening of a seminary, they nevertheless allowed the transfer of two old professors, Kolesnikov and Chetverikov, from Smolensk for the pastoral courses. The study in these courses was accelerated, and as soon as students acquired the basic knowledge, they received holy orders and were assigned to congregations. Usually such classes consisted of from twenty to thirty students. Frequently the congregations found candidates for the priesthood. Such candidates were brought to Minsk to be tested, and those who passed the examination were immediately consecrated, while the weaker candidates remained for further preparation. Under such an arrangement the investiture of priests and deacons took place every two or three days.

During the Archbishop's services, the Minsk churches were so full that it was impossible for members of the congregation to lift a hand to make the sign of the cross. Mass confessions were held in order to accommodate the great numbers who came to confess. Two excellent choirs, known respectively as the "metropolitan" and the "cathedral," were organized in Minsk. The cathedral choir consisted of members of the Odessa Opera Company which had become stranded during a guest performance in Minsk as a result of the German occupation. Attendance at services in the cathedral was as high as thirty-five hundred with fifteen hundred people finding places inside and the remainder standing outside.

Archbishop Filofei presents a vivid description of the pro-

[57]Kasiak, who describes the behind-the-scenes struggle for the Belorussification of the Orthodox Church, gives almost no information on the rise of religion among the population. He makes only one reference of this sort: on holidays the clergy of Minsk baptized up to ten thousand persons in a day. His information is apparently exaggerated. *Op. cit.*, p. 87.

cession on the feast of the Epiphany in 1944. A crowd of eighty to a hundred thousand of the faithful gathered from all churches in the city. Both shores of the Dnieper river were covered with people for a distance of three kilometers.

Thus, according to Archbishop Filofei's testimony, one can conclude that a true religious reawakening did occur, at least in part of Belorussia. Perhaps of equal interest is Archbishop Stefan's report written for Metropolitan Panteleimon to inform the latter on the situation in Smolensk. This document fully corroborates Archbishop Filofei's testimony. Because of its clarity and conciseness the report is given here in full:

> Condition of the Smolensk Eparchy from 20 December 1942, the day of Bishop Stefan's arrival there, to 1 January 1944. The Smolensk cathedral church was opened for divine services and blessed on 1 February 1942 by Protoierei P. Before this time the cathedral had been used as a storehouse for museum pieces, and Protoierei P. was custodian. In 1942 the churches in Smolensk were opened: the Okopnaia Church, on the side of the trenches of 1812, the Guz'evskaia Church as well as the Tikhvinskaia and Vsesviatskaia churches. The following deans were assigned to open the churches of other congregations in other centers: Archimandrite R. for congregations in the city of Krasnyi, Igumen A. for seven congregations in Roslavl', Archimandrite M. for twelve congregations in Briansk. Proteierei P. for five congregations in Mstislavl', Protoierei L. for eight in Viazma. There was one church each in the cities of Demidov, Dorogobuzh, Gzhatsk, Rzhev, and Karachev.[58]
>
> Courses were open to prepare persons who agreed to serve churches in the cities of Smolensk and Karachev.
>
> There were eparchial administrations in the cities of Mogilev and Vitebsk. Under the direction of Protoierei R. there were three congregations in Mogilev. In addition, there were deaneries in the cities. In the city of Orsha served by Protoierei V. there were ten congregations; in Shklov with seven congregations and in Borisov Protoierei S. with twenty-one congregations, and one congregation in the town of Berezino. There was also a monastery in the village of Belynichi.
>
> In Vitebsk, the eparchial administration was under the guidance of Archimandrite M. In the city itself there were two congre-

[58] As stated before, the authors have avoided using names that might implicate the priests themselves or their relatives. The full names appear on the document, however.

gations, and in the surrounding area, six. There was also a deanery in the city of Lepel' under Protoierei K. for nine congregations. There was a congregation and the Evfrosinievskii Convent in Polotsk under Father D. On 23 May 1943 the relics of Blessed Evfrosiniia were brought to Polotsk from Vitebsk, where they had been since 1925. . . .

Cadres of the clergy were filled mainly from those who had come from former Poland and from the repressed clergy who remained in the Soviet zone. Again, persons chosen and attested by congregations, mainly former teachers, were newly consecrated.

In regard to the moral level of the clergy, thanks to the Lord, despite the burden of the war all were, as they say, in their proper place. In regard to the people, one can only say good things about them: during the establishment of congregations the people themselves, without being ordered or coerced to do so, established them, undergoing sacrifice and effort to do so. Thus, when the question of the re-establishment of Orthodoxy was raised by the German authorities, I said and I shall maintain that it would be re-established tomorrow with the arrival of some authority acceptable to the people.

There were numerous baptisms and marriages. There were general confessions of the mass of the people. In witness to the morality of the population, one must note that Russians hid Jewish children, registered them into their own families, and baptized them with their own name.

Attested: Archbishop Stefan
March 24, 1954

Other witnesses interviewed for this project attest to the vital religious experience shared by the Orthodox of Smolensk. A priest, Father A., who was in the city immediately after the arrival of the Germans, testifies that there was one open church for the 150,000 inhabitants of Smolensk, and he is not certain whether services were conducted in it or not. The city had suffered greatly, mainly because for a long time the front had remained on the Dnieper river, which divided the city into two parts. Despite the fact that, as a result of evacuation and deaths, only approximately thirty thousand inhabitants remained under the Germans, four churches were opened in the city. However, other phenomena characterized this religious revival. Very typical was the mass baptism of children, ranging in age from infants to seventeen or eighteen years. Having christened all the city children, the priests began to go out into the country. They would stop at a village and baptize all the children in the surrounding area. On the average, they would remain in one place for about a week, performing 150 to 200 baptisms daily. Sometimes, around the houses in which the priests were staying, as many as 100 to 150 carts carrying believers would gather. Naturally, there were not enough clergy for the newly organized congregations. Eight or ten priests who had been hiding from the Soviet authorities were discovered in the Smolensk region. After Bishop Stefan's arrival, in the course of seven months, about forty priests were consecrated for the Smolensk region alone. In September 1942, 30,000 prayer books were printed. This supply ran out in one year.

According to authentic witnesses, in those places where the clergy could act freely, up to 75 percent of the pre-Revolutionary churches were opened, despite interference from the rapidly growing partisan movement. The Communist leaders of partisan units up until September 1943, when Stalin received Metropolitan Sergii Stragorodskii, harassed and killed Orthodox clergymen, and it was only after the beginning of a more favorable policy of the Soviet government toward the church that their relationships to the clergy in occupied territories changed sharply. It was at exactly this time that the eparchial administration was transferred to Borisov because of the approach of the front. It remained there until the spring of 1944, having activated about 70 percent of the pre-Revolutionary congregations.

Besides Smolensk and Borisov, in Polotsk also four Orthodox Churches ministered to a population of nearly fifteen thousand. The absence of accurate church statistics for this region during this troubled period forces us to rely more on the accounts of witnesses, and it is a consolation that after interviewing individuals representing different points of views the picture that emerges is devoid of contradictions. Mass christenings and baptisms and mass confessions as well as heavy attendance were typical phenomena in the newly opened churches. In the city of Polotsk, according to a former inhabitant, four churches were open—St. Nikolai's on the drill ground, the Cathedral of St. Sofiia, the Spaso Evfrosin'evskaia Church in the convent and St. Ioann Bogoslov beyond the Dvina.[59]

In the city of Vitebsk, according to a local inhabitant of long standing, much of the destruction was done by the local party and the NKVD with the help of special brigades. The city was fired from all sides. Three-fourths of the residential section burned for three days. All of this took place before the arrival of the German forces on 12 July 1941. Already before this fire, all Orthodox churches of Vitebsk were closed, and many of them were turned into storehouses. The Church of St. Antonii was turned into an antireligious museum. Incidentally, the relics of St. Evfrosiniia, Princess of Polotsk, were kept there.

After the retreat of the Red Army in August and September 1941, the Sviato-Pokrovskaia Church was tidied up completely and the first service took place on 14 October 1941. In November 1941, with the permission of the German authorities, the relics of St. Evfrosiniia were transferred to the Sviato-Pokrovskaia Church. In May 1944 the saint's relics were transferred to her native town, Polotsk. Repair of the Vitebsk Cathedral was to have begun in the fall of 1943, but military events interfered with this plan. Incidentally, it should be noted that the city of Polotsk was also set on fire by special detachments before the arrival of the German Army. Generally, the burning of cities during the retreat of the Red Army was conducted more or less according to plan. This is what a resident of Vitebsk at the time writes of the efforts to burn the churches that were still standing:

> Both the Sviato-Pokrovskaia Church and St. Nicholas' Church were saved from fire mainly because the Komsomol brigade consisting of young girls was destroyed before the plan could be realized.[60]

In the same way, churches in the city of Gorodok were saved miraculously when a young Komsomol girl who had been as-

[59]Data on Polotsk and its existence under the Germans are given in an article by Pavel Ilinskii, "Tri goda pod nemetskoi okkupatsiei v Belorussii; zhizn' Polotskogo okruga, 1941-1944gg" [Three years under German occupation: Life in the Polotsk area, 1941-1944], *Grani*. No. 30 (April-June, 1956), 85-122; No. 31 (July-September 1956), 94-127.

[60]Letter in the possession of W. Alexeev.

signed to burn the churches did not carry out her orders and committed suicide.

According to the same source, courses for pastors in which twenty persons participated were opened in Vitebsk in 1942. During the German occupation Orthodox churches were opened in all eleven of the counties of the former Vitebsk Guberniia, in the cities of Nevel, Gorodok, Polotsk, Drissa, Surozh, Velizh, Sebezh, and Liudin.

Finally, there is a detailed account by Father I. about Zaslavl in the Minsk Oblast. Father Porfirii, the last priest who was in charge of two congregations in Zaslavl, was sent to a peat factory near the city of Gomel, where he was killed by partisans in 1943. Since before 1939 Zaslavl had been only eight kilometers from the Polish border, all persons of doubtful loyalty were sent away. After the arrival of the German forces faithful religious believers obtained the sacred vessels, icons, and even the Antimins and the altar Gospels which had been hidden during the time of persecution, and opened a church on 2 November 1941. Bishop Filofei assigned a priest permanently to the city. Since in the preceding four years there had been no clergy in the region, at first it was necessary to perform as many as a thousand (later up to five hundred) baptisms daily. Afterward, on holidays there were regularly fifteen to twenty baptisms. On days of memorials for the dead, thousands of people gathered in the old and new city cemeteries. During 1943-1944 the Church of the Transfiguration, Na Valu, was repaired. Two icon painters executed eighty large icons and a new iconostasis was built surpassing in splendor the old one which had been destroyed by the Bolsheviks. Support for repairs came from collective farms in the form of grain which was brought in even from partisan areas.

Thus, one sees that in Belorussia, in the Smolensk and Briansk oblasts, the same thing occurred that took place in the area of the Pskov Mission's activities.

German police communiqués, mentioned above, fortunately give considerably more material on Belorussia than on the Pskov area. By a strange coincidence, they illustrate best of all the situation in Smolensk and Borisov, the areas about which we have information from Orthodox witnesses as well. Perhaps this can be explained by the fact that the eparchial administration of Archbishop Stefan was situated in these cities.

In a communiqué dated 5 July 1941, an incidental mention is made of the great number of worshippers in the town of Baranovichi. The same document tells of a similar situation in the Bilsk-Podlaski area.[61]

Four days later, another communiqué notes that apparently the population on the former Polish territory did not fall under the Communist influence during the Soviet occupation of that area, if one judges by church attendance there.[62]

A communiqué of 5 August 1941 is of interest, too. There is further discussion of the German fear, mentioned before, that the Polish intelligentsia, which composed the upper cultural layer of Belorussia, would again seize control over the Belorussian population. Furthermore, it repeats the already familiar information that Polish Catholic clergy are conducting intensive work among the Orthodox Belorussians by using their longing for religion, but adds certain details to the picture: Catholics sometimes take advantage of the absence of the Orthodox clergy and confiscate Orthodox churches for their own use. This communiqué also states that Catholic chaplains of the German forces participate in this activity.[63]

If one examines the same source further, it becomes obvious that the fear of Polish influence and the unwillingness of the local population to work with the civil administration created by the Germans forced the latter to rely almost exclusively on Belorussian émigrés who were brought in by the army and who, as seen above, in their turn were held in suspicion because of the great number of Roman Catholics among them. All this forced the occupation authorities to welcome the revival of the Russian Orthodox Church. In any case, members of the Orthodox Church were grateful for the relative religious freedom they enjoyed on occupied territory, and obviously expressed their gratitude publicly. For instance, the communiqué relates that in

[61]U.S. National Archives and Records Service, Reich Chief Security Office, *Ereignismeldungen. UdSSR*, No. 13 (5 July 1941), Roll 233.
[62]*Ibid.*, No. 17 (9 July 1941), Roll 233.
[63]*Ibid.*, No. 43 (5 August 1941), Roll 233.

Minsk where thousands gathered for Orthodox services and forty-five children were baptized, thanks were expressed to the Führer in the sermon.[64]

One month later, on 4 September 1941, an SD report speaks of the inadequacy of church organization in Belorussia in connection with the marked interest of Belorussians and Russians toward Orthodoxy. It notes that churches are opening, but there is need for priests and facilitation of clergy movement to areas of greatest need.[65]

One must note, however, that after the complete destruction by the Communists, it would have been difficult to expect a more organized church than that which was developed in occupied territories. In addition, the critical observations of the document cited above merely emphasize the spontaneity of the religious revival in occupied territories.

An interesting sidelight of this document is a statement that the German secret police hoped to secure information concerning the mood of the people, and also to be able to influence the population through the church. They conclude that "for this reason, a swift solution to the church question would be very desirable."[66]

References to the religious revival abound in the German documents. It is also clear that German officials in the area were aware of the mood of the population, and even though they could not influence or change the course of Rosenberg's and Hitler's Russian policy, they made some efforts to bring to the attention of policy makers the political possibilities which could be open to Germany in the event of a different attitude toward the population of occupied regions and to the Russian question in general. The feelings of such German officials can be illustrated by the report of Major O. W. Müller, "Beauftrager des Reichsministers für das Ostgebiet b. Kommand," addressed to the Minister of seized territories and dated 8 October 1942. Major Müller stated that the Russians constantly inquired

[64] *Ibid.*
[65] *Ibid.*, No. 73 (4 September 1941), Roll 233.
[66] *Ibid.* About September 1943 Stalin definitely came to this conclusion and, evidently with the same motives in mind, he allowed the resumption of a religious NEP in the USSR.

about their country's future, that is about Germany's aims in Russia. The prisoners of war were ready to fight against Communism. They believed the Germans, but they also loved their fatherland; they were ready to fight against Communism, but they wanted to see Russia free after the war. Major Müller went on to tell about the large attendance of churches, and even though he noted that the young people in towns were not interested in religion, he pointed out that the populace was restoring churches and that a bishop was needed for the central segment of the front to direct the religious revival. He further inquired if the Metropolitan of Minsk could be given permission to do this.[67]

One must remember that the Smolensk and Briansk oblasts were under the jurisdiction of the bishop in Minsk. In the remaining territories of the central part of the front which were in German hands for only a short time, church life was not organized with any regularity.

In another communiqué dealing specifically with the Orthodox Church in Belorussia (21 September 1941) there is again mention that in Vitebsk and Smolensk the Roman Catholic army chaplains served the native population. The SD checked the reliability of the clergy, but also in Vitebsk the clergy were allegedly attempting to conduct pro-Bolshevik services.[68] There is also an interesting testimony indicating the degree to which the occupation authorities feared the Orthodox Church which was organizing. The SD informed the military authorities of the undesirability of church unions above a strictly local level. Furthermore, the secret police found it essential to undertake a disbandment of any already existing unions on a higher level.[69]

A further glimpse into the attitudes of the population can be found in the SD communiqué of 8 October 1941, where mention is made of the situation in Smolensk. Representatives of the local intelligentsia put a number of typical questions to the representatives of the occupation authorities. These included questions about the relations between Russia and Germany in

[67]Document Occ E 3d-7, YIVO.
[68]U.S. National Archives and Records Service, Reich Chief Security Office, *Ereignismeldungen. UdSSR*, No. 90 (21 September 1941), Roll 233.
[69]*Ibid.*

the future, and the reasons for the German division of Russians into Ukrainians, Belorussians, and Great Russians.[70] Further, in the same communiqué one again finds mention of reports about the great participation of the populace in the Orthodox services, about mass baptisms of children and of parents with lack of information on their church marital status. One detail stands out in this document: in the town of Velizh the peasants dug up the dead and reburied them with church rites even though such reburials had been forbidden by the German authorities for sanitary reasons.[71]

Of particular interest is the 23 October 1941 secret police report which deals with the return of the population to the church in the city of Smolensk. At first only women and old men attended services. Gradually young people, including former Komsomol members, began to attend. Priests who had finished a theological seminary before World War I and who had not served in this capacity during the Soviet period were returning to the priesthood. As is known, such newly designated priests had to be cleared through the SD, who had hoped to use some of them as German agents.[72]

A very valuable communiqué is dated 12 December 1941, because it gives the results of a census of the Smolensk population, including the following religious categories:

Orthodox	24,100	94.6%
Catholics	849	3.4%
Lutherans	259	1.0%
Mohammedans	24	0.1%
No religion	201	0.8%

What is striking about the census is not only that Smolensk had been reduced from its prewar 150,000 population to about 25,000, but also the low figure among the survivors of those without religious affiliation.[73] It is hard to explain this fact as resulting solely from fear of the Germans, that is to say that an atheist could possibly be regarded as a Communist by the Ger-

[70]*Ibid.*, No. 107 (8 October 1941), Roll 234.
[71]*Ibid.*
[72]*Ibid.*, No. 122 (23 October 1941), Roll 234.
[73]*Ibid.*, No. 145 (12 December 1941), Roll 234.

mans.[74] The 1937 census in the Soviet Union was not published by the Bolsheviks, because more than 50 percent of the population were not afraid to indicate their religious affiliation. The results of a census taken at Borisov are also interesting because of their similarity to those obtained at Smolensk:[75]

Orthodox	19,317
Catholic	6,255
Evangelical	130
Mohammedan	23
No religion or belonging to other faiths	894

The last German document on the situation of religion in Belorussia is a monthly communiqué of *Oberkommando der Heeresgruppe Mitte*. Again, there is mention of heavy church attendance, and of four church and prayer-house openings, as well as a report on the Feast of the Epiphany in Bobruisk with a procession of five thousand faithful.[76] Despite the rise in partisan activity and the retreat of the German forces, the population continued to display its religion openly. Finally, in this communiqué there is information on a leaflet found near Lepel bearing the name of the Metropolitan of Moscow and Kolomna which accused the Germans of persecuting priests and destroying churches.[77]

Mention should be made here that the Metropolitan of Moscow and Kolomna was none other than Metropolitan Nikolai (Iarushevich), who became the chief representative of the Moscow Patriarchate at innumerable world conferences after the war. He died under suspicious circumstances in 1961 after the end of the temporary religious NEP introduced by Khrushchev. In November 1942, by a decree of the Presidium of the Supreme Council of the USSR, Metropolitan Nikolai was designated a

[74]The same phenomenon is noticeable in a census of Borisov where out of 20,000 only 1000 were listed as having no religious affiliation. U.S. National Archives and Records Service, Reich Chief Security Office, *Ereignismeldungen*. *UdSSR*, No. 180 (13 March 1942), Roll 235.
[75]*Ibid*.
[76]Oberkommando der Herresgruppe Mitte. Monatsbericht, für Februar, 1944, dated 13 March 1944, p. 5, Document No. 2006.
[77]*Ibid*.

member of the Extraordinary Government Commission on the determination and investigation of the crimes of fascist usurpers and their collaborators.[78] The appointment of Metropolitan Nikolai was the first assignment of a representative of the Orthodox Church in the USSR to an official government post. Soviet propaganda not only used the Orthodox Church for its own purposes but, with its capacity for boldness, totaled up on the German score the destruction of churches, a practice which the Soviet government itself had initiated and continued during the course of two decades. Such measures on the part of the Soviet government forced the occupation authorities to deal even more cautiously with the Orthodox Church. Thus, Orthodoxy became an extremely important factor in the propaganda struggle between the Nazis and the Communists.

Despite the less accurate figures available on Belorussia in comparison with the Pskov region, it is possible to conclude that the Orthodox faithful of Belorussia showed the same strong desire to reestablish Orthodoxy as did the Pskov believers.

The religious persecution of the Soviest by 1939 had made Belorussia almost a religious desert similar to Pskov. The reestablishment of 30 percent of the prerevolutionary churches in the Minsk eparchy under exceedingly difficult conditions of the war can be considered as much of a miracle as the opening of three hundred churches in the Pskov area where there had remained only one or two open churches. The mass baptizing of children attests to the same phenomenon, supported by the statistical data on the number of believers in Smolensk and Borisov.

In Belorussia, as in Pskov, with the reestablishment of church organizations the decisive role was played by the émigré clergy who had not been on Soviet territory before 1939. It is true that Metropolitan Sergii (Voskresenskii) in the Baltic was a Soviet citizen, but the missionaries he sent out were from the ranks of the clergy who had lived in the free Baltic states before 1940. In Belorussia the beginnings of the reestablishment

[78] V. Nikonov, "Vysokopreosviashchennyi Nikolai, Mitropolit Krutitskii i Kolomenskii" [Most Holy Nikolai, Metropolitan of Krutitsy and Koloma], *Zhurnal Moskovskoi patriarkhii*, No. 4 (1952): 9-21.

of an Orthodox hierarchy lay entirely on the shoulders of Metropolitan Panteleimon, who had lived in Poland before 1939.

In both instances, moreover, the Orthodox Church did everything in order to maintain its traditional canonical position. This was especially noticeable in Belorussia, where from the very beginning occupation authorities permitted the reestablishment of the Orthodox Church only as an autocephalous Belorussian church. But, as the Germans concluded, the Orthodox clergy outmaneuvered the occupation authorities and in place of a Belorussian Church created a Russian Orthodox Church.

Finally, one must note that all sources found by these authors were in complete agreement as to the factual side of the reestablishment of the Orthodox Church in Belorussia during the German occupation. The Belorussian chauvinist Kasiak admirably supplements the data of Archbishop Filofei, while neither one of these sources contradicts the information of the German secret police.

FIVE

 ## The Ukrainian Case

The reestablishment of Orthodoxy in the Ukraine during the German occupation took place with the same rapidity as it did in the Pskov region and Belorussia, but the organization of the church hierarchy was complicated by the struggle between the Ukrainian Autonomous and Autocephalous churches. The Autonomous Church based its canonical position on the decision of the All-Russian Church Council of 1917-1918 which provided for the creation of a Ukrainian Autonomous Church within the framework of the Russian Orthodox Church. The Autocephalous Church, on the other hand, had on principle severed every tie with the Russian Orthodox Church, as it was the product of Ukrainian separatists who had accepted without reordainment Lypkivs'kyi priests, or the so-called "self-consecrators," whom no Orthodox Church would consider as having been canonically ordained. As Armstrong points out, the Ukrainian Autocephalous Church

> ... was not recognized by any other body of the Orthodox Church, for the method of consecration of the new bishops was regarded throughout the Orthodox world as uncanonical, a violation of the essential principle of apostolic succession.[1]

[1]John Alexander Armstrong, *Ukrainian Nationalism, 1939-1945*, p. 189.

In order to appreciate the peculiar conditions surrounding the appearance of the Autocephalous Orthodox Ukrainian Church in occupied USSR territory in 1941 to 1944, one must be aware of the Ukrainian Autocephalous Church which existed in the USSR from 1919 to 1930, as well as the Ukrainian autocephalous movement in former Polish territory up to 1 September 1939, and in the German Government-General from September 1939 to 1941.

The Ukrainian Autocephalous Church in the USSR originated during the heat of the Civil War, and was formed in 1921, that is to say during the years of confusion when any improvization was possible.

In his monograph, *The Efforts of the Ukrainian Autocephalous Church in the Twentieth Century,* Fotiev dates the formal beginning of the Lypkivs'kyi schism to 29 June 1919, the day when the priest Lypkivs'kyi, with the cooperation of the Soviet authorities, received St. Sophia's Cathedral in Kiev and began services in it in the Ukrainian language, despite the prohibition issued by the ruling Orthodox Bishop.

> The Bolsheviks turned over St. Sophia's Cathedral on July 28 to the newly created Ukr. congregation and on the following day, the day of Sts. Peter and Paul, in St. Sophia's the first liturgy was conducted without the Bishop's blessing. When a delegation . . . had appeared before Bishop Nazarius for his blessing of the celebration of the Liturgy in St. Sophia's, he refused it. "Then," writes Lypkivs'ky, "we continued without his blessing." June 29 can be considered as the beginning of schism. The path into complete church illegality began at this moment.[2]

The fact that the Communist authorities helped Ukrainian nationalists should not come as a surprise. It was part of their policy to weaken the Russian Orthodox Church, which they considered their primary challenger, by fostering a series of schisms within the church's ranks, the first of which was the Ukrainian Autocephalous Church.[3] To quote Armstrong again "the phe-

---
[2]K. V. Fotiev, *Popytki ukrainskoi tserkovnoi avtokefalii v XX veke* [The efforts of the Ukrainian Autocephalous Church in the twentieth century], pp. 25-26.

[3]Friedrich Heyer, *Die orthodoxe Kirche in der Ukraine von 1917 bis 1945*, pp. 77-78.

nomenal growth of the new church was possible only because of the comparatively indulgent attitude shown by the Communist authorities who, at that time, were more antagonistic to the Russian church than to dissident bodies.[4]

In 1920, Lypkivs'kyi's group, with the active support of the triumphant Soviet government, again took possession of St. Sophia's Cathedral in Kiev for their use and created their own church council or *Rada*. In February 1921, priests who were members of the Rada were deprived of their holy orders by the Council of Ukrainian Bishops, and those of the laity associated with them were excommunicated. These measures did not stop the schismatics, however, and on 23 October 1921 their Rada, consisting of laity, deacons, and priests, consecrated Lypkivs'kyi as a Metropolitan by all participating in the action of laying on of hands on him, an act which violated the canons of the Orthodox Church. After this, adherents of Metropolitan Vasyl' Lypkivs'kyi began to be called "self-consecrators." During the NEP, the period of Lypkivs'kyi's success in the Ukraine, the number of Ukrainian congregations acquired by the schismatics reached approximately 11 percent of all congregations in the Ukraine.[5]

The Autocephalous Ukrainian Church remained active until 1930, when it, along with other bourgeois nationalist movements in the Ukraine, was liquidated by the Soviet authorities. By 1941, all of the so-called bishops of the Ukrainian Autocephalous Church had died. There remained only the priests consecrated by them who had been accepted, as duly consecrated, in the newly created Ukrainian Autocephalous Church, evidently more for political than for church considerations.

There also turned out to be a great number of Ukrainian

[4]Armstrong, *op. cit.*, p. 189.
[5]The historian of the Ukrainian Autocephalous Church, Ivan Vlasovs'kyi, gives the following figures for this church: in 1924, 1080; in 1926, 1040; in 1927, 1039. He states that there were 10,000 congregations in the Ukraine in 1917. Considering that during the NEP period churches were closed only rarely, one can easily figure that the percentage of autocephalous churches was approximately 11 percent of the number of Orthodox congregations in the Ukraine. See his *Narys istorii ukrains'koi pravoslavnoi tserkvy, XX St.* [History of the Ukrainian Orthodox Church, XX century], vol. IV, pp. 134-35.

separatists on Polish territory who had inspired self-consecration in the Ukraine. In 1941 they became the organizers of a newly created Ukrainian Autocephalous Church on territory in the Ukraine occupied by the Germans. In order to understand exactly how this occurred, a few words must be said about the Orthodox Church in Poland.

According to the Riga Treaty of 1921, there were approximately five million Orthodox persons on Polish territory. Of these, more than two-thirds were Ukrainians, about a third were Belorussians, and a very insignificant percentage were Great Russians. Until 1924 Polish Orthodox bishops were nominally subordinate to the Moscow Patriarchate and were included in the structure of the Russian Orthodox Church. But in 1924 the Polish Orthodox Church received its autocephality from the Patriarch of Constantinople. The Polish government not only sympathized with the separatists in the Polish Orthodox Church, but in fact played a decisive role in the separation. The next step was to weaken Russian cultural influence in the Polish Orthodox Church and to substitute ukrainization for it. In this question Polish national interests, in part, coincided with the interests of the Ukrainian separatists. The Ukrainian separatist political leader Simon Petliura was on Polish territory and was able to reach some mutual understanding with Marshall Pilsudski, the creator of independent Poland. This provided the opportunity to begin training a new cadre to found a Ukrainian Autocephalous Church. The new autocephalists differed from Lypkivs'kyi's adherents in that during the time of the existence of independent Poland, they were able to supplement their theological training or begin it anew and, most important, to receive the "legal" elevation of their candidates to the rank of bishop from the Polish Orthodox bishops.

The future head of the Ukrainian Autocephalous Church, Bishop Polikarp Sykors'kyi, head of the chancellory of Petliura's Council of Ministers during the Civil War, became Bishop of Lutsk in 1932.

The beginning of World War II did not suspend this preparation. According to Heyer's data,[6] in that part of Poland

[6]Heyer, *op. cit.,* p. 69.

which had been taken by the USSR in September 1939, there were 3,900,000 Orthodox and 1,200 parishes. In that part of Poland which went to Germany, there were about 300,000 Orthodox and ninety-eight parishes. Insofar as the head of the Polish Orthodox Church, Metropolitan Dionisii, remained in the German part of Poland (in the Government-General), the Polish Autocephalous Church also remained in the Government-General. The fate of those ninety-eight parishes which remained outside the USSR would be of no interest for the history of the Russian Orthodox Church on German-occupied territory if the large part of the Ukrainian separatists had not remained in the Government-General and if Metropolitan Dionisii had not dreamed of extending his influence not only into the Soviet part of the Ukraine but even over the entire Russian Orthodox Church. One already knows of analogous pretensions of the Metropolitan of Warsaw in regard to Belorussia and of the support given his claims by the head of Hitler's Government-General, Frank. From a historical standpoint, Metropolitan Dionisii had more basis for his claim to the Ukraine and Kiev, because it was the Kievan Orthodox Metropolitanate which, until 1686, had been subordinate to the Constantinople patriarchate, from which the Polish Orthodox Church had received its autocephality in 1924, and not to Moscow. However, German policy consisted of the greatest possible territorial dismemberment of the Orthodox Church in occupied territory; the remainder of Poland was not subservient to the Eastern Ministry created later, but remained a completely separate administrative unit (Government-General), isolated from other occupied territories in the east. Despite this, Ukrainian separatists using the name of Metropolitan Dionisii were able to influence the course of organization of the Orthodox Church in Ukrainian territory.

Immediately after the fall of Poland, Metropolitan Dionisii not only lost more than 90 percent of the parishes and congregations, but he was also subjected to house arrest by the Germans. This is in a way understandable, especially since at the beginning of the Polish-German war the head of the Polish Orthodox Church issued a patriotic and, consequently, an anti-German proclamation. Besides this, there was at the moment another Orthodox Metropolitan, Serafim of Berlin, to whom Metropolitan Dionisii was ready to subordinate himself at the first opportunity, but the peculiar situation of two metropolitans was even more unusual in that Metropolitan Dionisii, Russian by origin, represented a Polish Orthodox Church which had separated from Russia, and the Metropolitan of Berlin, Serafim, a German by birth, represented the Russian Orthodox Church Abroad, one that symbolized anti-Communism, Orthodoxy, and nationalist Russia. In such a situation Metropolitan Dionisii's subordination to Metropolitan Serafim could not last long and on 23 September 1940 the Metropolitan of Warsaw again became independent. Actually, he fell even more into the hands of the Ukrainian separatists. Heyer points out that General-Governor Frank wanted to make the Polish Orthodox Church a weapon for seizing the Russian Orthodox Church in Russian territory.[7] For this, a Ukrainian committee was created which raised to the rank of bishop two Ukrainian separatists, Ivan Ohienko, former Minister of Religion in Petliura's government, and Archimandrite Palladii (Vidibida-Rudenko), Petliura's former Assistant Minister of Finance. Afterward the two bishops were not allowed on Ukrainian territory, and therefore are of secondary interest here. However, at that time Stefan Skrypnyk (not to be confused with the deceased Ukrainian Commissar of Education), a future important figure in the Ukrainian Autocephalous Church in the occupied Ukraine, a nephew and former adjutant of Petliura, became Vice President of the Bishop's Council, and actually the leader of Orthodox Church policy in the Government-General. After the beginning of the Soviet-German War, Skrypnyk was able to get to the occupied territory, at first not as a religious but as a political figure.

To the chagrin of the Poles and Roman Catholics, the occupation authorities somewhat strengthened the Orthodox Church in the Government-General. Ivan Ohienko, who as a monk received the name Ilarion and became Archbishop of Kholm, was able to achieve much: a number of Orthodox churches which had been closed by the Poles were returned to him. As a matter

[7] *Ibid.*, p. 163.

of fact, Archbishop Ilarion was a candidate in some separatist circles for the position of Metropolitan of Kiev, and even that of a Ukrainian Patriarch, but he was not allowed on former Soviet territory. The political considerations that led Governor-General Frank and the Nazis in general to support the Ukrainian Autocephalous Church and the nationalist-separatists are entirely clear in view of the traditional German policy in regard to Russia at the end of the nineteenth and the beginning of the twentieth century. This policy of supporting Ukrainian separatists had its origins in the Austro-Hungarian monarchy and became especially noticeable during World War I.

At the beginning of World War II, Ukrainian separatists in emigration and in Polish territory, members of the OUN (Organization of Ukrainian Nationalists) split into two competing groups: followers of S. Bandera and followers of A. Mel'nyk. Both organizations openly collaborated with the Germans and created diversionary groups within the framework of the German Army. One of these groups, bearing the name "Nightingale" and under the control of Bandera, was later active in the L'vov area; another, known as "Roland," was under the control of Mel'nyk and active in Rumania.[8]

Representatives of both groups turned up in Soviet territory after the beginning of the war, and, to a large degree, seized the civilian administration created by the Germans. This was the situation in the Government-General on the eve of Hitler's invasion of the USSR. One must remember that Bishop Polikarp (Sykors'kyi) of Lutsk, former head of Petliura's Chancellory, had been on Soviet territory since 1939. Whether Polikarp recognized the jurisdiction of the Moscow Patriarchate or not remains a debatable question.[9] However, he stayed in his position as Vicar of Lutsk during the administration of Exarch Nikolai (Iarushevich), who had come from Moscow and who was at that time one of the supporters of the Moscow Patriarch-

[8]Collaboration of Ukrainian separatists with German counterintelligence began in 1939 when the OUN, not yet split as outlined above, organized a Ukrainian regiment for war against Poland and for preparation for an uprising in the rear of the Polish army. See Alexander Dallin, *German Rule in Russia, 1941-1945*, p. 115 and Armstrong, *op. cit.*, pp. 73-75.

[9]Heyer, *op. cit.*, p. 168.

ate's pro-Communist line. At the same time, Bishop Polikarp avoided a trip to Moscow (which would have emphasized his subordination to the Moscow Patriarchate) on the excuse of ill health. Despite such a manifestation of independence, Bishop Polikarp was not arrested. It is also interesting to note that at this time his future opponent, Archbishop Aleksii (Gromadskii), who was later to head the Ukrainian Autonomous Church, miraculously avoided death during his arrest by the Soviets and his deportation with the retreating Soviet troops in 1941 when he succeeded in escaping.

The policy of the Minister of Occupied Territories, Rosenberg, toward the Russian Orthodox Church was very close to that of Governor-General Frank. In his directive letter of 13 May 1942, cited above, addressed to the Reichskommissars, he stated unequivocally that the Ukrainians must have their own Orthodox Church, separate from the Russians, and that the main enemy of German policy on the dismemberment of Russia was the Russian Orthodox Church. The question arises as to how a pro-Russian Ukrainian autonomous church, and not simply a Russian church for Great Russians living in the Ukraine, was allowed to be created on Ukrainian territory. To answer this question it is necessary to note, though in briefest outline, the facts connected with the organization of two competing Orthodox churches in the Ukraine.

A week after the war began, on 30 June 1941, L'vov, the capital of Galicia and cradle of Ukrainian nationalism, was taken by the Germans. Ukrainians of the Nightingale detachment took part in the seizure of the city. Taking advantage of the confusion, they seized the L'vov radio station and announced the independence of the Ukraine. This action by the followers of Bandera frightened the German officers commanding the Nightingale detachment. The followers of Mel'nyk, the rivals of Bandera's group, were obviously disturbed by the successes of this competing group. According to Armstrong, among the numerous Ukrainian interpreters and "political reporters" who arrived with the SS *Einsatzgruppe* three days after June 30 there was an important representative of the Mel'nyk group. On July 9, most of the persons responsible for the announcement of independence were placed under "honorary arrest" At the same time Bandera and his closest coworkers were also arrested. After questioning in Berlin and their refusal to retract the announcement of independence, none of these individuals suffered further repression; on the contrary, while nominally under house arrest, they were allowed to carry on their political activities in Berlin, and one of the main leaders of the organization, "Stets'ko, was even able to go to Cracow, where he consulted with Lebed', whom he had secretly delegated to take command of all activities in the Ukrainian lands."[10]

Thus the German policy toward the Bandera group was one of restraining and not stopping their activities completely. At that time, when the chief leaders of the organization were restricted in their activities, other members of both the Bandera and Mel'nyk groups had, almost unhindered, penetrated occupied territory of the Soviet Ukraine either as interpreters and advisers, or independently. Armstrong states that there is even a map of the Ukraine on which are drawn the lines of movement of the Ukrainian separatist groups in occupied territories.[11]

On 26 July 1941, Stepan Skrypnyk was appointed representative of the Ostministerium with the group of the Armies South, and became a trusted person on the question of the organization of the civil government in the Ukraine.[12]

All this led to the rapid seizure of command posts in the civilian administration, created by the Germans, by members of the most extreme Ukrainian nationalist organizations. The seizure was complicated by the bloody struggle between the followers of Bandera and those of Mel'nyk.[13] This struggle made it possible for the occupation authorities to weaken both organizations, supporting the more tractable one at that time, or simply advancing others against the well-organized emigrants from the former Polish Ukraine—local public men of the eastern Ukraine who were pro-Russian and sometimes even those who were Russian by nationality. Evidently the policy of "divide and rule" was

[10]Armstrong, *op. cit.*, p. 83.
[11]*Ibid.*, p. 78.
[12]Heyer, *op. cit.*, p. 174.
[13]See below data from German SD political communiqués.

not always carried out in a sufficiently well thought-out and subtle way. In addition, the struggle between military and civilian authorities, as well as the general chaos in the German administration, created an opportunity for the most varied improvisations on the spot.

Such a situation somewhat equalized the position of the autonomous and autocephalous churches, though in theory (the general German aim to dismember Russia) and in practice (pressure of local administration, selected mainly from the chauvinists), the position of the autonomous church was much less favorable. It is no wonder that only supporters of the autonomous church appear on Heyer's list of bishops and priests who perished during the period of occupation.

On 18 August 1941, Orthodox bishops in Ukrainian territory occupied by the Germans gathered in council at the Pochaevsk Abbey. Those taking part in the council were Aleksii of Kremenets, an old Polish bishop who in 1941 had gone over to the jurisdiction of the Moscow patriarchate; Antonii (Marchenko), a retired bishop consecrated in Poland at the beginning of the 1920's; Simon Ivanovskii, an old bishop of the Polish clergy; Panteleimon (Rudyk) and Veniamin (Novitskii)— both consecrated in 1941 as bishops of the Moscow Patriarchate.

The council noted the significance of Volynia with its undestroyed religious life for the reestablishment of Orthodoxy in the entire Ukraine, which had, as yet, been free of persecutions. It offered Archbishop Aleksii (Gromadskii) the title of Metropolitan, and decided to organize a church on the basis of the decision of the All-Russian Local Council of 1918 which had granted the Ukrainian Church autonomy within the framework of the Russian Orthodox Church. Bishops Polikarp (Sykors'kyi) and Aleksandr (Inozemtsev) refused to take part in the council.

On 1 September 1941, in a district message to congregations, the elder bishop of this group, Aleksii (Gromadskii), explained his decision not to renew his fealty to Metropolitan Dionisii of Warsaw. In Heyer's interpretation, the statement of Metropolitan Aleksii suggested that since in 1939 Metropolitan Dionisii had refused, in writing, to head the Polish Orthodox Church and the Volynia eparchy (which had gone to the USSR), and since the Volynia eparchy recognized the jurisdiction of the Russian Orthodox Church in 1940, the highest ecclesiastical authority in the Ukraine now rested in the Council of Bishops of the Ukrainian Autonomous Church.[14]

On 25 November 1941 a new Council of Bishops in the Pochaevsk Monastery elected Metropolitan Aleksii (Gromadskii) Exarch of the Ukraine. Metropolitan Dionisii, on the other hand, did not recognize the arguments of Metropolitan Aleksii, having formed his own objections to the message of 13 November 1941.

At approximately the same time, Bishop Aleksii (Gromadskii) visited Kiev and there tried to come to an agreement with Ukrainian nationalist circles. As a compromise, it was suggested that the Ukrainian Orthodox Church should be headed by the Archbishop of Kholm, Ilarion (Ohienko), but this was never realized. About the same time, 29 September 1941, what remained of Lypkivs'kyi's followers were organized in Kiev, and the relations with them completely split the Ukrainian Orthodox Church.

Things continued to move rather rapidly. On 18 December 1941 Archbishop Panteleimon (Rudyk), a supporter of the Autonomous Church, arrived in Kiev and during transactions with Lypkivs'kyi's followers offered to include them in communion after a new ordination. On 24 December 1941 Metropolitan Dionisii appointed Bishop Polikarp (Sykors'kyi) administrator of the Ukrainian Church in the Ukraine. Things became complicated again when on 7-10 February 1942 there occurred in Pinsk a gathering of bishops who were in opposition to the Autonomous Church, namely, Aleksandr (Inozemtsev), a Russian by heritage, and Polikarp (Sykors'kyi), a Ukrainian. Bishops Aleksandr and Polikarp consecrated two Ukrainians as bishops and decreed that Lypkivs'kyi's priests perform their duties without a new consecration. Thus, the split between the Ukrainian Autonomous and Ukrainian Autocephalous churches was defined. From then on the rivalry between them was intensified. Both churches consecrated new bishops,

[14]Heyer, *op. cit.*, p. 176.

whose numbers soon rose to sixteen for the Autonomous Church and fifteen for the Autocephalous Church.[15]

There was an effort to unite these two branches on 8 October 1942. The head of the Autonomous Church, Metropolitan Aleksii (Gromadskii) and two bishops of the Autocephalous Church, Mstislav and Nikanor, met in the Pochaevsk Abbey. Bishop Mstislav was none other than Petliura's nephew, already known as a person trusted by the Germans under the name of Stepan Skrypnyk before his consecration as bishop. Skrypnyk had been promoted from the rank of a monk to that of a bishop in great haste. The agreement reached by him and Metropolitan Aleksii was not accepted by the bishops of the Autonomous Church, because it placed the Autonomous Church under the control of the Autocephalous Church, and did not satisfactorily solve the canonical question of Lypkivsk'yi's followers. Here it must be borne in mind that Reichskomissar Koch advocated an all-German policy which encouraged divisions between the churches. Koch expressed the direct opinion that it was necessary to support divisions and conflicts between the autonomous and autocephalous churches.[16]

Shortly after the rupture of the Pochaevsk agreement, Metropolitan Aleksii was killed by unidentified persons on a forest road. The death of the head of the Autonomous Church was not the only instance of terror toward pro-Russian clergy. As mentioned by Heyer, there is a long list of clergy of the Ukrainian Autonomous Church who were killed by Ukrainian nationalists. Some of the murders took place during holy services. In some cases entire families of priests displeasing to the partisan nationalists were liquidated. Bishop Manuil, formerly of the Autocephalous Church, who had broken with it and gone to the Autonomous Church, was also kidnapped and hanged in a forest.[17]

It was in the midst of such terrible conditions that the religious revival in the Ukraine took place. Despite the political opportunism of some of the leaders, the people returned to the

[15]For the list of bishops, see Heyer, *op. cit.,* pp. 181-82.
[16]See Harvey Fireside, *Icon and Swastika,* p. 219, note 105.
[17]*Ibid.,* p. 155; Heyer, *op. cit.,* p. 220.

faith as had those in the Pskov area and Belorussia and the Ukrainian experience serves as a brilliant chapter in the history of the Orthodox revival during World War II.[18]

This revival started almost immediately as the Red Army evacuated before the German advance. In almost all cities of the Ukraine there were priests living there as deportees or employed as skilled workers. These priests appeared before the local *kommandatura* and received permission to organize church communities, and began to make use of the various remaining church buildings scattered in the region. Most frequently these were cemetery churches which had been closed since 1937. The first religious services were usually conducted a few days after the arrival of the German Army. In Kamenets-Podol'sk an old priest conducted services in July 1941 in the Church of St. Peter. A priest who had come from Galicia with the Germans began services in the City of Proskurov. On 4 August in that same city, a local priest was also serving in the cathedral. In Vinnitsa an old priest, who before the arrival of the Germans had hidden in the basement of a cemetery church, began services, to be joined soon by three more priests. When on 1 September 1941, connection was established with the Volynia episcopate, the three priests had already opened two new churches. In the city of Zhitomir, the first church community was created by a German Catholic military chaplain. So anxious were people to resume their religious practices that in the beginning they overlooked ecclesiastical differences.

Priests who belonged to the catacomb church took advantage of these changes and began organizing their own Orthodox parishes. The best example was Archimandrite Leontii (Filipovich), who was soon consecrated bishop and who thereafter entered the hierarchy of the Autonomous Ukrainian Church. Similar incidents occurred in Odessa and Poltava where priests spontaneously began holding services. In Poltava, the first priest who began services had worked as a mason under the Bolsheviks and conducted his first service the day of the German arrival. The last church closed by the Bolsheviks, that of

---

[18]*Ibid.*, p. 200. German secret communiqués are very illuminating on this matter.

St. Makarius', was in good condition so that services could be held in it. But soon there were five churches open in Poltava, and eighteen priests had emerged from the underground to perform liturgies.

Heyer notes that the faithful met the arrival of the Germans as God's punishment for falling away from the faith. Many peasants crossed themselves upon seeing the white crosses on the German tanks which served, alas, only as identification marks for the German forces.

A religious fervor permeated the atmosphere. The people streamed into the opened churches from all sides. Heyer notes the large number of baptisms. For example, the priest who had opened the first church in Poltava baptized 2500 children during the first sixteen months. There were cases of mass baptisms ranging in numbers from twelve to 130 children. Often young men and women as well came on their own to be baptized. Sometimes the baptisms were conducted in a river. Celebration of the important Orthodox holidays was reintroduced, generating great enthusiasm. On the Feast of the Epiphany, 19 January 1942 in all Ukrainian towns, especially those along the Dnieper, religious processions and blessing of the waters attracted crowds of people. In Poltava, some five thousand gathered. On the Feast of Pokrov, celebrated on 14 October new style, on the streets of Kamenets-Podol'sk, one constantly met peasants with horse carts bringing in pilgrims from the surrounding villages. Right before the New Year, children again began to go from house to house caroling. In the large industrial city of Dnepropetrovsk about sixty thousand believers gathered on the Feast of the Epiphany in 1943. At Easter, the churches could not hold all those who wished to attend services.[19]

Needless to say, there was a growing demand for the organization of church life. Heyer quotes Bishop Nikanor of the Autocephalous Church who stated that the requests for priests from all corners of the eparchy were innumerable. Sometimes as many as a hundred persons a day came to ask for priests and that services be organized. In three months under Bishop

[19] *Ibid.*, pp. 170-172.

Nikanor 518 parishes were organized anew, and soon six new bishops were added to assist him. The number of parishes in the Kiev diocese under the jurisdiction of the Autocephalous Church increased to 298. The number of priests appointed by Bishop Nikanor in his own and in other dioceses reached 455; 226 of them were old priests who had been working in civilian jobs, and 136 were newly ordained. The Autonomous Church, according to Heyer's conclusion, fully supported by German secret documents, soon exceeded the growth of the Autocephalous Church in the Kiev eparchy. Toward the end of 1942, in the Kiev diocese there were 410 autonomous parishes with 434 priests.[20]

The Autonomous Church continued to grow. During the first two months of 1943, the number of priests exceeded six hundred. Thus, during the German occupation, after combining the 410 Autonomous and the 298 Autocephalous parishes, the total of newly organized parishes was 708 or 350 times greater than in 1939. According to information provided by Archbishop Panteleimon, by 1943, there were in the eparchy 500 as contrasted to 410 churches as indicated by Heyer for the end of 1942. If this latter figure is added to the number of Autocephalous churches, then the figure rises to approximately 800 churches—slightly fewer than half of those active before the Revolution. If one considers the number of priests available, the picture becomes even more impressive. Heyer speaks of 600 priests of the Autonomous Church and 434 priests of the Autocephalous Church, as compared to the prerevolutionary figure

[20]Heyer, *op. cit.*, p. 206, introduces an interesting table which characterizes the position in the Kiev diocese before the Revolution, during Communist rule, and during the German occupation. The figures given in the 1942 column include the Autonomous Church only.

	Pre-Revolution	Under Communism	1942
Churches	1710	2	318
Monasteries	23	—	8
Priests	1435	3	434
Deacons	277	1	21
Sacristans (readers)	1400	2	86
Monks and nuns	5193	—	387
Parishes	?	2	410

of 1435 priests. This indicates that during the occupation 72 percent of the prerevolutionary number of priests were restored. Such was the situation in the Kiev diocese.[21]

The large percentage of churches opened in the Kiev diocese was not equalled by other dioceses. In the Poltava eparchy, for example, there were about twelve hundred parishes before the Revolution; at the beginning of 1943, 140 Autonomous parishes had been reinstated with approximately the same number of priests. Of this number, twelve priests were newly consecrated and six had come from Volynia. The Autocephalous Church had 102 priests, of whom twenty were newly ordained. Thus in the Poltava eparchy only 20 percent of the prerevolutionary parishes were reinstated; if one counts one priest to a parish, one must agree with Heyer when he states that 20 percent of the number of prerevolutionary churches served immeasurably more parishioners than the corresponding number of churches before the Revolution. In 1941-1943, churches were usually overflowing with worshippers. "The huge marketplace in Poltava," continues Heyer, "was overflowing with many thousands of peasants every Sunday." And only very few of them did not also attend the church which stood, nearly completely repaired and painted, not far from the marketplace. In Poltava itself, there were six Autonomous and four Autocephalous churches.[22]

On the other hand, in Podol'e only 20 percent of the prerevolutionary church edifices remained intact. This may be partly due to the fact that this eparchy was for a long time a border zone of the USSR, thus experiencing religious persecution at its worst. Only ten surviving priests were found in the whole Podol'e area. Despite these difficulties, a bishop Damaskin of the Autonomous Church was able to organize some six hundred parishes in the eparchy. This number is significant, if one keeps in mind that there were 1500 parishes in the eparchy before the Revolution. There is information on the composition of priests in a part of the Podol'e eparchy, the Vinnitsa region where, 350 new priests, deacons, and readers were ordained.

[21]*Ibid.*
[22]*Ibid.*, pp. 206-7.

In the city of Vinnitsa itself, five churches belonged to the Autonomous and two churches to the Autocephalous jurisdiction.[23]

In the Synod of the Russian Church Abroad, there are preserved some of the files of Bishop Evlogii of Vinnitsa who occupied this post during the German occupation and at that time belonged to the Autonomous Church. In these files there is a "List of Priests of the Orthodox Slavic Church of the Vinnitsa Eparchy." Unfortunately it is not dated, but according to the Secretary of the Synod, Protopresviter Father Georgii Grabbe, the list was compiled in 1941. There are 223 names on the list. Thus, the Autonomous Church in the Vinnitsa eparchy alone had 223 priests.

In the Zhitomir eparchy, according to Heyer's data, there were 800 parishes before the Revolution. By the summer of 1943, approximately three hundred Autonomous and a hundred Autocephalous parishes had been organized there. Thus it would appear that 50 percent of the prerevolutionary parishes had been restored. Thirty old priests were found to serve these congregations, and the bishop of the Autonomous Church alone ordained about two hundred priests who had completed a short course there.[24]

Bishop Leontii of the Autonomous Church, who headed the Zhitomir eparchy during the occupation, not only confirms Heyer's figures on the opening of three hundred parishes of the Autonomous Church, but also supplements it. For example, he speaks of the newly opened Bogoiavlenskii Monastery where ten new brothers were active. In the convent of Ovruch there were forty-five nuns and in Liubarskii fifteen, besides the twenty nuns who stayed at two hermitages. No less than twenty thousand persons took part in the religious procession on the Feast of Epiphany in 1943 in Zhitomir.[25]

The Autonomous Church opened 318 parishes in the Dnepropetrovsk eparchy. In Dnepropetrovsk itself, which had twenty-seven churches before the Revolution, the Autonomous

[23]*Ibid.*, p. 207.
[24]*Ibid.*
[25]Letter in the possession of W. Alexeev.

Church reopened ten churches. Heyer gives no data on the number of Autocephalous churches in the eparchy,[26] and it is unlikely that anyone is now in a position to do so. The collected material on the whole confirms Heyer's information regarding Zhitomir and Vinnitsa, and supplements it somewhat with regard to Kiev. It is characteristic that his data relate to that part of the Ukraine which was under occupation for a long time. The eastern part of the Ukraine—Kharkov, for example—actually remained a "front" belt all the time. The Germans took it late, remained there for a short time or, more accurately, occupied and cleared it out several times, thereby creating a very unstable atmosphere. All this instability had its impact on the number of reopened churches; for example, one can judge by scanty and not too accurate data collected from Kharkov refugees that before the Revolution there were thirty churches in his city. Only one remained at the beginning of the war. After the city was taken by the Germans, two more were opened. Fortunately, secret communiqués of the German SD provide, comparatively speaking, a wealth of material on the Ukraine.

Official information on the religious mood of the population of the Ukraine is first given by the communiqué of 17 July 1941. It describes the situation on territory which had been part of Poland up to 1939, but which nonetheless had undergone two years of Communist rule. The communiqué notes that attendance at church services was very great. The churches raised the question to the German military authorities about the return of property seized by the Communists, to which the military authorities gave individual permission.[27] Characteristically it was emphasized that the German Army immediately took upon itself the responsibility, and returned to the faithful the property that had been appropriated by the Soviet authorities.

Information on the situation in the Zhitomir region is provided by an SD report dated 18 July 1941. According to this

[26]Heyer, op. cit., p. 208.
[27]U.S. National Archives and Records Service, Reich Chief Security Office, Ereignismeldungen. UdSSR, No. 25 (17 July 1941), Roll 233.

communiqué, the appearance of the Germans in Zhitomir was accompanied by the opening of religious gatherings attended by a great number of young people. Churches in the city had either been destroyed or turned into warehouses. After the evacuation of the Communists, the city was half empty.[28]

At the same time plans for the creation of a separatist Ukrainian church were made in Poland. According to the communiqué of 22 July 1941, Ohienko (evidently Archbishop Ilarion Ohienko) had prepared, on the territory of the Government-General, about two hundred persons for missionary work in territory of the Soviet Union with the hope of creating a Ukrainian Church independent of Moscow, but the Germans would not permit these people to pass through to former USSR territory.[29]

The general situation in Zhitomir is further discussed in a communiqué dated 29 July 1941. This source states that at the beginning of the war there were 98,000 inhabitants in the city, of whom 30,000 were Jews. After the evacuation, 65,000 inhabitants remained, 500 of whom were Jews. Thus, if these figures are compared with the data of Bishop Leontii, it would seem that there were about ten thousand inhabitants for each church. This explains why the churches could not contain all the worshippers and the priests had to conduct services from morning till evening.[30]

Further, this communiqué states that the Ukrainians—at least the older generation—were very religious. During the Soviet period churches had either been destroyed, closed, or converted into various public buildings. Despite this, especially in the villages, there were itinerant priests who served the population. The longing of the people for religious satisfaction was very great, and on the basis of impressions from occupied regions of the USSR, the antireligious propaganda had had little effect.[31]

The failure of antireligious propaganda in Zhitomir is again

[28] *Ibid.*, No. 26 (18 July 1941), Roll 233.
[29] *Ibid.*, No. 30 (22 July 1941), Roll 233.
[30] *Ibid.*, No. 37 (29 July 1941), Roll 233.
[31] *Ibid.*

noted in the communiqué of August 1941. Only a small part of the Komsomol showed activity in antireligious propaganda before the Germans came. After this observation the source discloses important evidence on religiosity even among members of the Communist Party. "Even among the old convinced Party members one often observes that they pray before their execution."[32]

A communiqué of 5 August 1941 describes conditions in the city of Iampol' on the Dnieper river. Of 6000 inhabitants of the city, 4000 were Orthodox. Before the Revolution there had been two Orthodox churches and one Roman Catholic church in the community. Two Orthodox priests had been shot by the Bolsheviks. Three had fled. One Orthodox church was used for grain storage, the other as a stable. As a result, religious life could develop only in private homes. This, however, did not extinguish religious practices. The first question directed to the Germans was: When can we again attend church? This was considered a typical question by the majority of Ukrainians who, despite religious persecution, preserved their faith.[33]

Some discrepancies exist in some of the communiqués about the state of religious revival in the Ukraine. Some of them, like the one dated 7 August 1941, point out that only some of the women and older men were truly religious. The youth and people of middle age were indifferent; however, they were not hostile, but rather sympathetic toward religion.[34] This picture is overbalanced by the next communiqué (14 August 1941), which stresses the desire of the Ukrainians to reestablish the Orthodox Church with sermons in the Ukrainian language and services in Church-Slavic. It contradicts the opinion that the youth of the village were apathetic toward religion, and that this attitude applied chiefly to children of city dwellers. Admittedly, Orthodox consciousness had weakened somewhat during the interwar years, but it preserved nevertheless "a primitive catacomblike spirit."[35]

[32]*Ibid.*, No. 40 (1 August 1941), Roll 233.
[33]*Ibid.*, No. 43 (5 August 1941), Roll 233.
[34]*Ibid.*, No. 45 (7 August 1941), Roll 233.
[35]*Ibid.*, No. 52 (15 August 1941), Roll 233.

Still this did not reduce the complexity of the religious situation in the Ukraine with which the occupation authorities had to deal. On the one hand, they feared the penetration of Roman Catholics and Uniates, while on the other, their efforts to disseminate Ukrainian separatism met with complete apathy in circles of the Orthodox clergy and could find substantial support mainly among the Uniates, whom as symbols of Catholicism and the Pope the Germans feared and hated. German policy, to be sure, aimed at separating the Ukraine from Russia, and had hoped to utilize the separatist movement for this objective. This did not mean, however, that the Germans wanted to create an independent Ukraine. Similarly, even though they aimed at separating the Ukrainian from the Russian Church, they did not want to create a strong independent Ukrainian church either.

The connections between the Ukrainian separatist-nationalists and the Autocephalous Church became especially complicated in Galicia (the center of the separatist movement, at one time Austrian and later Polish territory) where propaganda for an independent Ukraine conducted by Bandera's extreme group partially used religious holidays for their political purposes. This development evidently disturbed the Germans, as did the situation in the Pinsk area. Pinsk was a Belorussian city which had been annexed to the Ukraine by the occupation administration. It turned out that followers of Bandera operated among the population of this region, though without much success. It is especially noted that here, also, the Bandera group used church holidays for their purposes. This group distributed leaflets, one of which included the text of a proclamation by the head of the Autocephalous Church, Bishop Polikarp. And in Lutsk an open swearing-in of members of the Bandera group took place during religious services in connection with a memorial to the victims of Bolshevism.[36] Lutsk was the residence of the head of the Ukrainian Autocephalous Church, Metropolitan Polikarp.

The efforts of the Ukrainian Autocephalous Church to

[36] *Ibid.*, No. 78 (9 September 1941), Roll 233.

Ukrainianize even non-Ukrainians, including Belorussians of the Poles'e eparchy, by replacing the Church Slavonic language used in religious services with Ukrainian is related in a communiqué dated 10 September 1941. According to this source, a message to that effect was sent by Metropolitan Dionisii from the Government-General (from Warsaw) to Bishop Polikarp of Brest and to Aleksandr of Poles'e on former Soviet territory. This communiqué notes a struggle between the Belorussian Bishop Venedikt and the Ukrainian Bishop Polikarp for the Belorussian parishes in the Brest region, which had been annexed to the Ukraine.[37]

But when all is said and done, the German reports conclude that there was no Ukrainian nationalist movement among the masses in the Ukraine. In fact, there was even no thought of an independent Ukrainian state and all the people aspired to was improvement of their material lot.[38]

The dissent noted between the followers of Bandera and the occupation authorities elicited a sharp struggle between the various groups of separatists, mainly between the Bandera group who stood fast on the eve of 30 July 1941 (the announcement of the Independent Ukraine made in L'vov) and the Mel'nyk group who were more inclined to compromise. The Ukraine was filled with alarming rumors in connection with the terrors perpetrated by the Bandera group against the Mel'nyk group. The slaughter of a hundred followers of Mel'nyk was reported, and the representatives of the old intelligentsia proposed arresting the whole leadership of the Bandera group and liquidating the main culprits (of terror).

During a requiem service organized by followers of Mel'nyk for two of their dead in the Government-General, i.e., Poland, leaflets were passed out which openly accused the Bandera group of murders. The well-known Uniate Metropolitan Sheptyts'kyi who was in Poland was on the Mel'nyk side.

The Uniate Church in its own way was preparing for action on the German-occupied territory of the USSR. The Uniate

[37]*Ibid.*, No. 79 (10 September 1941), Roll 233.
[38]*Ibid.*, No. 81 (12 September 1941), Roll 233.

Church, according to the information received from several parish priests, remained outside the struggle between the Bandera and Mel'nyk political groups. Furthermore, the whole behavior of the Uniate Church indicated that it would never consent to a break with Rome.

The terror of the Bandera group against the Mel'nyk group was also extended to other enemies of Ukrainian extreme separatism: to the clergy of the Ukrainian Autonomous Church. The pro-German pronouncement of the Uniate Metropolitan Sheptyts'kyi can be explained by the complexity of his position. At the time of the announcement of Ukrainian independence at L'vov, he supported the Bandera group, who took this decisive step against the wishes of the German government. Later, during the heightening of the struggle between the Bandera and Mel'nyk groups, the Germans began to prefer the more amenable Mel'nyk group and the aged Metropolitan had, in some way, to isolate the Uniate Church which he headed from the terrorist activities of the followers of Bandera.

The preparation of the Uniates, based on L'vov, which had gone into the Government-General, for action on Soviet territory remained only in the initial phase. Beside the policy of separation of the Government-General from the occupied Ukraine, the Nazis could not reconcile themselves to the fact that the Uniate Church was under direct subordination to Rome. Both facts were sufficient for the occupation authorities to prohibit Metropolitan Sheptyts'kyi from attempting to extend his influence on occupied territories of the Ukraine.

The struggle between the Bandera and Mel'nyk groups continued, the former executing some six hundred political murders in Galicia alone. But even though the Mel'nyk group was beginning to win politically, both groups were generally rejected by the population.

Of particular interest is the communiqué dated 20 September 1941, which describes in detail the struggle with religion in the Ukraine during the Soviet period and which divided the struggle into two periods—before and after 1931. Up to 1931 persecution was reflected in the fact that the church was separated from the government. The consequences of this separation were liquidation of church property, high taxes assessed against the clergy, and antireligious education of youth. Religion was thus preserved only among the peasants and city dwellers who had recently moved from the country. According to the author of the communiqué, in the large industrial cities situated in the bends of the Dnieper the majority of the workers were not completely bolshevized, although in these cities there was apathy toward religious questions. The second period of suppression, according to the author of the communiqué, was characterized by the persecution of individuals for their religious beliefs. The character of religious persecution was different in different places. For example, in Novoukrainka traditional religious funerals were forbidden very early, while in other places such as Vinnitsa and Nezhin there was some fluctuation in policy toward them. In the second period of religious oppression there was a general liquidation of the clergy, destruction of religious monuments, and persecution of believers together with prohibition of religious customs: "It is all the more surprising that the popular tradition has remained practically unaltered."[39] It is further noted in the communiqué that religious holidays (Easter, Christmas, Epiphany, Ascension, St. Andrew's Day, St. Nikolai's Day), continued to be celebrated by the people despite prohibition by the authorities. Later on in the communiqué mention is made of the secret baptism of children, sometimes by others than priests.

Perhaps of equal interest is a communiqué dated 1 October 1941 in which the situation of the church on Ukrainian territory occupied by Rumanian troops is described. The communiqué notes, not without envy, that the Rumanians took advantage of the inability of the Communists to break up religion and transported priests to Bessarabia. An archbishopric had been created at Tiraspol. Further, it reports that in the USSR up to 1933 even Communists had their children baptized. It was only after that year that real religious persecution began. In the Anan'evskii Okrug there had been no church services since 1935.

[39] *Ibid.*, No. 86 (17 September 1941); No. 87 (18 September 1941); No. 89 (20 September 1941), Roll 233.

After the Red Army retreated, three churches were opened, and local priests were found for them. Soon another church opened. Six hundred children up to the age of eighteen had been baptized. Many people also wanted to have church weddings.[40]

In the next SD report which deals with religion (13 October 1941), large attendance at churches in the Ukraine is again mentioned, as well as the opening of new churches, although the communiqué speaks of certain apathy toward religion by some of the youth. Then the author of this document introduces a rather interesting detail: the fact that the people are strangers to anti-Semitism in the racial "ideal" sense of the word.[41]

The rebirth of Orthodoxy in Russia was of such magnitude that it warranted serious reconsideration by the occupation authorities. One is impressed by the careful reports which they prepared and in which they tried to summarize the religious situation in the area under the Soviets, such as the one dated 20 September 1941 and the one of 18 October 1941, describing the religious scene as the Germans found it. It is also quite remarkable how knowledgeable despite inaccuracies the German reporters were on Orthodox matters. Thus they could distinguish between the various religious groups they encountered: Old Orthodox—Tikhon Church; Autocephalous—Ukrainian Church; Living Church; various sects; Schismatics (Old Believers); and Roman Catholics.[42]

There is an interesting report in a German communiqué of the dual relationship of the clergy and laity to the *Locum Tenens* Metropolitan Sergii. On the one hand, the majority were against the "concordat"; on the other, it was a time of war which very easily could end with the downfall of communism, and it could mean the freeing of the Moscow Patriarchate from the oppression of a godless regime. Under such conditions, Metropolitan Sergii would become a person who could unite

[40]*Ibid.*, No. 100 (1 October 1941), Roll 233. Mention of the use of the religious revival by the Rumanians is also made in *Ibid.*, No. 113 (14 October 1941), Roll 234.
[41]*Ibid.*, No. 112 (13 October 1941), Roll 234.
[42]*Ibid.*, No. 117 (18 October 1941), Roll 234.

the reemerging Orthodox Church. Evidently, many representatives of the Autonomous Churches of the Ukraine and Belorussia created in occupied territory were prepared to close their eyes on the past sins of the aged Metropolitan and see in him only the heir of Patriarch Tikhon.

Unfortunately, however, in October 1941 Metropolitian Sergii was under complete control of the Communist authorities, and was not able to take part in the rebirth of the church in the Pskov region, in Belorussia, and in the Ukraine. Further on in the communiqué now under discussion, a text of one of Metropolitan Sergii's proclamations directed against the Germans is quoted. It is suggested that the proclamation was written with the help of the NKVD. It is interesting that the author seems to reassure his readers by saying that the problem of Metropolitan Sergii, in his opinion, is a Moscow problem and not a Ukrainian one, that the Autocephalous Ukrainian Church is hostile to Moscow, and that its hierarchy is anti-Communist and under the influence of Ukrainian separatists. Furthermore, in Kiev there was a tendency toward the union of the Ukrainian Autonomous and the Autocephalous churches. His reaction to this is positive. According to him, in the case of union the Autocephalous Church would become canonical and would lose its sharply nationalistic character. He feels that both Ukrainian churches encompass 95 percent of the population of the Ukraine: 55 percent belong to the pro-Russian Autonomous Church and 40 percent to the Autocephalous. It is interesting that, as in the Baltic states in 1944 when Exarch Sergii (Voskresenskii) refused to speak out against *Locum Tenens* Sergii who became the Moscow Patriarch, so in the Ukraine in 1941-1944 the occupation authorities were forced to become knowledgeable in the canons of the Orthodox Church. And though the German secret police did not become an authority in this question, it is significant that it also considered the Ukrainian Autocephalous Church as a noncanonical church. It is no less interesting that even according to German figures in the Ukraine, 40 percent of the people were in the separatist Ukrainian Church at the time that 55 percent were in the pro-Russian Autonomous Church. As far as is known, the above figures are the only available statistics of this kind. In general, they agree with the above-cited data of Heyer which relate to the number of autonomous and autocephalous parishes.

As far as the Living Church was concerned, the Germans connected it with the Communist regime and, not surprisingly, suppressed its services, especially in the city of Berdichev. But neither the Living Church nor the other sects were significant factors. The latter were found where German colonists had settled since the eighteenth century. All this again underscores the overwhelming significance of the Orthodox Autonomous and the Autocephalous churches.

The German reports on the religious situation in the Ukraine must have been written by different individuals who often times disagreed as to the level of the population's religious mood and behavior. What is significant, however, is that they all attest to the vitality of religion in general and Orthodoxy in particular under Soviet rule. And even though they may disagree among themselves about the periodization of these happenings their emphasis is often helpful in that they reveal what they or their informers considered as landmarks in the history of Orthodoxy during this period.

Thus, for example, the report dated 21 October 1941 does not consider the influence of Orthodoxy on the Ukrainians as significant as some of the other reports do. And its periodization of religious and especially Orthodox persecution in the USSR differs from the rest. Up to 1924, it maintains, there was practically no persecution. Obviously the author was thinking in comparative terms, for, as is known, following the law of 1918 concerning separation of church and state and of the school from the church, there was considerable confiscation of church valuables, as well as execution of clergy and laity. In any case, the first period was followed by the years 1924-1926, which he describes as years of scientific-atheistic propaganda and the beginning of persecution. Open persecution began with 1927, resulting in the arrest of the clergy who did not accept the "concordat" between Metropolitan Sergii and the Soviet authorities.

A systematic persecution of the believers began in 1931. Almost all churches were closed, even though many Communists secretly baptized their children. By 1941 the older generation staunchly stood for Orthodoxy and among them 70 to 80 percent were believers. These estimates are more conservative than the report of October 18, which claimed that 95 percent of the population belonged to the Orthodox Church. But all the reports are in agreement as to the multitude of worshippers that attended the first services after the Germans arrived.

As we turn to the situation of church affairs in Volynia, we must keep in mind that the Orthodox Church in that area was subordinate to the Metropolitan in Warsaw before the division of Poland between Stalin and Hitler in September 1939. The clergy consisted of Ukrainian priests, with a significant admixture of Russians.

After the Bolsheviks occupied this region in September 1939, they did not immediately begin to close the churches, but instead placed them in difficult material straits through high taxes, assuming that the churches would thus be obliged to close. This, however, did not lead to the desired results, because much to the surprise of the authorities the parishes raised the necessary funds. Then an effort was made to place the church under Communist control by subordinating it to the Moscow Metropolitan. According to the German reports (dated 14 November 1941) the Moscow clergy only had to pretend that they governed the church. Furthermore, a part of the Moscow clergy was to have been placed in the services of the NKVD. The directive on subordination to the Moscow church administration was immediately carried out by a part of the Volynia clergy, but a smaller group expressed opposition to it. The former were left to perform their duties, while the latter were removed. Among them was the Bishop of Lutsk (Polikarp Sykors'kyi) who was formally subordinate to the Moscow Patriarchate but who avoided making the trip to Moscow. It is obvious that the information given in the communiqué is not altogether reliable.

The author of the communiqué stated that at the time it was not known to whom the Orthodox Church in Volynia was subordinate. An eparchial council was to meet in the city of Kholm to decide this problem, but it was sure to encounter great difficulty because the clergy of Ukrainian nationality stood for the Autocephalous Ukrainian Church. (At the head of the Kholm eparchy stood Archbishop Ilarion Ohienko, an active Ukrainian separatist, formerly minister of faiths in the Petliura government.) At the same time, the other part of the clergy wanted to unite with some Orthodox church. The political commitments of the clergy were not the same. The impression was that sympathy for the moderate Levits'kyi predominated. Nonetheless, up to that time the clergy had refrained from any display of sympathy for either one or the other political school. The author of the communiqué stated that it was most likely that the Orthodox Church of the Eastern Ukraine would extend its influence over the entire Ukraine, but it was not clear at the moment whether this unifying tendency of one church would be limited only to ecclesiastical activity.[43]

It seems that if the Kholm area was included in the Polish Government-General, then according to the plan of the occupation authorities it should have been separated from the Eastern Ukraine. Evidently the writer of this communiqué knew nothing of this plan.

The communiqué of 5 December 1941 throws some light on the life of the Russian (Autonomous) Church in Kiev.[44] The author of the report was disturbed by the fact that the church administration occupied the former building of the NKVD. Meetings took place in the building, and it was suspected that these were held in connection with the work of Soviet agents. At the meeting of 7 November 1941 forty-nine priests and ninety-five lay individuals participated. The chairman was an archbishop (evidently Aleksii Gromadskii). Two priests who took part in the meeting turned out to be Soviet agents, according to the information of the author of the communiqué. A proclamation signed by *Locum Tenens* Sergii was found on one of them. Arrests were made, and the head of the Autonomous Church, Archbishop Aleksii (Gromadskii), was among those arrested.

[43] *Ibid.*, No. 133 (14 November 1941), Roll 234.
[44] *Ibid.*, No. 142 (5 December 1941), Roll 234.

Then the communiqué gives certain biographical details of Archbishop Aleksii's life.

After 1939 he was on Polish territory that had gone to the USSR and subordinated himself to Moscow. In March 1941 he visited the Soviet capital. Later he was arrested by the NKVD who wished to remove him from the path of the advancing German forces; however, the old bishop collapsed on the way, thereby avoiding evacuation. Then he became the head of the Autonomous Ukrainian Church. The military authorities, the writer of the communiqué continues in a dissatisfied tone, gave the Archbishop a pass to visit Zhitomir and Berdichev. In Kiev Archbishop Aleksii wanted to appoint Archbishop Panteleimon; this was done on 18 December 1941.

The two priests who had been arrested, Aleksandr Vishniakov and Pavel Ostrinskii, upon questioning admitted to being NKVD informers who had been assigned to ascertain the mood of the population and to influence it. Both were shot. The SD took signatures from the other people who had attended the meeting attesting that they had not participated in activities hostile to the Germans.

The communiqué dated 8 December 1941 has a good deal to say about the complicated relations between the occupation authorities and the Ukrainian separatists.[45] While the Germans themselves had brought separatist émigrés into Belorussia, new OUN agents (followers of Bandera) were, contrary to German wishes, continually penetrating from former Polish territory into the occupied Ukraine. They systematically seized command posts in the civilian administration organized by the Germans, eliminating the so-called "Easterners" (local Ukrainians) from the Soviet part of the Ukraine and carrying on their own politics. This information in the communiqué was based on questioning of arrested Ukrainian nationalists. Thus the policy of the Bandera group became increasingly more anti-German. They collected Soviet arms found in the forests and attempted to create their own partisan detachments, using their position in the German administration in occupied regions. When these detachments were set up sufficiently well, including the Bandera

[45] *Ibid.*, No. 143 or 144 (8 December 1941), Roll 234.

militia, adds the communiqué, they could be used against the German forces. The ruling circles of the OUN did not believe the Germans would be victorious, and considered that their appearance must be timed for the moment when the Germans and Russians (the Ukrainian separatists did not differentiate between Russians and Communists) would exhaust themselves to the point where they could offer no serious resistance. The independence of the Ukraine would then be won at that moment.

The communiqué reports concrete cases of the penetration of separatist-westerners into Ukrainian cities. Four such agents were arrested in Zhitomir. The Bandera group first arrived in Zaporozh'e on 8 October 1941. Fifteen western Ukrainians were registered, and it was established from the attitude of nine of them that they were members of the OUN. These men tried to penetrate the leadership of the civilian administration created by the Germans. The author of the communiqué adds that because of transportation difficulties the return of the separatists to their home land in the western Ukraine had not yet been accomplished.

As already mentioned, it was in December 1941 that the Autocephalous (separatist) Ukrainian Church was organized. One can assume that because of the occupation authorities' everincreasing suspicions regarding the separatists' activities, the church did not receive the support which might have been expected from the occupation authorities in view of the German religious policy.

The communiqué of 14 January 1942 again contains a statement about the separatist-westerners and their activities and tactics. All of the Bandera followers were Galicians (western Ukrainians). The penetration of Galicians into the eastern Ukraine influenced the disbandment of the Ukrainian Legion by the German command (after the announcement of Ukrainian independence in L'vov). Former legionnaires were dispersed throughout German units as interpreters, which immediately gave them the opportunity to occupy a series of key positions in the administration of the occupied regions. Having these key positions, the Bandera followers used them to organize the penetration of their supporters from the western into the eastern

Ukraine. The author of the report then reverts to the plans to create a Ukrainian army and passes on to the question of the connection between the Autocephalous Ukrainian Church and the Ukrainian political separatists.[46]

The communiqué of 4 February 1942 also deals with the delicate question of the occupation authorities' loss of faith in the Ukrainian nationalists, in this instance accusing them of having ties with the NKVD. It notes that in the Kiev area the anti-Communist struggle was turning into a struggle against nationalist bands and that the latter's connections with the NKVD were "close and complicated." The author of the report also felt that the local Ukrainian populace in former Soviet territory was beginning to react more and more negatively toward the western Ukrainians from former Polish territory. He further pointed out their preference for the Mel'nyk over the Bandera group. According to him, no kind of agreement could be made with the latter, and they should be completely exterminated. In addition, he once more emphasized that, in the final summation, the extreme nationalism of both groups was utterly unaccepable to the occupation authorities.[47]

The communiqué then lists a series of Ukrainian organizations on occupied territory which had been seized by nationalist groups and goes on to the question (important for this work) of the Autocephalous Church, which the author considered to be an instrument of the nationalist-Ukrainian politicians. He considered Bishop Ilarion of Kholm to be the leading representative of this movement, more a politician than a prince of the Church, who had hopes of becoming the Metropolitan of Kiev. He did not know how close Archbishop Ilarion's ties to the Mel'nyk group were, but information had been received from trusted individuals (agents) on the connection between the Bishop of Kholm and the NKVD. This latter supposition evidently seemed daring to the author, and he pointed out that there really was no direct proof of this connection with the NKVD, though, judging from the Archbishop's character, one could not consider such a connection improbable.

[46]*Ibid.*, No. 155 (14 January 1942), Roll 234.
[47]*Ibid.*, No. 164 (4 February 1942), Roll 234.

All these suppositions and suspicions are interesting because they paint a behind-the-scenes picture of the relationship between the occupation authorities and the Ukrainian nationalists who supported the Ukrainian Autocephalous Church; they also indirectly explain why the Autonomous (pro-Russian) Church still had the possibility of developing despite the purposes, discussed above, of German policy, which had set a stake on Ukrainian separation. The relationship between the occupation authorities and the Ukrainian nationalists soon deteriorated.

Two months later, on 10 April 1942, the SD report again deals with the Bandera problem, stating that in 1939-1941 the NKVD recruited many followers of Bandera into its ranks. It goes on to say that the mayor of Kiev, who was connected with the Mel'nyk group, transferred gasoline which had been released for city needs to the nationalists. Using automobiles which were at his disposal, he sent people to the Government-General and thus maintained connections with Metropolitan Dionisii in Warsaw and Archbishop Ilarion in Kholm on the question of the appointment of the Metropolitan of Kiev. Under the guise of a religious section created in the city government (*Abteilung für Glaubensbekenntnisse*), in actual fact a Ukrainian church council, substituting for the dispersed national council, was created. The representatives of the designated organization, two Ukrainian emigrants, adherents of Mel'nyk, had already visited Bishop Panteleimon of the Autonomous Church for the purpose of exerting pressure on him in favor of the Ukrainian nationalists and threatening him in the event of his refusal.[48]

The information on the Orthodox Church in the Ukraine breaks off on this note. By this time the formation of the two Ukrainian churches had been finished, and the religious revival defined. No further events of special interest to the occupation authorities in this area occurred and their attention began to be directed increasingly toward the growing partisan movement, which found detailed description in SD communiqués.

The question of monasticism, which occupies a central place in the life and organization of the Orthodox Church, also needs

[48]*Ibid.*, No. 191 (10 April 1942), Roll 235.

to be discussed briefly. High-ranking ecclesiastics, such as bishops, must be monks or widowed priests who have accepted monasticism. A lack of monks can therefore strike very hard at the church hierarchy. On the other hand, an ample supply of monks means that the Church has the possibility of creating a strong episcopate. As we know, monks were subject to the severest repression at the hands of the Soviets. During the German occupation monasticism was reestablished, though in the face of several difficulties. Heyer notes that the occupation authorities on Ukrainian territory did not permit monasteries to accept new monks on the grounds that many Ukrainians could evade the labor responsibilities in this way. Because of this, the central role in the reestablishment of monasteries was left to monks who had survived the Communist oppression. It was natural that the greatest number of monks who had been saved were on former Polish territory. In the largest and best-known monastery, the Pochaevsk Abbey, festive services were reintroduced, attracting large numbers of the laity. The monastery in the City of Kremenets played a similar role, though on a smaller scale. There were only seven monks in this monastery, but they were extremely active. The Archbishop lived in the monastery, which also housed a seminary.

The head of the monastery in the city of Dubno was Archimandrite Iosaf, a man who had experienced Soviet exile. He had been sent to build Soviet fortifications in the Dubno area at the beginning of the war and had been taken prisoner by the German forces. In addition to Archimandrite Iosaf there were eight monks in the monastery, most of them Great Russians. There were 300 monks in the Zagajec monastery, fifteen in the Melec monastery, and five in the Kazachie Mogily monastery. The Derman monastery, with sixty monks, and the small monastery near Rovno had gone over to the Autocephalous Church. In addition, a convent of 130 nuns had been preserved at Korec on the Soviet-Polish border of 1939. Monasteries were organized in various places in the former Soviet Ukraine. The number of nuns naturally exceeded that of the monks significantly.

At the famous Kievo-Pecherskii monastery which had been

turned into a museum in Soviet times and then blown up after the arrival of the Germans, twenty-five elderly monks gathered and gradually their number increased. In Kiev, at the "Ionaskloster, there were ten monks. In the Mikhailov monastery there were thirty. In the Convent of St. Flor there were 250 nuns; in the Pokrov, 200 nuns; in the Vvedenskii, 150 nuns. In the Kozelshchina convent, some sixty kilometers from Poltava, there were ninety nuns, and in Poltava itself, at the Krestovozdivizhenskii monastery, there were three monks. In Dnepropetrovsk, in the Tikhvinskii convent, sixty nuns had gathered. In Kamenets (Podol'e) there were three monks. One convent opened in Zhitomir with approximately one hundred nuns.

In the convent near the city of Ovruch there were fifty nuns. In the Vinnitsa eparchy there was a convent at Brailov with a hundred nuns, and one at Nemirov with eighty nuns. All these monasteries belonged to the Autonomous Church. According to Heyer's information, Archbishop Nikanor of the Autocephalous Church once announced, concerning this, that the Ukrainian Autocephalous Church had no monasteries. The Belevskii and Dermanskii monasteries in Volynia transferred to the Autocephalists later. The reason for the almost complete absence of monasteries in the Autocephalous Church, according to Archbishop Nikanor, was that monks considered that the bishops and priests of the Autocephalous Church were not canonical. The monks, evidently to an even greater degree than the ordinary faithful, felt that the reasons for the creation of the Autocephalous Church lay not in the religious but in the purely political area.[49]

Previously, in describing the religious revival in the Ukraine, we referred to the SD communiqué of 18 October 1941. This report was written by a person who understood the essentials of the process of religious revival which developed in occupied territory. In this same communiqué an opinion of considerable interest is expressed. According to the unnamed author, neither Roman Catholicism nor the émigré movement of the Orthodox Church, which set off the church against the government, had any influence in Russia. Evidently the old movement of Ortho-

[49]Heyer, *op. cit.*, pp. 202-4.

doxy, whose ideal was "symphony" in relations between the church and the government, was predominant. It is curious that such a view was noted in the Ukraine. It must have been connected with the pro-Russian Autonomous Orthodox Church. It is true that formally the Ukrainian Autocephalous Church supported the same view, substituting the old idea of Russian statehood for the idea of Ukrainian independence; but then the separatist movement, at its base, rested on the Uniate Church and was half Roman Catholic. It is not without reason that the majority of Ukrainian monks and laity recoiled from this movement which contradicted the thousand-year-old Orthodox tradition. In addition, and this Heyer also notes, the connection of the Autocephalous Church with the followers of Lypkivs'kyi extended the accusation of self-ordainment to the former. The self-ordination of Lypkivs'kyi's priests was connected with the first years of the Revolution, with that movement which, in the Russian Orthodox Church, was cast in the form of the Living Church. Interestingly enough, the Living Church was not able to revive under occupation conditions.

Thus, in 1941-1943, the majority of the people longed for the reestablishment of the conservatism of traditional Orthodoxy. Even the outer manifestations of modernism repelled the faithful. Heyer notes that such incidents as the visit of Bishop Nikanor (a bishop of the Autocephalous Church) to the Kiev Opera had an adverse effect on the population's opinion. In addition, wide circles of the populace held it against the Autocephalous Church that its priests appeared in Ukrainian embroidered shirts instead of the traditional frocks, and that the priests cut their hair short—another break with tradition.

It is from this same standpoint that the question of the exchange of the Ukrainian language for Church Slavonic in church services must be considered. In their time, the renovators tried to do the same in exchanging Russian for the Church Slavonic language. The believers did not accept this reform. In Poland and the Government-General the Ukrainian language was used in part for services, but the experiment was short-lived.

As Heyer suggests, before the division of Poland in 1939, one-third of the Orthodox parishes in Volynia had transferred to the Ukrainian language for their services. After the Soviet occupation at Volynia the Ukrainian language was abandoned in some parishes apparently because some of the priests were afraid to demonstrate separatist tendencies, and partly because the Ukrainian chauvinists, who had formerly insisted on the introduction of the Ukrainian language, were not the truly religious segment of believers, and under new conditions had separated themselves from the church.

In this way modernism in the Ukrainian Autocephalous Church not only repelled almost all Ukrainian monks, but it also repelled the majority of the laity. The frequently quoted communiqué assessing the influence of the Autonomous and Autocephalous churches in the Ukraine gave, on 18 October 1941, approximately the relationship of 55 percent and 40 percent of the population to the advantage of the Autonomous Church. In October 1941 the Germans were just concluding their occupation of the Ukraine; thus, the specific weight of the western part, in which the Autocephalous Church was strongest, was at that time exaggerated. On this point Heyer arrives at an interesting conclusion, according to which the farther one went to the east, the less developed was the nationalistic fanaticism and, therefore, the less prepared was the ground for an Autocephalous movement. In the diocese of Poltava 80 percent of the faithful considered themselves to be part of the Autonomous Church. In the Diocese of Dnepropetrovsk seventy-six Autonomous and only ten Autocephalous churches were opened. In the Diocese of Chernigov the Autonomous clergy successfully prevented an attempted schism.[50]

With the population in such a mood, it is clear why the extremist groups of Ukrainian nationalists had to revert to terrorism. It is also clear why some of the clergy belonging to the Autonomous Church perished during the occupation. Several German communiqués were introduced above to illustrate this situation in the Ukraine. These showed the methods used by the Ban-

[50]*Ibid.*, pp. 189, 194. See also Fireside, *Icon and Swastika* and Alex Inkeles and Raymond H. Bauer, *The Soviet Citizen: Daily Life in a Totalitarian Society* (Cambridge, Mass.: Harvard University Press, 1959), who reach the conclusion that the Autonomous Church in the Ukraine had twice as many members as the Autocephalous Church.

dera group in the struggle with their opponents, the followers of Mel'nyk, both equally Ukrainians and both preponderantly from the western Ukraine. Naturally, the same methods were employed against members of the Autonomous "pro-Russian" Church. For example, an SD communiqué of 10 April 1942 relates that Ukrainian chauvinists from the Kiev City Council used direct pressure on one of the most influential bishops of the Autonomous Church, Bishop Panteleimon (Rudyk); and such a situation was more or less the same throughout the entire occupied Ukraine.[51]

A description of the methods by which members of separatist Ukrainian groups acquired influence in the Ukraine can be found in a communiqué dated 14 January 1942. This source states that members of the Bandera organization in the former Soviet Ukraine consisted of Galicians who had penetrated to the east after the disbanding of diversionary detachments which had been created before the beginning of the war by the German *Abwehr,* and disbanded as a result of the announcement of Ukrainian independence in L'vov. Former ranks of Ukrainian units, after the disbanding, were dispersed among German military units to act as interpreters, which gave them the opportunity to extend their influence in the entire occupied Ukraine.[52]

It is difficult to generalize about the situation of the Autonomous and the Autocephalous Churches in the Ukraine because of the complexity of the matter and the emotional intensity of the period. The picture that emerges is a rather peculiar one. In the first period, the influential Archbishop Aleksii (Gromadskii), the future head of the Autonomous Church, headed the Orthodox Church in Volynia and by his personal authority restrained the very pronounced show of Ukrainian chauvinism in this region; on the other hand, in 1941, on former Soviet territory, agents of Bandera and Mel'nyk who had penetrated there with the German Army acted freely. From the end of 1941, the great independence of these agents, especially

[51]U.S. National Archives and Records Service, Reich Chief Security Office, *Ereignismeldungen, UdSSR,* No. 191 (10 April 1942), Roll 235.
[52]*Ibid.,* No. 155 (14 January 1942), Roll 234.

the Bandera group, forced the occupation authorities to take extremely decisive, but not entirely regular, measures. In some places these measures hampered their interference in the struggle between the Autonomous and Autocephalous Churches, and in other places suspended it. By 1943 an open struggle between the German command and Soviet and Ukrainian nationalist partisans had developed. The Soviet part of the Ukraine began to go over into Communist hands, and the occupied territory was reduced to the former Polish border, where there were Ukrainian partisans in the forests. A significant part of the Autonomous and Autocephalous clergy poured into this territory, and it was there that the most intensive terror by extreme Ukrainian nationalists developed.

Despite these confusing political events the evidence suggests that there was an undeniable religious, and Orthodox at that, revival in the Ukraine during the German occupation, as was the case in the Pskov area and in Belorussia. Between 1941 and 1943, in the Ukraine, there were baptisms of children and adolescents who had not been baptized during the Soviet period, and there also took place the restoration of about 40 percent of the churches. The impact of the religious revival in the three major sectors of German occupied territories will persist far into the postwar period.

SIX

Miscellany
Transnistria and the Front

The study thus far of the three major regions under German occupation makes it abundantly clear that religious developments occurred on at least three levels. Firstly, and most significantly, there was the spontaneous resumption of religious practices by thousands of people from all walks of life and of all ages, as if the interlude of twenty years of Soviet antireligious persecution was a faint memory of the distant past. This was followed by the opening and restoration of numerous abandoned churches, a task usually undertaken by the believers themselves. This activity undoubtedly constituted the heart of what can be described as the Orthodox revival of these years. At a different but closely related level was the creation of the appropriate ecclesiastical apparatus with its hierarchs for the expressed purpose of ministering to as well as administering the flock. The phenomenal growth of the number of clergy is in itself a measure of the great revival. But it was at this level that the religious experience was beginning to be colored by political rivalries and intrigues, as practically all hierarchs involved could be thought of as having some political purposes either by the occupying powers or by nationalist groups within the occupied territories. The latter, as we have seen, was especially true in the case of the Ukraine.

Despite a variety of differences, the regions discussed thus far had certain uniform characteristics resulting from the relatively long duration of German occupation in the area. This is not altogether true of the areas that will be discussed in this chapter, namely Transnistria, that part of the Ukraine which had been occupied by Rumanian troops, and certain regions in the South where major cities were experiencing no stability whatsoever because of their proximity to actual fighting and which for purposes of this study we call the "front" areas, although the interplay of political and religious issues manifested themselves here as well, especially in the case of Transnistria.

Transnistria became a unique case in this religious revival because of the involvement of Rumania. In order to compensate Rumania for her participation in World War II, Hitler proposed to return Bessarabia and Transnistria—the region between the southern Bug and the border of Bessarabia—which had been taken from her by the Soviet Union in 1940. In terms of ecclesiastical jurisdiction, the Russian Orthodox Church of Transnistria included an important part of the historical Kherson eparchy with Odessa as its capital.

The fact that Rumania was an Orthodox country meant that ecclesiastically as well as politically Transnistria became or could become an integral part of that country. And it was natural that the reestablishment of Orthodoxy would be undertaken by Rumanian clergy. One might add that in the case of Bessarabia they simply restored the pre-1940 order. What complicated matters in the case of Transnistria was that the ecclesiastical mission sent from Rumania embarked upon a double project. Besides restoring Orthodoxy, they also sought to promote rumanization of the region.

Literature for the study of this problem is, as can be sur-

[1]Heyer, *Die orthodoxe Kirche in der Ukraine,* Chapter VI, "Der kirchliche Auflau Transnistriens unter der Miseunea romana," pp. 209-12.

mised, scarce. Fortunately, besides Heyer,[1] there is the "Report of the Rumanian Orthodox Mission to Transnistria, from 1 April to 30 June 1942," drawn up by Archimandrite Anfim, assistant to the head of the Rumanian Orthodox Mission,[2] and a typescript provided especially for this project by Archbishop Vissarion (later Metropolitan), Head of the Rumanian Ecclesiastical Mission in 1943.[3] The rest of the information consists of scattered references.

Unfortunately Metropolitan Vissarion's typescript is not as informative as it could be. He seems to rely heavily on Heyer's work although he corrects the latter's figures occasionally. More disappointing is the sketchy description of the activities of the mission. Archimandrite Anfim's report, on the other hand, is precise and informative and amplifies Heyer's material usefully.

The Rumanian Patriarch sent the mission by a special Rumanian decree on 8 October 1941, soon after the city was taken. The same mission was also in charge of the Orthodox Church in Transnistria. The head of the mission was Archimandrite Julius Skriban, who had come from Bucharest. At the beginning of 1942 (6 December 1942 according to Metropolitan Vissarion's correction), the Archimandrite was replaced by Bishop Vissarion. The latter was well prepared for work in Russia; he had graduated from the Kiev Theological Academy in the tsarist period and spoke Russian well. He was replaced a year later by the young Archimandrite Anfim (Nika).

The basic church policy of the mission was one of gradual rumanization. But it must be mentioned that they allowed fol-

[2]Archimandrite Anfim, "Otchet Rumynoskoi pravoslavnoi missii v Transnistrii s 1 aprelia do 30 iiunia 1942 goda" [Report of the Rumanian Orthodox mission in Transnistria from 1 April to 30 June 1942], translated from the Rumanian by L. Stepanova, and published in the newspaper *Pravoslavnaia Rus'* [Orthodox Russia] (Vladimirova, August 15 Old Style August 28 New Style, 1942).

[3]The typescript was evidently made by the Archbishop himself, in French, and titled "L'archevêque Roumain Vissarion en Transnistrie (Ucraine) en 1943." There are thirteen pages in the manuscript. Corrections in the text were made by the Metropolitan. The script is not dated, but an accompanying letter is dated 18 September 1958. (Bishop Vissarion at that time was an émigré in France and headed the Rumanian Church Abroad with the rank of Metropolitan.)

lowers of the late Patriarch Tikhon, that is to say the local clergy, to participate in the religious activity which followed.

According to Metropolitan Vissarion, Transnistria was divided into three eparchies: (1) the northern eparchy, with its temporary center in Zhmerinka; (2) the central eparchy, with its center in Balta; (3) the southern eparchy, with its center in Odessa. Archimandrite Anfim was placed at the head of the northern diocese, Bishop Vasilii Stan at the head of the central one, and Metropolitan Vissarion remained as the head of the one in Odessa. According to Vissarion's typescript, it was chiefly Rumanian clergy who were used in Transnistria. They came from Rumania for six months, and then were replaced by new priests. Archimandrite Anfim considers this policy of replacing prelates so frequently as one of the mission's major faults, limiting its effectiveness considerably.

Before the Revolution, there were 1150 parishes in Transnistria, but one has to calculate in the context of what had ocurred elsewhere under Soviet rule in order to have an idea what happened in this region. The Mission opened thirty churches in Odessa (twenty-five, according to Vissarion's correction) and soon approximately 350 churches were functioning in the entire region, that is, as in other places, about 35 percent restoration of the prerevolutionary situation.

The work must have progressed satisfactorily, for a year later, according to Archimandrite Anfim's account, there were 500 newly consecrated churches in Transnistria, but only 411 individuals with holy orders. Of these latter 287 were priests, eighteen were deacons, and 106 were readers. Keeping Heyer's prerevolutionary figures of 1150 churches in mind, 500 churches constitute 40 percent of the prerevolutionary churches even though there must have been less than 25 percent of the priests, even counting one priest for every church. But this did not limit the activity of the Rumanian clergy. An indication of their energy and resourcefulness was the opening of a seminary in Dubossary for eighty students on 30 November 1942. Also during the occupation, twelve monasteries were opened in Transnistria.

Part of the rumanization policy of the mission was the introduction of the Rumanian language, which was met with displeasure among the parishioners. It is hardly possible that this policy had any lasting effect anyhow. The majority of the Rumanians had left for Rumania with the approach of the front, and the parishioners rejoiced that "Slavic" priests were again serving them. Other Rumanian activities, according to Archimandrite Anfim's report, included the distribution of land to churches, five to ten hectares per church, and the publication of a newspaper *Pravoslavnaia Zhizn'* [Orthodox Life], by the Mission. Several priests began to establish cultural circles in a number of villages. This cultural activity was remarkable and in many respects unique. There is no evidence that such activity occurred anywhere else except in the zone of Rumanian occupation.

Of course all this activity supplemented mass baptisms of children and marriages, a trend noticeable throughout the occupied territory. Religious instruction was begun in all schools, and "the certain coolness began to melt." The mission conducted regular meetings of the clergy and published a calendar for 1942 in Russian. The insufficient number of priests created many crises, especially as the mission was besieged by delegations from parishes who came not only from Transnistria but also from beyond the Bug (from the German-occupied Ukraine with the request that it provide them with priests. In this connection, the Rumanian Synod issued a decree to ordain local Russian priests from persons having the necessary education. An excerpt from Archimandrite Anfim's report suggests the seriousness with which the Rumanians assumed the task of providing priests for the occupied territory:

> The missionary work here is very responsible and full of difficulties. The priest here must be gentle, sympathetic to all, full of love toward the laity, and must be without pretensions. The priest does not need so much intellectual development as he does religious zeal, and most of all, exemplariness, virtue in life, and moral purity. In this regard the people are very demanding. Many of our missionaries enjoy the love of all the people and are valued by the people, as bearers of the seal of grace, and some even of martyrdom.

The priests who come here from Rumania must bring the highest understanding of their mission, enthusiasm and great pastoral tact. Older priests are preferred over the younger ones here. Those who come here must understand the surrounding conditions, understand the people here, their customs and language.[4]

Archimandrite Anfim's last observation is especially valuable and testifies to the depth and seriousness of the religious revival which preserved the population's faith after almost twenty-five years of religious persecution.

The policy of rumanization of the population of Transnistria with the help of the Rumanian Orthodox Church is mentioned casually in an SD communiqué dated 18 September 1941.[5] A more detailed one, however, dated 1 October 1941 describes the situation in territory occupied by the Rumanians in some detail, pointing out that Rumania took advantage of the inability of the Bolsheviks to destroy religion during the interwar years. It confirms the fact that priests were brought to Bessarabia from Rumania, that an archiepiscopate was created in Tiraspol, and that generally the Rumanian activity contributed to the religious revival.[6]

Even though religious developments in Transnistria were on a smaller scale in comparison with the three major sectors of the Baltic, Belorussia, and the Ukraine, in some respects they were more impressive. The spiritual quality of the Orthodox population made an indelible impression on the Rumanian hierarchs and rumanizing projects had little or no effect. Finally, as far as restoration of the churches was concerned, here too, as in the other occupied areas, they managed to reach approximately 35 percent of the prerevolutionary number.

Probably the most difficult aspect of the revival to assess is that which took place at the "front" regions. The instability of the front created instability among the population and available evidence is at best fragmentary, although some accounts by survivors are quite useful.

[4] Archimandrite Anfim, *op. cit.*, p. 7.
[5] U.S. National Archives and Records Service, Reich Chief Security Office, *Eriegnismeldungen*. UdSSR, No. 87 (18 September 1941), Roll 233.
[6] *Ibid.*, No. 100 (1 October 1941), Roll 233.

In one of the largest cities in the south of Russia, Rostov on the Don, for example, according to the testimony of a long-time inhabitant of the city, at the beginning of World War II only one church remained open for 600,000 inhabitants. After the Germans arrived, three more churches were opened for the 400,000 inhabitants who remained.

In an article, "From Memoirs of Church Life in the USSR under German Occupation," Abbot Georgii significantly expands the picture given by the long-time inhabitant. Rostov was occupied by the Germans in July 1942, writes Abbot Georgii, and the people immediately began to think of the restoration of their churches:

> On the third or fourth day after the capture of the city, seven or eight parishioners of All Saints' Church came to me with the proposal to survey the church and to begin getting busy immediately on strengthening it for communal use and for conducting religious services.[7]

It turned out that the church had been smashed by bombs and was strewn with metal shavings—inherited from the workshop which had been installed in it by the Communist authorities. There was so much trash that, according to Abbot Georgii, 300 horses and carts were needed to cart it away. In the absence of any kind of transport, all undertakings seemed to him to be impracticable, and he told the parishioners this, but they persisted in their demands. The next day, beginning at five o'clock in the morning, there were already 300 people working on cleaning out the building. In the most primitive manner, with sacks and hand carts, the church was cleaned. The church was not only cleaned, but it was also repaired in the course of two days, and one old man brought forth religious vessels which had been buried in the ground eight years. At the first service the church, which held 2000 persons, was literally overcrowded, the worshippers occupying the church yard as well.

[7]See Igumen Georgii, "Iz vospominanii o tserkovnoi zhizni pri nemetskoi okkupatsii" [From memoirs of church life in the USSR under German occupation], *Vestnik Instituta po izucheniiu SSSR*, No. 2 (23) (April-June, Munich, 1957): 105.

> Daily services began, always with an overcrowded church, filled not only with old men and women, . . . but also with young boys and girls who had been born and raised under Soviet reality. These young people, who had heard of God only in the sense of His negation, not having an idea of the Church, not knowing the basic truths of religion, nor any kind of prayer, had been seized by the general religious rebirth and revitalization, filled the churches, and begged: "We want to pray but we are not able to; teach us!"[8]

In all, according to Abbot Georgii, not four as claimed by the Rostov inhabitant, but eight churches were opened. In the case of Polotsk in Belorussia, even the local bishop did not know how many churches had been opened—such were occupation conditions. Soon Archbishop Nikolai arrived from the city of Eisk, where he had survived "in retirement." A Rostov deanery and consistories were organized. "Daily there arrived both priests and lay delegates from the provinces (the Don and Kuban regions) with joyful tidings of the opening of churches, the organization of parishes, with requests for priests to be designated." There were not enough priests, and Archbishop Nikolai "after a short testing of knowledge of services, reading, singing, the basic truths of the Orthodox religious doctrines, ordained such simple, devout individuals who came with the delegations. In a comparatively short time sixty parishes were organized and their number continued to grow."[9] The liturgy was celebrated in all Rostov churches twice a day, at 7 and 9 o'clock in the morning. There were two priests and two readers in each church. There were many services of all kinds. From twenty to thirty persons were baptized daily, beginning with infants and ending with eighteen-year-old men and women.

> There were many instances of the performance of marriage for people of a mature age who had lived in civilian spousehood many years. But especially numerous were the so-called "sealing of the dead," *i.e.*, performance of the burial office for those long dead (murdered, tortured in prisons and camps, and exiled).[10]

[8] *Ibid.*, p. 106.
[9] *Ibid.*, pp. 106-7.
[10] *Ibid.*, p. 107.

In October 1942, Abbot Georgii visited the Cossack village of Kushchevskii in the Kuban oblast. where he blessed a church and served until the permanent priest arrived. During the first week he served from morning till night, performed a great many services, and on the first Sunday baptized from 100 to 125 children and young people who had gathered from other villages. After the liturgy, Father Georgii asked the parents why they were in such a hurry with the baptismals at a time when their permanent priest was expected to arrive. The characteristic answer was, "Every day is dear, Father, who knows, maybe before the priest arrives 'our people' will again come and again it will be the end of the church."[11]

In another city of the Don region—in Novocherkassk, according to an authentic witness, a priest, interviewed for this project, only one cemetery church existed until the Germans arrived.

> When the Germans occupied the city in June 1942, in a few days all the churches in the city were already open. In the marketplace church closest to us (it appears to be the Holy Trinity Church), I came across some women cleaning it. Since all the ikons had been taken down, the people brought their own and soon all the walls were hung with small ikons, sometimes in two rows. From somewhere there appeared church banners, vessels, etc., and services began. In the first month there were many requests, baptismals, marriages, etc., not only of city dwellers but also from surrounding villages. Simultaneously there were opened the cathedral, the church near the city (Ataman's) garden (it seems to be the Church of Transfiguration), the Cemetery Church, and one on Kolodeznaia Street. . . .
> There turned out to be religious people among the teachers of the middle schools and even of the local institutions of higher learning (there were five institutions of higher learning and *technikums* in Novocherkassk) whom I met in church after that; among them were even such "Soviet public workers" of whom I never could have thought this. One history instructor, for example, even dreamt of ordination into the priesthood.

This same priest gives some interesting data on Taganrog:

> I had not been in Taganrog in those years, but I had ties with the faithful there. In addition, the last bishop, Iosif of Taganrog (Chernov), was concurrently with me in the Ukhto-Pecherskii

[11]*Ibid.*, p. 108.

concentration camp from 1936 to 1940. At the beginning of 1941 he returned to Taganrog, but immediately went underground, hiding in a village near. . . . There he was not alone; he performed services and nourished his parish.

When the Germans took Taganrog, Bishop Iosif appeared in the city and received the right to administer his diocese. He was given his bishop's house with a church, served, supplied the bishopric, and so forth. I cannot say which churches were open at that time, but many from Rostov and Novocherkassk traveled to him to take Communion.[12]

According to the information of Cossack D. from the Cossack village of Mitiakinskaia, Donetsk Okrug, before the Revolution there were ten churches in the village. By 1937 they had all been closed by the Soviet authorities. After the Germans came, three churches were reestablished.[13]

In Orel, a town of 180,000 inhabitants, according to the report of one of those who lived in this city, of twenty-four pre-revolutionary churches, when the Germans came only a small shrine in a cemetery, large enough to hold fifty people, remained. After the arrival of the Germans, four churches were opened immediately. All of the open churches were filled with worshipers. On the Feast of the Epiphany, several thousand persons took part in the procession.[14]

In an SD communiqué of 12 December 1941, it was stated that the Rumanian clergy who accompanied the Rumanian troops into the Crimea by 12 December 1941 baptized 200,000 persons, and the Rumanian soldiers acted as godfathers. These baptisms took place in the Karasubazar. It is unfortunate that there is no elaboration as to the type of people who were baptized. It is very probable that the figure includes not only children or young people, but Red Army prisoners of war.[15] In any event, mass baptisms must have been common, judging from frequent reportings on the matter as in SD communiqué of 2

[12]See Protoierei S. Shch, "Sostoianie Pravoslavnoi tserkvi pered 2-i Mirovoi voinoi" [The state of the Orthodox Church before the Second World War]. Notes are held in the files of W. Alexeev.
[13]A record with D's words is contained in the files of W. Alexeev.
[14]There is a record of an old inhabitant's words in the files of W. Alexeev.
[15]U.S. National Archives and Records Service, Reich Chief Security Office, *Ereignismeldungen. UdSSR.* No. 145 (12 December 1941), Roll 234.

January 1942.[16] And the communiqué of 9 October 1942 makes references to the spontaneous openings of churches in the Don region. The manifestation of the religious zeal of the population depended on the availability of priests and other equipment needed for churches was readily supplied by the population. It seemed that icons had been preserved since prerevolutionary days in nearly all the houses. Services were attended by elderly people, women, and children.[17] In many cases, the church services or the opening of churches were followed by solemn processions through the city with thousands of people participating as was the occasion following the opening of the Cathedral in Novocherkassk. During these days the priests enjoyed high prestige with the population, especially those priests who had suffered the most under the Soviet rule (communiqué, 16 October 1942). Joy at the opening of churches was so great that often German soldiers were asked to become godfathers of the children being baptized.[18]

Similarly impressive developments occurred in the area of the Northern Caucasus.[19] In the majority of the district centers (*Ortschaften*) and cities there was not only a revival but also a stabilization of traditional church life which, among other things, gradually replaced the remnants of the Living Church in the area. As may be remembered, the Living Church came to existence in the early 1920s as a rival to Patriarch Tikhon, especially at the time (1922) when the latter was under arrest. The Living Church was supported by the regime and was tolerated until 4 September 1943, when Stalin and Molotov met with the three Metropolitans representing the traditional Russian Orthodox Church. At that time, as a gesture of conciliation to the latter, the Living Church was dissolved. But many adherents of the Living Church could still be found scattered througout the occupied territories. Reference was made to their activity in the Ukraine, but generally speaking, as religious revival was set-

[16]*Ibid.*, No. 150 (2 January 1942), Roll 234.
[17]U.S. National Archives and Records Service, *Meldungen aus den besetzten Ostgebieten*, No. 24 (9 October 1942), Roll 236.
[18]*Ibid.*, No. 25 (16 October 1942), Roll 236.
[19]*Ibid.*, No. 34 (18 December 1942), Roll 236.

ting in, the position of the followers of the Living Church known as the *Obnovlentsy* was becoming increasingly unenviable. Not only were they not recognized organizationally, but in some cases they became the object of derision by the population as was the case with the two Living Church priests in Piatigorsk and in Prokhladnaia who were accused of having been agents of the NKVD. Living Church followers tried to convince the German authorities that they had not been favored by the Soviet régime and that in fact they, too, had suffered, especially after 1937 when their clergy was equally persecuted, and their church shut down. So they tried to hold onto what they had and if possible acquire some more property. It was a desperate struggle between them and the *Tikhonovtsy* or followers of Tikhon. In Krasnodar, for example, they fought for possession of a cathedral and two city churches. The population supported the *Tikhonovtsy* and the verdict was in their favor, but in Prokhladnaia the Living Church followers managed to hold onto their cathedral.

Participation of believers in religious services followed the same pattern as in other occupied territories. Adults as well as children attended regularly. In Kislovodsk two thousand Orthodox believers were joined by members of the local German administration and the burgomaster in a moving occasion to celebrate a Thanksgiving service.

There are indications in the German reports that the religious revival had spread in the Cossack villages between the Don and the Manych river and that young people were becoming a common sight at religious gatherings. In fact the same reports stress not only the revival but the religious character of the Russian people, factors which, if properly utilized, they maintained, could serve the occupation authorities well.

Undoubtedly there must be a relation between individual or national crises and preoccupation with metaphysical or religious issues or, more specifically, return to religion for consolation. The experience of Soviet citizens under Stalin's rule, especially in the thirties, and World War II provided numberless crises of this sort. And nowhere were Soviet citizens more aware of the transience of life than in the so-called "front" regions where the fluidity of the situation added an element of insecurity as to who the ruler of the region might be the next day. This may explain the intensity of the religious fervor which was witnessed at the front regions. But what is still more astonishing is the speed with which large sections of the population acted in resuming their traditional forms of worship publicly and thus making their contribution to the Orthodox revival at large which was taking place throughout the territories occupied by the Germans.

Epilogue

The main purpose of this study is to tell the story of the religious revival in the Russian Orthodox Church which took place during World War II in the Soviet Union and especially in that part of it occupied by the German forces. This revival, which has been described as "the second baptism of Russia," was of such great proportions that both the Soviet and German authorities had to reckon with it seriously and pragmatically. This was especially true of the Soviet leaders, who until the outbreak of the war had adopted a systematic and thorough antireligious policy. The study also shows how World War II, with its heavy toll of human lives and its disastrous effect on the economy, nevertheless gave the Russian Orthodox Church a badly needed opportunity to reemerge as a significant religious and social institution. The church's supportive role during the war years was undoubtedly largely responsible for the Soviet regime's willingness and indeed readiness to accommodate the Church on a more respectable basis than had been the case since the Bolshevik Revolution. Some viewed this change in church-state relations as .part of a broader process of social readjustment in progress in the USSR since the mid-thirties and which sought to stabilize social relations in the country. In other words, in an effort to reduce intergroup tensions and internal conflicts wherever possible and necessary, the Soviet authorities embarked upon a calculated policy of conciliation toward the Church since the latter had in principle and in practice gradually transformed itself into an ally of the state. This "strange alliance" has been the subject of an endless controversy, as many observers maintain that for all practical purposes it set the pattern for a coexistence of long duration between the Orthodox Patriarch and the Communist Party. This view was expressed by such an astute student of Soviet society as Alex Inkeles in a report he wrote on the subject in 1949, a view he reiterated twenty years later in his excellent study, *Social Change in Soviet Russia*.[1]

The record certainly supports the view of a calculated coexistence. And even though it is naive to insist that the Party, ideologically at least, significantly changed its attitude toward religion, it nevertheless made several practical gestures which could and indeed were interpreted as suggesting a fundamental reversal of policy toward the Orthodox Church. For fifteen years after the war the Orthodox Church enjoyed a spiritual NEP. Its administrative apparatus was reestablished by a special *Sobor* held in the beginning of 1945 (31 January-2 February), during which time the Church could boast nearly fifty consecrated bishops, elected its new Patriarch Aleksii, and adopted Forty Eight Paragraphs entitled "Situations of the Administration of the Church";[2] two theological academies (in Moscow and Leningrad) and eight seminaries were reopened; the same was true of numerous churches throughout the land; the *Journal of the Moscow Patriarchate* continued to be published regularly; several *Sobors* to which foreign church dignitaries were invited were held in the Soviet Union; and the Soviet press toned down its attack on the Church and quite frequently praised their wartime loyalty and linked the Patriarch with the government in a common effort to reconstruct the country.

[1] pp. 228-29.
[2] William B. Stroyen, *Communist Russia and the Russian Orthodox Church 1943-1962*, pp. 46-47 and 136-40 which contain the entire text of the 1945 Regulations.

Equally impressive was the Orthodox Church's intense activity abroad. Whereas up to World War II contact between the Russian and Western religious leaders and thinkers was almost nonexistent, the postwar years brought Russian Orthodoxy and its chief spokesman into direct contact with notable religious personalities from all over the world. The Russian hierarchs became actively involved in the Peace Movement and the World Council of Churches and traveled extensively throughout the world. Patriarch Aleksii himself, with an impressive entourage, visited the Eastern Patriarchates (except that of Constantinople) in an effort to strengthen the relations between the Russian Church and the Orthodox East, but also in the hope of claiming for himself the role of the "Ecumenical Patriarch," traditionally enjoyed by the Constantinople Patriarch, at that time His All Holiness Athenagoras. The Old Russian Orthodox Palestine Society was revived in 1952 and serious efforts were made to reactivate the religious and cultural influence which the Russians had enjoyed in the Near East during the nineteenth century.[3] In short, the Church seemed to provide useful service, supplementing the State's diplomatic and cultural activity abroad. In return, the Church was allowed to enjoy certain privileges at home. This ecclesiatical activity both at home and abroad favorably impressed many Western observers accustomed to or acquainted with the dark days of the Orthodox Church's experience. They began to describe it as a religious renaissance with its origins in the war years. True, as we have seen, the restoration of the Church administrative apparatus was a result of the war readjustments. Even after Khrushchev's open attack on the Church in 1959, the official Church continued to function and deal with the state through the Council for Russian Orthodox Church Affairs, itself a product of the war experience.

There are those, of course, who maintain that in reality nothing changed substantially as far as the official status of religion in general and Orthodoxy in particular is concerned. In a careful analysis of the *Journal of the Moscow Patriarchate* contents as well as other pertinent Soviet publications for the

[3]Spinka, *The Church in Soviet Russia*, pp. 121-23.

period 1943-1962, William B. Stroyen has demonstrated convincingly that on the domestic front the Church's role narrowed in contrast to its broad range of activity in the foreign field.[4] In the crucial areas of theological education and religious publications, the result remained at best poor and frequently comic. Obviously the regime was interested in training not theologians but "theological technicians," quite unversed in Western theology despite the increased contacts with the West. As far as the religious publications were concerned, they were generally devoid of any significant theological or social content. With some exceptions, the best known (and some of those referred to in this study) amount to political statements on the relationship between secular and religious authorities within the Soviet Union and in international affairs. Among such publications are: *The Truth About Religion in Russia* (1942); *Patriarch Sergii and His Spiritual Heritage* (1947); *The Russian Orthodox Church in the Fight for Peace* (1950); *The Russian Orthodox Church: Organization, Situation and Activity;* and the two-volume edition of the notes from the 1948 meeting celebrating the 500th anniversary of the autocephaly of the Russian Orthodox Church, *The Acts and Conferences of Heads and Representatives of the Autocephalous Orthodox Churches* (1948).

In contrast to the above unimpressive publication list, there continued an active and rather subtle antireligious publication drive carried on by the Party's organs and appointed committees. The leading newspaper and journals, popular and scholarly, gradually began to echo the traditional hostile position toward religion. As early as 1949, this campaign sought to direct the reader's attention to the incompatibility between science and religion:

> Our system of society fosters the development and strengthening of a scientific world outlook and the liberation of Soviet citizens from religious persuasions. . . . The entire system of communism is scientific and hence antireligious, for science is the opposite of religion. . . . One cannot be a progressive, fully aware fighter for communism . . . if he believes in life after death, just as it is impossible to be a consistent champion of science, if one is

[4] Stroyen, *op. cit.,* pp. 69-97.

not free of science, if one is not free of scientific antireligious convictions.[5]

One might argue that similar positions are common among intellectuals in the technologically advanced West. The difference is not only the fact that, in the case of the Soviet Union, we are dealing with official state antireligious policy, but also that open religious "propaganda" is not allowed the believer. Specialized journals and monographs dealing with various aspects of religion, atheism, and antireligious propaganda circulated in large editions. And of course there was the creation of well-displayed museums of religion and atheism in every major city, exposing the corruption and reactionary attitude of the Church through the centuries. And all this during the so-called religious NEP when Western observers spoke of an understanding between the Patriarch and the Party and of "religious renaissance."

Then came Nikita Khrushchev's open attack on the Church in 1959 and the fear that the "thaw" was over and that persecution years might be repeated in order to continue "the eradication of Christian religion and morality," as Solzhenitsyn put it.[6] But despite Khrushchev's attacks and those of his successors, the alliance between the Soviet regime and the Orthodox Church continues pretty much on the lines predicted by Professor Inkeles. As a matter of fact, Khrushchev's policy of repression (1959-1964) was abandoned somewhat by his successors in favor of a détente in the Church political situation. And in keeping with tradition, the new Russian Patriarch Pimen, who succeeded in 1971 after Aleksii's death, proceeded to announce his loyalty to the regime and urged the faithful to do likewise. Maybe, as it has been repeatedly pointed out, the Russian Orthodox Church has no choice. If it wants to survive it has to compromise and serve the state as Orthodoxy has done historically from Byzantium to the Soviet experience. Or, as another student has put it, "The Russian Orthodox Church and almost all other religious communities in the Soviet Union start in their own self-understanding from the unspoken premise that religion is

[5] Quoted in *ibid.*, pp. 83-84.
[6] Aleksandr I. Solzhenitsyn, *Letter to the Soviet Leaders*, p. 28.

quite compatible with the present social order and with any future one; but they avoid any open confrontation with atheism."[7]

The survival and reconstruction of the Orthodox ecclesiastical machinery is therefore significant for the perpetuation of the faith and can indeed be viewed as part of the revival of Orthodoxy in the Soviet Union. It, after all, provides all the agencies, services, and symbols meaningful to Orthodox believers from Patriarch to peasant.

An important question is, however, whether the accommodations of the Church by the state were the result of farsighted policy on the part of the latter (as suggested by some observers) or the inevitable result of the religious revival which had taken place during the war and which the Soviet leaders could not ignore either during the war or after. In other words, the religious revival exercised greater pressure on the Soviet leadership than is generally assumed. This is the line generally followed by Soviet dissidents and émigrés to the West, including such prominent figures as Aleksandr Solzhenitsyn; they feel that the Soviet Union yields to pressures from within as well as from without. There is no doubt that the Soviet authorities were realistically aware of the political explosiveness of the religious revival both in German-occupied territories and within the rest of the USSR during the course of the war. The fear of defection to the Germans by Russian hierarchs as well as common believers forced the Soviet authorities to court the Church and seek to reconcile as much as possible their hitherto irreconcilable differences.

This émigré view, sometimes supported by Western scholars, emphasizes the dynamic role of Orthodoxy in effecting church-state relations. The existence of an underground church throughout most of the Soviet period, for example, must have forced the Soviet authorities to consider the reality that uninterrupted persecution of the church might lead to even greater numbers of crypto believers, making their surveillance exceedingly difficult. The Orthodox underground church in the Soviet Union has not been sufficiently researched or discussed, but its existence and dynamism are attested to by several observers of the

[7]Gerhard Simon, *Church, State and Opposition in the U.S.S.R.*, p. 95.

Soviet religious scene. The present study, concentrating on the great religious revival during the war years, also supports the view of Orthodoxy's dynamic role. The evidence is certainly impressive. As we have seen, during approximately three years of German occupation, under conditions of hunger, devastation, and deprivation, the Russian Orthodox Church reestablished itself in the Pskov region with the reopening of 300 churches in contrast to a couple of churches which were functioning there before the war. Similarly, Belorussia, described in 1939 as a religious desert with a handful of open churches, witnessed the reestablishment of nearly 40 percent of the number of pre-Revolutionary churches. In addition, a church organization was created which preserved its ties with the Russian Orthodox Church despite efforts by the occupation authorities and by some Belorussian nationalists brought from former Poland to obstruct it. Only in the Ukraine did the German administration and Ukrainian nationalists who had come mainly from the territory of former Poland manage to weaken the Ukrainian Autonomous church which had preserved its loyalty to the Russian Orthodox Church. This they did by setting up the Ukrainian Autocephalous Church. Even there, the majority of the population remained faithful to the autonomous pro-Russian church and after the retreat of the German Army, the Autocephalous Ukrainian Church on Russian territory disappeared. What is even more significant is the fact that in the Ukraine, as in Belorussia, up to 40 percent of pre-Revolutionary churches were restored and mass baptism of children was a common phenomenon. The occupied territory on which this religious rebirth occurred encompassed more than one-third of the population of the USSR. The number of reopened churches, rising up to 20,000 as opposed to 3000 in the entire USSR before the war, necessitated an increase in the number of priests and bishops in order to staff the new and fast expanding ecclesiastical machinery on the region. This must have been a major factor in Stalin's decision on 4 September 1943 when, along with Molotov, he held that historic meeting with the three metropolitans remaining in the Soviet Union, headed by the *Locum Tenens* Metropolitan Sergii. The meeting was followed by a hastily convened council of Bishops four days later which elected Metropolitan Sergii Patriarch. By this time the war was almost won, and the help of the church was not really essential in the struggle against Hitler, and under the *Locum Tenens* the Moscow patriarchate continued to do everything required of it by the Soviet authorities. It is clear that in 1943 the goverment needed the Moscow Patriarch to lead the official branch of the Russian Orthodox Church, which had organized church life on occupied territory into a controllable channel. Fifty percent of the episcopate of the rapidly expanding Moscow patriarchate was sent into reoccupied territory. This had also been done in 1939 and 1940 on territories of former Poland and the Baltic states. One can safely conclude that it was the dynamics of the religious revival during the war which forced the Soviet government to retreat and allow the religious NEP of the forties and fifties. This, after all, was a period of consolidation of the reincorporated territories lost to the Germans during the war.

The "strange alliance" between Church and State, understandable perhaps during the war and early postwar years, became less so during the early sixties when Khrushchev unleashed his attacks on religion. Sensitive Russian Orthodox believers, lay and ecclesiastic, found the close collaboration between Church and State a constant source of disillusionment and embarrassment which gradually led to a serious crisis within the Russian hierarchy.

Western observers of the Russian religious scene have recently begun assessing the seriousness of this crisis and its implications for the survival of Orthodoxy. It reached its high point of expression in December 1965, when two Russian priests, Iakunin and Eshliman, leveled criticisms against the then Patriarch Aleksii who as official head of the Russian Orthodox Church had continually overlooked the unfortunate condition of his flock and who in effect approved the Soviet government's policy on religion. Aleksii did not answer the questions asked by the inquisitive priests and neither did his successor Pimen, who was enthroned on 2 June 1971. In fact, the Christmas greeting of the new Patriarch left no doubt in the mind of the listeners that he had no intention of deviating from the policy of his predecessors. Nevertheless, serious repercussions resulted from these incidents, damaging further, among other things, the credibility of the upper echelons of the Russian hierarchy. It developed into what Michael Bourdeaux described as a duel between the Russian priests on the one hand and the Patriarch on the other, reminiscent of the Old Testament "conflict between the established cultic religion as personified by the priest and the explosive calls to repentance from the prophet."[8] What is significant, of course, is the courage of individuals like Iakunin and Eshliman who were becoming surprisingly numerous and the spirituality to which their lives and pronouncements attested. Their stand also reflected a broader spiritual base in the persons of the Russian Orthodox believers whom they wanted to champion and who numbered anywhere from 25 to 40 million. This, in other words, suggests that the great revival of the war years persisted into Khruschev's and Brezhnev's Russia and, despite persecutions, the body of believers increased in numbers and improved in quality. This certainly is the general impression responsible visitors to the Soviet Union have been conveying, and it was reaffirmed as recently as April 1975 by the American Chaplain to Moscow, the Rev. Raymond Oppenheim, who also emphasized the fact that the number of young believers attending church increased considerably during the last five years.[9] This should not suggest a religious activity or revival as it is known among Protestant evangelistic circles in the West. It rather demonstrates that the consequences of the Orthodox revival from the war years are readily noticeable in the body of Orthodox Christians in Russia even as these lines are being written. In this respect, the significance of the "Great Revival" takes on a special meaning. To put it in another way, not only did it infuse the Orthodox community with a new lease of life, but it convinced them that in fact they could survive any form of persecution and indeed triumph. Its story is probably the greatest story of Christian triumph in the twentieth century. It was an Orthodox spiritual revival which went beyond the confines of the politics of the Russian hierarchy.

[8] Michael Bourdeaux, *Patriarch and Prophets*, preface and pp. 189-237.
[9] Interviewed by Professor Stavrou in Athens, Greece on 22 April 1975.

The "Great Revival" also contributed toward the supplanting of Communist ideals which by the time of Stalin's death were losing their appeal to a large section of Russian society, especially the intelligentsia. One of the most amazing characteristics of a substantial percentage of the Soviet intelligentsia has been its religious orientation. Significant writers and poets, such as Anna Akhmatova, Boris Pasternak, and Aleksandr Solzhenitsyn, to mention just the most prominent ones, disclosed themselves as Orthodox Christians, and religious motifs abound in their writings. It is, as has been pointed out, a "formidable paradox" that "in the countries where Christian Churches thrive there are practically no genuinely Christian novels. Truly Christian writing has had to come from Russia where Christians have been persecuted for several decades."[10] This again attests to the vital spiritual revival that Orthodoxy experienced in the midst of organized persecution. It may also attest to the efforts of Russian intellectuals to recover the prerevolutionary cultural heritage of which Orthodoxy is an essential part. Or, in the final analysis, it may be an expression of the conviction of some of them who "see Christianity today as the only living spiritual force capable of undertaking the spiritual healing of Russia."[11] Not all Russian writers or artists with a religious message are necessarily Orthodox. But even those who are not Orthodox oftentimes identify themselves with Orthodoxy as a symbolic gesture of their opposition to an undemocratic materialistic, and avowedly atheistic regime. Even Roy Medvedev, the celebrated Soviet dissident residing in Moscow, who rejects religion as a solution for his country's problems and in fact laments the fact that social and political realities in the Soviet Union make religion a haven for "many oppositionally minded people," admits that an increasing number among the Soviet intelligentsia is turning to religion. In his own words: "One characteristic feature of our cultural life has been the rising interest among a considerable section of our intelligentsia in religion and the church, church history, and theological problems in general. It is not just that

[10]Czelslaw Milosz, "On Modern Russian Literature and the West," *California Slavic Studies* VI (1971), pp. 171-72.
[11]Solzhenitsyn, *Letter to the Soviet Leaders*, p. 57.

it has suddenly become fashionable to collect icons. We hear powerful voices demanding an improvement in the wretched condition to which the church is at present reduced. Many distinguished representatives of the intelligentsia are outspoken in their protest about the wholesale destruction of church buildings that took place not only in the early years of the Revolution and in Stalin's time, but also in the first half of the sixties. An intellectual who is a believer no longer arouses scorn but is more likely to inspire a certain respect."[12]

Aleksandr Solzhenitsyn has, of course, been a most articulate, and in certain cases an extreme, spokesman of the role of Christianity and Orthodoxy for the future of Russia. He reached that position after careful reflection on the evolution of the Soviet regime—a regime whose objective was the eradication of religion. And, like the priests Iakunin and Eshliman, he reacted strongly to the Patriarch's servile attitude toward the Soviet authorities. He expressed his views in a letter to the Patriarch written during Lent, 1972. The letter is probably the most eloquent yet succinct statement on the fate of religion in the Soviet Union and at the same time a testimony of the indomitable spirit of Orthodoxy.[13] The very existence of a Solzhenitsyn and a number of others like him in the Soviet Union in 1972 attests to the reality that religion in general and Orthodoxy in particular have demonstrated remarkable resilience and are far from insignificant in the lives of appreciable numbers of believers representing various social strata and professions in the Soviet Union.

In the introductory remarks of this study we related the experiences of Nikos Kazantzakis, who had visited the Soviet Union several times during the interwar years, and whose report on the state of religion in that country was gloomy and full of pessimism about the future. It was his conviction and that of many of his contemporaries that religion was dying fast and that it was being replaced by a new religion—Communism—with its

[12] Medvedev, *On Socialist Democracy*, pp. 75-76.
[13] The letter can be found in Gerhard Simon, *op. cit.*, pp. 202-5; see also the special edition of Solzhenitsyn, *A Lenten Letter to Pimen Patriarch of all Russia*, pp. 5-8.

own set of dogmas and truths. If Kazantzakis were alive today and could visit the Soviet Union he would be able to determine for himself that his prophecy was not fulfilled. And the result would have pleased him, not so much because Orthodoxy survived as because in its survival he would have detected the insubordination of the human spirit which assumed unbelievable dimensions in the case of the believers. To quote Solzhenitsyn again, "For the believer his faith is supremely precious, more precious than the food he puts in his stomach."[14] Kazantzakis would also rejoice upon discovering that his own *The Greek Passion,* which had caused so much uproar in Greece and almost led to his excommunication by the Greek Orthodox Church, had been translated into Russian and read by intellectuals and devout Christians as well as being circulated for anti-religious propaganda purposes.[15]

All this certainly speaks of greater religious ferment in the Soviet Union than could have been anticipated a generation or so earlier. And even though one should not exaggerate the extent of this ferment, one cannot ignore it either. It is, in any case, a climate of religious feeling toward which the "Great Revival" during World War II made a significant contribution.

[14]Solzhenitsyn, *Letter to the Soviet Leaders,* p. 44.
[15]The Russian translation of Kazantzakis' *Greek Passion* appeared in Moscow in 1962 under the title *Khrista raspinaiut vnov* [Christ Recrucified] which approximates the Greek title, by Iannis Mochos and Igor Postupalskii, in an edition of 150,000 copies.

Bibliography

A Note on Sources

This study is based largely on accounts of numerous individuals who had witnessed the religious revival in German occupied territories and who emigrated to the West after World War II. Many clergymen and almost the entire episcopate of the Ukrainian and the Belorussian Orthodox Churches left the USSR. Not only were many of these individuals interviewed, but oftentimes they submitted special memoranda which they had prepared for personal use. Many of these interviews and reports are in the personal files of W. Alexeev. The picture provided by the interviews and reports of the Orthodox clergy was corroborated by documents prepared by the German occupation authorities. The Yiddish Scientific Institute (YIVO) in New York possesses an excellent collection of German secret documents which reflect Hitler's policy toward the Russian Orthodox Church and corresponding Nazi legislation in the area. Documents prepared for the Nuremberg trials proved very useful too. Over 200 communiqués of the SD (German secret police), which were of secondary value for the Nuremberg trials, proved exceedingly helpful for this study because they describe in great detail conditions in Russian territory occupied by the Germans. Many of these 20 to 25-page communiqués provide a great deal of information on religion, the Orthodox Church, and the morals of the people in occupied areas. These clearly written and informative reports were classified as secret and served only as information for the heads of Hitler's governmental apparatus. Since an effort has been made to place the religious revival in the context of the general fate of the Russian Orthodox Church during the Second World War, and indeed the Soviet period, we have also utilized official Russian sources, especially the pronouncements of the representatives of the Moscow Patriarchate, as well as pertinent memoirs.

The bibliography includes only works which have been cited in this study.

Primary Sources
Unpublished
Interviews and Correspondence

A . . . . A priest from Smolensk. 17 July 1956, at Jordanville, N.Y.

D . . . . A Cossack from the Cossack village of Mitiakinskaia. 20 January 1954, at New York City.

Filofei (Narko), Archbishop. 23 and 24 March 1964, at New York City.

Former employee of Kievo-Pecherskaia Lavra [Monastery] in Kiev. 17 June 1957, at Minneapolis, Minnesota.

Former inhabitant of the city of Orel. 15 January 1955, at New York City.

I . . . . A priest. 25 July 1953, at New York City.

Ionov, Aleksei, Protoierei. 21 and 22 August 1952, at Sea Cliff, Long Island, N.Y.

M . . . . 20 May 1965, at New York City. Discussion of the religious situation in Kiev after her visit to Kiev in 1965.

Oppenheim, Rev. Raymond, American Chaplain to Moscow. 22 April 1975 at Athens, Greece.

Panteleimon (Rudyk), Archbishop. Fall of 1954, at New York City.

Protoierei from Polish territory which was under Soviet rule between 1939 and 1941. Summer of 1956, at Chicago.

Sh . . ., Mrs., from Polotsk. 20 November 1954, at New York City.

Letters from Father Iosif Grinkevich, 15 February 1955; Bishop Leontii (Filippovich), 5 April 1954; and M . . . 20 and 21 November 1955.

BIBLIOGRAPHY 215

Document Collections

U.S. National Archives. Der Chef der Sicherheitspolizei und des SD [Chief Security Police and the SD] Ereignismeldungen UdSSR, Nos. 1-195 (June 1941-April 1942). Meldungen aus den besetzten Ostgebieten, Nos. 1-55 (May 1942-May 1943). Microfilms, Washington, D.C.: The American Historical Association, Committee for the Study of War Documents (1960), Rolls T175-233, 234, 235, 236.

Leibbrandt, Lieutenant. Leutenant Dr. Leibbrandt an den Reichsminister für die besetzte Ostgebiete. November 1941. Königsberg, Bericht No. 8. Document Ng-4435.

Russian Orthodox Church Outside of Russia. Archives.

"Spisok sviashehennikov pravoslavnoi tserkvi Vinnitskoi eparkhii" [List of priests of the Orthodox Church of the Vinnitsa diocese]. Unsigned. File of Bishop Evlogii of Vinnitsa [1941].

Yiddish Scientific Institute (YIVO). New York City, New York.

In this Institute sixteen files with documents are deposited under the following codes: OccE (Ch)-1; OccE (Ch)-2; OccE (Ch)-3; OccE (Ch)-4; OccE (Ch)-5; OccE (Ch)-6; OccE (Ch)-7-8; OccE (Ch)-10; OccE (Ch)-11; OccE (Ch)-12; OccE 4-11; OccE 18-19; OccE 3a; Occ 3a (Bar.); 3a-14; 3a 22. Most of these documents contain information concerning Russian Orthodox Church on territory of Russia occupied by the Germans. Of these the following documents were quoted in this work: II Politik Nr. 2456/42 . . . 19. November, 1942. An den Herrn Generalkommissar in Reval. Betrifft: Ammeldung der Religionsgesellschaften. Bezug: Mein Erlass vom 26. 10. 1942. Document OccE (Ch)-1 YIVO.

II Politik Tgb. - Nr. 2456/42g. Bu./Ko. . . . 26. Oktober, 1942. An den Herrn Generalkommissar in Reval. Betrifft: Anmeldung der Religionsgesellschaften. Bezug: Mein Erlass vom 25. August, 1942. Document OccE (Ch)-1. YIVO.

Abteilung Ost [das Reichsministerium für Volksaufklärung und Progaganda] Ref. Dr. Kurtz. Herrn Dr. Mehne, Abt. Pro. Berlin, den 13. Januar 1944. 26/44g (1). Signed by Doctor Kurtz. Document OccE (Ch)-3, YIVO.

Der Befehlshaber der Sicherheitspolizei und des SD Ostland. Abt. IV B3 Tgb. Nr. 524/43g. An den Reichskommissar f. d. Ostland, Abt. I. Politik, z. Hd. von Herrn Ministerialrat Burmeister, in Riga. Betr.: Stellungnahme des Exarchen Sergii (Voskresenskii) zur Wiener Resolution gegen den Moskauer Patriarchen. Instead of a signature, i. A. gez. Unterschrift SS-Sturmbannführer. Abschrift. Document OccE (Ch)-3, YIVO.

Major O. W. Müller's report, No. 21, addressed to the Minister of seized territories and dated October 8, 1942. Document OccE 3a-7, YIVO.

Wehrmachtsbefehlshaber Ostland Ic. 14222, den 22. VIII, 1942. Betr.: Stimmungsbericht aus Weissruthenien. Document OccE 3a-14, YIVO.

Soobschcheniia i rasporiazheniia Vysokopreosviashchennieishago Serafima, Mitropolita Berlinskago, Germanskago i Sredne-evropeiskago Mitropolich'iago okruga. Mitteilungen und Verfügungen des orthodoxen Metropoliten des Mitteleuropäischen Metropolitankreises und orthodoxen Bischofs von Berlin und Deutschland Seraphim, Rundschreiben. Berlin-Chbg., den 27 October 1943. Document OccE (Ch)-4. YIVO.

Der Reichskommissar für das Ostland. Abt. II Politik RR Tr./KoTgb. No. 2239/428. "*Vermerk.* Am 18. Juni 1942, 11, 30 Uhr fand bei Ministerialdirektor Leibbrandt eine Besprechung betreffend den Religionserlass statt." Riga, den 19. Juni 1942. Document OccE (Ch)-4, YIVO.

Rosenberg, Alfred. "Der Reichsminister für die Besetzten Ostgebiete an a) den Herrn Reichskommissar für das Ostland Gauleiter Heinrich Lohse, Riga; b) den Herrn Reichskommissar für die Ukraine Gauleiter Erich Koch, Rowno," Berlin W 35, 13. Mai, 1942, Rauchstr. 17/18. Typescript signed by Rosenberg. Document OccE (Ch)-4, YIVO .

[Sergii (Voskresenskii), Metropolitan] "Denkschrift betreffend die Lage der Orthodoxen Kirche im Ostland. Riga, November 12, 1941. Typescript copy. Document OccE (Ch)-6, YIVO.

Moscow, Sachbearbeiter. Abt. II Politik 2230/42. "Ergebnisse meiner Besprechung von 12.-16. Mai in Berlin, Ostministerium Rauchstrasse, Abteilung Kulturpolitik," Riga den 20. Mai 1942. Document OccE (Ch)-7-8, YIVO.

Private Documents

Shch . . ., S., Protoierei, "Sostoianie Pravoslavnoi tserkvi pered 2-i mirovoi voinoi" [The state of the Orthodox Church before the Second World War].

A report signed by Protoierei Shch . . . on 16 March 1954, in W. Alexeev's personal archives.

Stefan, Archbishop. "Sostoianie Smolenskoi eparkhii s 20 dekabria 1942 goda, so dnia pribytiia v g. Smolensk Episkopa Stefana, po 1 ianvaria 1944 goda [The condition of the Smolensk Eparchy from 20 December 1942, the day of Bishop Stefan's arrival in Smolensk, to 1 January 1944]. This is an account written for Metropolitan Panteleimon of Belorussia. A copy of this report signed by Archbishop Stefan in March 1954 exists in W. Alexeev's personal archives.

[Vissarion], Archbishop. "L'archevêque roumain Vissarion en Transnistrie (Ucraine) en 1943." A typescript of thirteen pages describing the activity of Archbishop Vissarion in Transnistria. Unsigned with corrections made by Archbishop Vissarion. Accompanying letter is dated 18 September 1958. In W. Alexeev's personal archives.

Published

Public Documents and Privately Published Documents

Brautingam, Otto. "Secret Note by Brautingam," 25 October 1942. Document 294-PS, TMWC, XXV (Nuremberg, 1947), pp. 331-42.

Gidulianov, Pavel Vasil'evich (ed.), *Otdelenie tserkvi ot gosudarstva v S.S.S.R.; Sbornik dekretov i.t.d.* [The separation of Church and State in the U.S.S.R.; Collection of decrees, etc.]. Moscow, 1924; third edition, 1926. Republished with supplement, 1928.

Meyer, Alfred, ed. *Das Recht der besetzten Ostebiete: Estland, Lettland, Litauen, Weissruthenien und Ukraine; Sammlung der Verordnungen, Erlassen und sonstigen Vorschriften über Verwaltung, Rechtspflege Wirtschaft, Finanzwesen . . .* Munich and Berlin: C. H. Beck, 1943.

"Osuzhdenie izmennikov vere i otechestvu" [Condemnation of betrayers of the Faith and Fatherland, *Zhurnal Moskovskoi patritrayers* [Journal of the Moscow Patriarchate] No. 1 (1943):16.

Pravda o religii v Rossii [The truth about religion in Russia]. Moscow: Moscow Patriarchate, 1942.

"Questioning of Rosenberg," Tuesday, 16 April 1946. TMWC, XI (Nuremberg, 1947), pp. 460-524.

Rosenberg, Alfred. "Vermerk über eine Unterredung mit dem Führer in Führer-Hauptquartier am 8.5.42." Document 1520-PS, TMWC, XXVII (Nuremberg, 1948), pp. 283-94.

Russkaia Pravoslavnaia Tserkov' i Velikaia Otechestvennaia Voina; sbornik tserkovnykh dokumentov [The Russian Orthodox Church

and the Great Patriotic War; collection of church documents].
Moscow: Moscow Patriarchate, 1943.

Sergii (Stragorodskii), *Locum Tenens.* "Opredelenie No. 27 ot 22 sentiabria 1942 goda . . . po delu mitropolita Sergiia Voskresenskogo s drugimi [Position paper No. 27 of 22 September 1942 . . . in regard to Metropolitan Sergii Voskresenskii and others] in *Russkaia Pravoslavnaia Tserkov' i Velikaia Otechestvennaia Voina; sbornik tserkovnykh dokumentov.* Moscow: Moscow Patriarchate, 1943, pp. 35-36.

Sergii (Stragorodskii), *Locum Tenens.* "Poslanie . . . 22 sentiabra 1942 goda" [Message . . . of 22 September 1942] in *Russkaia Provoslavnaia Tserkov' i Velikaia Otechestvennaia Voina; sbornik tserkovnykh dokumentov.* Moscow: Moscow Patriarchate, 1943, pp. 32-34.

Memoirs, Accounts by Contemporaries, etc.

Anfim, Archimandrit. "Otchet Rumynskoi pravoslavnoi missii v Transnistrii s 1 aprelia do 30 iiunia 1942 goda [Report of the Rumanian Orthodox Mission in Transnistria from 1 April to 30 June 1942]. Translated from the Rumanian by L. Stepanova. Vladimirova: *Pravoslavnaia Rus'* [Orthodox Russia] August 15 old style [August 28 new style], 1942, p. 7.

Fevr, Nikolai. *Solntse voskhodit na Zapade* [The sun rises in the West]. Buenos Aires: Novoe Slovo [The New Word], 1950.

Georgii, Igumen (Abbot). "Iz vospominanii o tserkovnoi zhizni v SSR pri nemetskoi okkupatsii" [From memoirs of church life in the USSR under German occupation]. *Vestnik Instituta po izucheniiu SSSR* [Herald of the Institute for Study of the USSR] No. 2(23; April-June 1957):103-10.

Hitler, Adolf. *Hitler's Table Talk, 1941-1944;* With an Introductory Essay on the Mind of Adolf Hitler, by H. R. Trevor-Roper. London: Weidenfeld and Nicolson, 1953.

Iljinsky, Pavel. "Tri goda pod nemetskoi okkupatsiei v Belorussii; zhizn' Polotskogo ohruga, 1941-1944gg" [Three years under German occupation; Life in the Polotsk area]. *Grani,* No. 30 (April-June 1956):85-122; No. 31 (July-September 1956):94-127.

Ionov, Aleksii, Protoierei. "Zapiski missionera (Pskovskaia missiia)" [Notes of a missionary (Mission of Pskov)]. *Po stopam Khrista* [Following the steps of Christ] No. 50 (September-October 1954): 11-16; No. 51 (November-December 1954):13-20; No. 52 (January-February 1955):11-16; No. 53 (March-April 1955):15-20.

Kasiak, I. *Z historyi pravoslavnai tsarkvy belaruskago narodu* [From the history of the Orthodox Church of the Belorussian people]. New York: Belorussian Central Council, 1956.

Venedikt, Archbishop. "B.A.P.T.S.'—novaia sektantskaia gruppirovka v Belorusskoi tserkvi v emigratsii" [B.A.O.C. — a new sectarian grouping in the Belorussian church in emigration]. *Tserkovnaia zhizn'* [Church Life] Nos. 3-4 (March-April 1952):48-60; Nos. 5-6 (May-June 1952):84-95.

Secondary Sources

Monographs

Alexeev, Wassilij. *Russian Orthodox Bishops in the Soviet Union, 1941-1953: Materials for the History of the Russian Orthodox Church in the U.S.S.R.* New York: Research Program on the U.S.S.R., 1954. (Mimeographed Series No. 61. In Russian.)

_____. *The Foreign Policy of the Moscow Patriarchate, 1939-1953.* New York: Research Program on the U.S.S.R., 1955. (Mimeographed series No. 70. In Russian.)

Anderson, Paul. *Russia's Religious Future.* London, 1935.

_____. *L'église et la nation en Russie soviétique.* French translation by C. Wilzkovoski from English of the classic *People, Church and State in Modern Russia.* Paris:Calmann-Levy, 1946.

Armstrong, John Alexander. *Ukrainian Nationalism, 1939-1945.* New York: Columbia University Press, 1955.

Balevits, Z. *Pravoslavnaia tserkov v Latvii pod sen'iu svastiki, 1941-1944* [The Orthodox Church in Latvia under the shadow of the swastika, 1941-44]. Riga: Zinatne, 1967.

Bogolepov, Aleksandr. *Tserkov' pod vlast'iu kommunisma* [The Church under the rule of Communism]. Munich: Institute for the Study of the U.S.S.R., 1958.

Bourdeaux, Michael. *Opium of the People: The Christian Religion in the USSR.* London: Faber and Faber, 1965.

_____. *Patriarch and Prophets: Persecution of the Russian Orthodox Today.* New York: Praeger Publishers, 1970.

Briem, Efraim. *Kommunismus und Religion in der Sovietunion; ein Ideenkampf.* Einzig berechtigte Uebersetzung aus dem Schwedischen von Edzard Schaper. Basle: Verlag Friedrich Reinhard, n.d.

Chrysostomus, Johannes. *Kirchengeschichte Russlands der neusten Zeit.* Munich and Salzburg: Anton Pustet, 1965, 1966, 1968. 3 vols.

Conquest, Robert, ed. *Religion in the USSR*. New York: Frederick A. Praeger, 1968.
Cooke, Richard Joseph. *Religion in Russia under the Soviets*. New York: Abingdon Press, 1924.
Curtiss, John Shelton. *Church and State in Russia, 1900-1917*. New York: Octagon Books, 1965.
———. *The Russian Church and the Soviet State, 1917-1950*. Boston: Little, Brown and Co., 1953.
Dallin, Alexander. *German Rule in Russia, 1941-1945: A Study of Occupation Policies*. London: Macmillan & Co.; New York: St. Martin's Press, 1957.
Fireside, Harvey. *Icon and Swastica: The Russian Orthodox Church under Nazi and Soviet Control*. Cambridge, Mass.: Harvard University Press, 1971.
Fletcher, William C. *The Russian Orthodox Church Underground, 1917-1970*. London: Oxford University Press, 1971.
———. *Nikolai*. New York: Macmillan Co., 1968.
———. *A Study in Survival: The Church in Russia, 1927-1943*. New York: Macmillan, 1965.
Fotiev, K. V. *Popytiki ukrainskoi tserkovnoi avtokefalii v xx veke* [The efforts of the Ukrainian Autocephalous Church in the twentieth century]. Munich, 1955?
Gsovski, Vladimir, ed. *Church and State Behind the Iron Curtain: Czechoslavakia, Hungary, Poland, Romania, with an Introduction on the Soviet Union*. New York: F. A. Praeger, 1955.
Gustafson, Arfved. *Die Katakomben Kirche*. Stuttgart: Evangelisches Verlagswerk, 1954.
Heyer, Friedrich. *Die orthodoxe Kirche in der Ukraine von 1917 bis 1945*. Cologne: R. Müller, 1953.
Inkeles, Alex. *Social Change in Soviet Russia*. Cambridge, Mass.: Harvard University Press, 1968.
Institut zur Erforschung der UdSSR. *Religion in the USSR*. Munich, 1960.
Kazantzakis, Nikos. *Taxidevontas Rossia* [Travelling Russia] (third edition). Athens, 1960.
———. *Khrista raspinaiut vnov* [Christ recrucified] Moscow, 1962.
Kolarz, Walter. *Religion in the Soviet Union*. New York: St. Martins Press, 1961.
McCullagh, Francis. *The Bolshevik Persecution of Christianity*. New York: E. P. Dutton, 1924.
Medvedev, Roy A. *Let History Judge: The Origin and Consequences of Stalinism*. New York: Alfred A. Knopf, 1971.

_____, *On Socialist Democracy.* New York: Alfred A. Knopf, 1975.

Patriarkh' Sergii i ego dukhovnoe nasledstvo [Patriarch Sergii and his spiritual heritage]. Moscow: Publication of the Moscow Patriarchate, 1947.

Polskii, M. *Kanonicheskoe polozhenie Vysshei Tserkovnoi Vlasti v SSR i Zagranitsei* [The canonical position of the highest church authority in the USSR and abroad]. Jordanville, N.Y.: The Holy Trinity Monastery, 1948.

Raevskii, S. *Ukrainskaia avtokefal'naia tserkov'* [The Ukrainian Autocephalous Church]. Jordanville, N.Y.: Publ. House of St. Iov of Pochaev in Holy Trinity Monastery, 1948.

Simon, Gerhard. *Church, State and Opposition in the U.S.S.R.* London: C. Hurst & Company, 1974.

Solzhenitsyn, Aleksandr I. *The Gulag Archipelago: 1918-1956.* New York: Harper & Row, 1974.

_____. *Letter to the Soviet Leaders.* New York: Harper & Row, 1974.

_____. *A Lenten Letter to Pimen, Patriarch of All Russia.* Minneapolis: Burgess Publishing Company, 1972.

Spinka, Matthew. *The Church in Soviet Russia.* New York: Oxford University Press, 1956.

_____. *The Church and the Russian Revolution.* New York: 1927.

Stratonov, I. *Russkaia tserkovnaia smuta* [The Russian church confusion]. Berlin: Parabola, 1932.

Stroyen, William B. *Communist Russia and the Russian Orthodox Church 1943-1962.* Washington, D.C.: Catholic University Press of America, 1967.

Struve, Nikita. *Les Chrétiens en U.R.S.S.* Paris: Editions du Seuil, 1963. (English translation, *Christians in Contemporary Russia.* New York: Charles Scribner's Sons, 1967.)

Svitich, Aleksandr. *Pravoslavnaia tserkov' v Pol'she i ee avtokefaliia* [The Orthodox Church in Poland and its autocephality]. Buenos Aires: Nasha Strana, 1959.

Thorwald, Jurgen. *Wen sie verderben wollen.* Stuttgart: Steinberg-Verlag, 1952.

Timasheff, N. S. *Religion in Soviet Russia, 1917-1942.* New York: Sheed & Ward, 1942.

Vlasovs'kyi, Ivan. *Narys istorii Ukrains'koi pravoslavnoi tserkvy, xx st* [History of the Ukrainian Orthodox Church, XX century]. New York: Ukrainian Orthodox Church in the U.S.A., 1961. T. IV, Ch. 1 [v. IV, p. 1]

Werth, Alexander. The Year of Stalingrad. London, 1946.

Articles

Alexeev, Wassilij. "Le drame de l'exarque Serge Voskresenskij et l'élection du patriarche de Moscou," *Irénikon,* xxx (2e Trimestre, 1957): 189-202.

————. "Smert' Ekzarkha Sergiia Voskresenskago i vybory Moskovskago Patriarkha v svietie niemetskikh sekretnykh dokumentov" [The death of Exarch Sergii Vosresenskii and the elections of the Patriarch of Moscow in the light of German secret documents]. *Tserkovnaia Zhizn'* [Church Life] 7-12 (July-December 1958): 108-119.

Dimitrii (Gradusov), Archbishop. "Poslaniia Sviateishego Patriarkha Sergiia" [Messages of His Holiness Patriarch Sergii] in *Patriarkh Sergii i ego dukhovnoe nasledstvo* [Patriarch Sergii and his spiritual heritage]. Moscow: Publication of the Moscow Patriarchate, 1947, pp. 77-91.

Kishkovskii, A. "W. Alexeev, Russian Orthodox Bishops in the Soviet Union, 1941-1953. Materials for the history of the Russian Orthodox Church in the USSR. Mimeogr. Series No. 61. Research Program on the USSR, New York, 1954." Review in *Vestnik Instituta po izucheniiu SSSR,* No. 4 (21, October-December 1956): 97-104.

Milosz, Czeslaw. "On Modern Russian Literature and the West," *California Slavic Studies,* VI (1971): 170-76.

Nikonov, V. "Vysokopreosviashchennyi Nikolai, Mitropolit Krutitskii i Kolomenskii" [Most Holy Nikolai, Metropolitan of Krutitsy and Koloma]. *Zhurnal Moskovskoi patriarkhii* [Journal of the Moscow Patriarchate] No. 4 (1952): 9-21.

Smirnov, A. R., Protoierei. "Moskva v Ulianovske" [Moscow in Ul'ianvosk] in *Patriarkh Sergii i ego dukhovnoe nasledstvo* [Patriarch Sergii and his spiritual heritage]. Moscow: Publication of the Moscow Patriarchate, 1947, 237-45.

Index

A

A...priest from Smolensk, 135
Afanasii (Martos), bishop of the Belorussian Church, 113, 114, 118, 120, 122, 123, 124 n., 127, 128, 129, 132
Agafangel, Metropolitan of Iaroslavl, named as *Locum Tenens* by Patriarch Tikhon, 16
Akhmatova, Anna Andreevna, poetess, 210
Aleksandr (Inozemtsev), Bishop of Poles'e and Pinsk, later Metropolitan, 46 n., 47, 112, 130, 131, 156, 157, 168
Aleksandr, bishop in Latvia, 89 n.
Aleksandr, Metropolitan of Estonia, 48, 71, 76, 77, 87, 88
Aleksei (Ionov), Protoierei, 99, 100, 120
Alexeev, Ludmila, xvi
Alexeev, Wassilij, xiii n., xvi, xiii n., 27 n.
Aleksii (Gromadskii), Archbishop of Voly'n and Kremenets, 46 n., 47, 154, 156, 157, 158, 175, 176, 184
Aleksii (Simanskii), Metropolitan of Leningrad, later Patriarch, 22, 41, 54, 55, 56, 58, 60, 84, 202, 203, 205, 208, 209
Anan'evskii Okrug, 170
Anastasii (Gribanovskii), Metropolitan, head of the Russian Orthodox Church Abroad, 90, 129
Anderson, Paul, xv, 30, 43
Andrii (Sheptyts'kyi), Metropolitan, 1865-1944, 168, 169
Anfim (Nika), Rumanian Archimandrite, the head of the Rumanian Orthodox Mission in Transnistria, 189, 190, 191, 192
Antireligioznik (Antireligious), 24
Antonii (Marchenko?), Bishop of Kamenets Podol'sk, 46 n.
Antonii (Khrapovitskii), first head of the Russian Orthodox Church Abroad, 12
Antonii (Marchenko), Bishop of the Ukrainian Autonomous Church, 156
Archbishop of Canterbury, 18
Archbishop of York, 94
Armes, Keith, xi n.
Armstrong, John Alexander, 147, 148, 154, 155
Athanasius the Great, 78
Atheist (Bezbozhnik), antireligious weekly journal, 4, 15, 24
Athenagorus, the Ecumenical Patriarch, 203
Autocephalous Church in the Ukraine, 55, 56. See also under Ukraine
Autocephalous National Church in Belorussia. See under Belorussia
Autonomous Church in the Ukraine, 65. See also under Ukraine
Autonomous Orthodox Church in Belorussia. See also under Belorussia
Avgustin, Metropolitan of Latvia, 48, 71, 76, 77, 87, 88, 89 n.

B

Balai, priest in Belorussia, 126
Balevits, Z. xii n., 102 n.
Baltic countries, 51, 67, 75, 76, 107, 126, 208
Baltic Sector, administrative division of the Orthodox Church by the Germans, 65, 71-106. See also under Pskov Mission and Exarch Sergii Voskresenskii
Bandera, Stepan (1909-1959), 153, 154, 155, 167, 168, 169, 176, 177, 178, 179, 183, 184, 185
Baranovichi-Novogrudok, 118
Bednyi, Demian (pseud. of Pridvorov, Efim Alekseevich), Soviet poet, 43 n.
Belevskii monastery, 181
Belorussia:
  administrative division of the Orthodox Church by the Germans, 65, 107-146, 147
  Autocephalous National Church in, 112ff, 117, 119, 123ff
  Autonomous Orthodox Church in, 107ff
  Catholic and Polish activities in, 108, 109-112
  German policy in, 107-116
  religious revival in, 132-145
Belynichi, 134
Berezino, 134
Berdichev, 173, 176
Bessarabia, 170, 188
Bialystok, 118
Bogoiavlenskii Monastery, 163
Bolshevik Revolution, x, xii, xiv, 1, 7, 8, 9, 17, 25, 52, 115, 201
Borisov, 134, 136, 138
Bourdeaux, Michael, Rev., 6 n., 209, 42 n.
Bormann, Martin, 61, 62
Brailov, 181
Brest-Litovsk, Treaty of, criticized by Patriarch Tikhon, 10
Brest eparchy, 130, 168
Brezhnev, Leonid Il'ich, 209
Briansk, 65, 111, 128, 134, 138, 141
Bukharin, Nikolai Ivanovich, 13

C

Catacomb or Underground Church, xiii n., 5 n., 22, 26-27, 206
Cers, Janis, xvi
Chernigov, Diocese of, 183
Chetverikov, Professor, 133
Communism, Soviet and religion, xii, 2, 15, 201-212
Constitution of the USSR, ix, 11, 23, 25, 57
Council for the Affairs of the Russian Orthodox Church, 59, 203
Cracow, 155
Crimea, 196
Chrysostomus, Johannes, 12 n., 14 n.
Curtiss, John Shelton, xii, 15 n., 41
Curzon, George Nathaniel, Lord — British Foreign Secretary, 18

D

Danilov Monastery, 73-74
Decree of Separation of Church and State, 9-11, 26
D.... Cossack from the village of Mitiakinskaia, 196
Dallin, Alexander, xv
Damaskin, bishop of the Ukrainian Autonomous Church, 162
Derman Monastery, 180
Deutsch, Harold C., Professor, xv
Dionisii (Vabedinskii), Metropolitan, head of the Autocephalous Polish Orthodox Church, 113, 114, 115, 116, 125, 151, 152, 156, 157, 168, 174, 179
Dmitrii Donskoi, Prince, 55
Dnepropetrovsk eparchy, 163, 181, 183
Drissa, 138
Dubno, 180

E

Eastern Patriarchates, 203
Ecumenical Patriarchate, 47-48, 83, 203
Elevferii, Metropolitan of Lithuania, 47 48, 76, 77
Ermachenko, Ivan, member of Belorussian Committee in Warsaw under Metropolitan Dionisii (a trusted person attached to the Department of Culture and Politics in Generalkommissariat of Belorussia), 114, 125, 127
Eshliman, N.I., priest, 208, 209, 211
Estonia, 47, 48, 49, 65, 72, 76, 77, 82, 83, 85, 86, 87, 88
Evlogii (Markovskii), bishop of the Autonomous Ukrainian Church, 163
Evfrosiniia of Polotsk, Saint. and Cathedral of, 115, 135, 137
Evstaf'ev, Vasilii, priest, 78

F

Fedor, bishop who lived in the Danilov Monastery in Moscow, 73, 74

INDEX

Feodosii, bishop of Vil'no and Lida, 46 n.
Feofan (Protasevich), Archimandrite, 113
Fevr, Nikolai, Russian émigré journalist, 101
Filofei (Narko), Archbishop in Belorussia, 112 n., 113, 114, 115, 116, 117, 118, 119, 120, 121, 122, 123, 124, 125, 126, 127, 129, 130, 131, 132, 133, 134, 138, 145
Fireside, Harvey, xiii n.
Fletcher, William C., xiii n.
Fotiev, Kiril, 148
Frank, Hans, Governor of Poland, 114, 151, 152, 153, 154
Fraser, Alexander K., xvi
"Front regions" of the religious revival, 192-198

G

Galicia, 159, 177
Georgii, Abbot (Igumen), 193, 194, 195
Georgii (Grabbe), Ver. Rev., later Protopresbyter, xv, 163
German attack on the Soviet Union, 53
German fascism xii
  attitude toward the Orthodox Church, xii, 60-66, 90-99
German-Soviet Pact, 27, 41, 44
Germanos, Archbishop, Exarch of Patriarch of Constantinople in London, 83
Gomel, 129, 138
Gorodok, 137, 138
Grigorii, Bishop of Gomel and Mozyr, 129, 132
Grodno, 111, 118, 121, 122
Gsovski, Vladimir, 10 n.
Gdov, 100, 101

H

Heyer, Friedrich, xii, xiii, xv, 47, 75, 150, 152, 156, 158, 160, 161, 162, 163, 164, 172, 180, 182, 183, 188, 189, 190
Hitler, Adolf, xii, xiv, 44, 53, 60, 61, 62, 63, 64, 89, 109, 140, 151, 153, 156, 174, 188
Holy Governing Synod of the Russian Orthodox Church, 6-7
Holy Trinity Cathedral, Pskov, 103

I

I..., priest in Zaslavl, 138
Iakunin, Gleb, 208, 209, 211

Iaroslavskii, Emel'ian, leader of the Union of the Militant Godless, 24, 26, 28, 42
Ilarion (Ohienko), Archbishop, 152, 157, 165, 175, 178, 179
Iampol', 166
Inkeles, Alex, 202, 205
Ioann, Archbishop of Latvia, 76
Ioann (Lavrinenko), Bishop of Brest, 129, 130
Ionov. See under Aleksei
Iosaf, Archimandrite of Pochaevskaia Lavra, 180
Iosif, Bishop of Taganrog, 196
Iosif, Metropolitan of Leningrad, 23
Ivashkevich, priest in Belorussia, 126

J

Jews, in Zhitomir, 165
Journal of the Moscow Patriarchate, 22, 59, 202, 203
Julius (Skriban), Rumanian Archimandrite, first head of the Rumanian Orthodox Mission in Transnistria, 189

K

Kamenets-Podol'sk, 159, 160, 181
Kaminskii, General Bronislav, organizer of Russian Liberation People's Army (RONA), 98
Karachev, 134
Karasubazar, 196
Karlovtsy Conference, 12-13, 15, 18, 19, 90, 92, 95
Karpov, G.G., head of the Council for the Affairs of the Russian Orthodox Church, 59
Kasiak, I., Belorussian nationalist, engineer, 112 n., 114, 119, 120, 125, 126, 127, 128, 131, 132, 145
Kazachie Mogily Monastery, 180
Kazan Cathedral, Leningrad, as Antireligious Museum, 24
Kazan Theological Academy, 115
Kazantzakis, Nikos, on religion in the Soviet Union, 1-5, 24, 211-212
Kharkov, 164
Kherson eparchy, 188
Kholm, 174, 175, 177, 178, 179
Khruschchev, Nikita Sergeevich, 143, 203, 205, 208, 209
Kiev, 157, 161, 162, 164, 172, 175, 176, 178, 179, 181, 184, 189
Kiev Theological Academy, 189

Kievo-Pecherskii Monastery, 180
Kishkovskii, Aleksandr Ivanovich, 46 n.
Kislovodsk, 198
Koch, Erich, Reichskomissar of the Ukraine, 111 n., 158
Kolarz, Walter, 58
Kolesnikov, Professor, 133
Korec, 180
Kozelshchina convent, 181
Krasnitskii, priest, 17
Kremenets, Theological Seminary in, 44, 47, 156, 180
Krestovozdivizhenskii Monastery, 181
Kube, Wilhelm, Generalkomissar of Belorussia, 116, 117
Kurtz, member of the East Section of the Ministry of Propaganda, 93, 96, 97, 98
Kushchevskii, village in the Kuban oblast, 195
Kushnir, priest in Belorussia, 120

L

Lapinski, N., Belorussian priest, 120, 132
Latvia, 47, 48, 49, 65, 71, 72, 76, 77, 81, 82, 85, 86, 87, 88, 89
Lebed', Ukrainian nationalist, 155
Leibbrandt, Georg, Ministerialdirektor in Ostministerium, head of the Main Dept. I: Political, 72, 104, 108
Lenin (Ul'ianov), Vladimir Il'ich, x, xiii, 3, 4, 8, 10
Leningrad, 53, 55, 56
Leningrad Ecclesiastical Academy, 202
Leontii (Filipovich), Archimandrite, later Bishop of the Autonomous Ukrainian Church, 159, 163, 165
Levits'kyi, Dmytro, Ukranian nationalist, 175
Liady, 119, 124
Lithuania, 65, 71, 72, 76, 77, 86, 89
Liubarskii, 163
Liudin, 138
Living Church (Zhivaia Tserkov), 15-19
Journal of, 16, 22, 59, 171, 173, 182, 197, 198
L'vov, 153, 154, 168, 170, 177, 184
Luga, 101
Lutsk, 167, 174
Lypkivs'kyi, Vasyl', Ukrainian Metropolitan, 147, 148, 149, 150, 157, 158, 182

M

Manuil (Tarnovs'kyi), Bishop of Autocephalous, later of Autonomous Ukrainian Church, 158
Marshall, R., 5 n.
Martindale, Don A., Professor, xv
Marx, Karl, and Marxism, ix, x, xi, 1, 2, 4, 8
Medvedev, Roy, x, 24, 210-211
Mehne, Propaganda Section of the German Ministry of Propaganda, 93, 97
Melec Monastery, 180
Mel'nyk, Andrii, Ukrainian nationalist, 153, 154, 155, 168, 169, 178, 179, 184
Mikhailov Monastery, 181
Minsk, 108, 109, 113, 116, 117, 118, 119, 120, 121, 122, 124, 125, 126, 130, 132, 133, 138, 141
Mir, 110
Mitiakinskaia, Cossack village, 196
Mogilev, 118, 122, 134
Molotov (Skriabin), Viacheslav Mikhailovich, xiii, 58, 89, 197, 207
Moscow, 53, 55-56
Moscow Patriarchate, 7ff, 19, 20, 21, 22, 27, 41, 45, 46 n., 47, 48, 49, 51, 56-59, 71, 76, 77-78, 80, 81, 82, 84, 85, 90, 95, 107, 129, 171, 208
Moscow Theological Academy, 202
Mozyr, 129
Mstislav (Skrypnyk), Stepan, Ukrainian nationalist, later Archbishop of Autocephalous Ukrainian Church, 152, 155, 158
Müller, O.W., Major, "Beauftrager des Reichsministers für das Ostgebiet b. Kommand," 140, 141

N

Narkombog or Narkomopium (nickname of the Council for the Affairs of the Russian Orthodox Church), 59
Nazarius, (Nazarii), Bishop, 148
Nezhin, 170
Nektarii, chief housekeeper of the Pochaevsk Abbey, 47
Nemirov, 181
NEP, Religious, xiii and n., xiv, 19, 74, 143, 149, 202, 208
Nevel, 138
Nikanor (Abramovich), Bishop of the Ukrainian Autocephalous Church, 158, 160, 161, 181, 182
Nikolai, Archbishop in Rostov on the Don (from Eisk), 194

INDEX

Nikolai (Iarushevich), Archbishop of Novgorod and Pskov, later Metropolitan of Kiev and Galicia, Exarch of Ukraine, 41, 45, 46, 54, 55, 56, 57, 58, 107, 116, 143, 144, 153
Nikol'skii, antireligious lecturer, 51
NKVD, 50, 73, 75, 78, 84, 93, 137, 172, 174, 175, 176, 178, 179, 198
Novgorod eparchy, 45
Novocherkassk, 195
Novogrudok, 122
Novoukrainka, 170

O

Odessa, 159, 188, 190
Opochka, 99, 101
Oppenhein, Raymond, Rev., American chaplain in Moscow, 209
Orel, 196
Orsha, 134
Orthodox Church, Russian, x, xii:
  administrative divisions by the Germans, 65-66
  Belorussia, 107-146
  and church relations, ix-x, 1-30
  during World War II, 41-66
  and German policy, xii, 60-65, 90-99
  in the Baltic region, 71-106
  statistics, xi, xiv, 7, 24, 29-30, 44-48, 49-50, 76, 102, 132-136, 142-143, 149 n., 151, 161-166, 172, 174, 180ff, 190, 192, 207
  Transnistria and the front, 187-208
  Ukraine, 147-185
Ostrinskii, Pavel, priest of the Ukrainian Autonomous Church, 176
Ostrov, 100, 101, 102, 103
Ostrovskii, Rodoslav, President of the Central Rada in Belorussia, 130, 131
OUN (Organization of Ukrainian Nationalists), 153, 176, 177
Ovruch, 163

P

Palladii (Vidibida-Rudenko), Ukrainian bishop of Autocephalous Church, 152
Pankratii, Archimandrite, Vicar of the Pochaevsk Abbey, 47
Panteleimon (Rozhnovskii), Archbishop. Former Bishop of Pinsk. Metropolitan of Belorussia, 46 n., 112, 113, 114, 115, 116, 117, 118, 119, 120, 121, 122, 123, 124, 125, 126, 127, 128, 129, 130, 131, 132, 134, 141, 145

Panteleimon (Rudyk), Archbishop of the Ukrainian Autonomous Church, 156, 157, 161, 176, 179, 184
Pasternak, Boris, 210
Paul, Apostle, 98
Pavel, Bishop of Briansk, 128, 129
Pavel, Bishop of Narva, 88
Peace-Movement, The, and the Russian Orthodox Church, 203
Peter the Great, 7
Petliura, Simon Vasil'ovich, Ukrainian nationalist, 152, 158, 175
Petr (Polianskii), Metropolitan of Krutitsy, later *Locum Tenens,* 20, 23, 25, 74
Petrograd Theological Academy, 73
Piatigorsk, 198
Pilsudski, Joseph, Marshall, the creator of independent Poland, 150
Pimen (Izvekov), Patriarch, x, xi, 205
Pinsk, 111, 167
Pochaevsk, Abbey, 47, 180
  Council of Bishops, (1941), 156-158
Podol'e, 162
Pokrov, 181
Poland, xiv, 44, 45, 46 n., 46, 51, 76, 108, 109, 110, 115, 127, 150, 151, 164, 168, 174, 176, 178, 207, 208
Polikarp (Sykors'kyi), Bishop of Lutsk, later Metropolitan of the Ukrainian Autocephalous Church, 46 n., 54, 150, 153, 154, 156, 157, 167, 168, 174
Pole'se, 65, 130, 131, 168
Polotsk, 115, 118, 135, 136, 137, 138, 194
Poltava, 118, 159, 160, 162, 181, 183
Porfirii, priest in Zaslav', 138
Porkhov, 101, 103
Porokhovo, 65
Po Stopam Khrista (In Christ's footsteps), 99
Pravda o religii v Rossi (the truth about religion in Russia), 56, 57, 57 n., 204
Prokhladnaia, 198
Proskurov, 159
Protoierei, 49, 50, 51
Provisional Government, 7
Pskov eparchy, 45, 71
Pskov, city, 65
Pskov region, 67, 107, 144, 147, 159, 185, 207
Pskov Ecclesiastical Mission, 73, 84, 99-105, 138, 144

Q

R

Raevskii, S., 114
Ranovich, A., 29
Rasputin, Grigorii, 20
Red Army, xiv, 49, 50, 51, 110, 115, 132, 137, 159, 171, 196
Redikul'tsev, former bass of the Bolshoi Theater, 98
Religious revival in the Soviet Union:
  definition, ix-xv
  evaluation of, 201-212
  in the Baltic sector, 65, 71-106
  in Belorussia, 132-145
  in the "front" region, 192-198
  in Transnistria, 187-192
  in the Ukraine, 159-166, 171-185
Revel, 87, 88
Riga, 45, 78, 79, 83, 87, 97, 98, 104
  Treaty of, 150
Roman Catholic Church 45, 63, 152, 166, 167, 171, 181
Rovno, 180
RONA (Russian Liberation People's Army), 99
Rosenberg, Alfred, head of the Ministry of Occupied Territories, Ostministerium, 61, 62, 63, 64, 71, 86, 107, 140, 154
Rostov on the Don, 193, 194
Rumania, 66, 170, 188
Rumanian Orthodox Church in Transnistria, 66
Rumanian Orthodox Mission in Transnistria, 188-192
Russian Church in North America, 8
Russian Orthodox Church Abroad, 12-13, 90-91, 129, 131, 132, 152, 163
Russian Orthodox Palestine Society, 203
Russian Civil War, 11, 13, 150

S

St. Flor, Convent of, 181
St. Sophia's Cathedral in Kiev, 148
Schapiro, Leonard, 8 n.
Sebezh, 138
Serafim (Lade), Metropolitan of Berlin (of the Russian Orthodox Church Abroad), 90, 97, 152
Sergii (Stragorodskii), 1867-1944.
  Locum Tenens, later Patriarch, 60, 74, 76, 78, 79, 80, 81, 82, 83, 89, 90, 91, 92, 93, 94, 95, 96, 97 n., 117, 119, 121, 136, 171, 172, 173, 175, 176, 207, 208
  becomes Patriarch, 58-59
  the Declaration of 1927, 21-23, 27, 74, 76, 90, 91
  death, 60
  early relations with the Bolsheviks, xi, 20-28
  his policy during World War II, xiii, 30, 41, 45, 53-57
  meeting with Stalin, 58
Sergii (Voskresenskii). Metropolitan, Exarch of the Baltic countries:
  biography and characterization of, 73-78ff
  Exarch of the Baltic countries, 41, 45, 46, 55, 65, 71-106, 107, 115, 121, 144, 172
  his memorandum on the Orthodox Church, 27-28, 47-49, 82-88ff
  his mysterious death, 98
Shch....S., Protoierei, 196 n.
Shklov, 134
Simon (Ivanovskii), bishop of the Autonomous Ukrainian Church, 46 n., 156
Smirnov, Aleksandr, Protoierei, 80
Smirnov, Dmitrii, famous singer, 98
Smolensk, 65, 111, 118, 122, 133, 134, 135, 136, 138, 141, 142
Smolitsch, Igor, 7 n.
Sobor (Council), All-Russian, 7, 17, 91
Solzhenitsyn, Aleksandr Isaevich, x, xi, 205, 206, 210, 211, 212
Spasski Monastery, 24
Spinka, Matthew, 20
Stalin (Dzhugashvili), Iosif Vissarionovich, x, xiii, xiv, 19, 25, 26, 43, 44, 45, 52, 54, 55, 57, 58, 64, 89, 91, 93, 94, 95, 96, 98, 129, 136, 174, 197, 198, 207, 210
  Reception of the ecclesiastical triumvirata, xiii
Stalingrad, 53
Stavrou, Freda L., xvi
Stavrou, Theofanis G., Professor, xi, xvi, 1
Stefan (Sevbo), formerly Protoierei Simeon, later Bishop of the Belorussian Orthodox Church, 118, 119, 122, 123, 124, 126, 127, 130, 131, 132, 134, 135, 136, 139
Stein, Dora, xvi

INDEX

Stets'ko, Iaroslav, one of the leaders of the Bandera organization, Ukrainian nationalist, 155
Stratonov, I., 16
Struve, Nikita, Professor, xii
Supreme Church Council of the Living Church, 17
Supreme Russian Ecclesiastical Administration Abroad, 12, 13
Surozh, 138
Svitich, A., Russian journalist from Poland, 113, 114

T

Taganrog, 195, 196
Tikhon (Belavin), Patriarch:
confrontation with the Bolsheviks, 10-18
his confession and testament, 18-19, 20, 21-22, 74, 76, 172, 189, 197, 198
Tikhvin, Mother of God miraculous icon, 103
Tikhvinskii convent, 181
Tiraspol, 170
Transnistria:
Orthodox Administration Division transferred to Rumania, 66, 187-192
Rumanian Orthodox Mission and policy in the region, 188-192
Trotsky, Lev Davidovich, 10

U

Ukraine:
administrative division of the Orthodox Church by the Germans, 65, 147-185
Autonomous Church of, 147, 157-159, 161f, 173, 175, 176, 179, 181, 182, 183, 184, 185, 207
Autocephalous Church of, 147-153, 171-173, 175, 177, 178, 179, 181, 182, 183, 184, 185, 207
religious revival in, 159-166; 171-185
struggle between the Ukrainian Autonomous and Autocephalous Churches, 147ff, 157-158, 171-173ff
Ulianovsk, Evacuation of Patriarchal *Locum Tenens* to, 55, 56, 80 n., 89.
Uniates, 44-45; 167, 168-169
Union of Militant Godless, 24, 29, 42, 52, 59
Uspenskii, Cathedral, 8

V

Vasilii (Stan), Rumanian bishop in Transnistria, 190
Ielizh, 138, 142
Venedikt, Archbishop, 92, 112, 113, 115, 116, 118, 121, 122, 123, 125, 127 n., 129, 130, 132, 168
Veniamin, Metropolitan of Petrograd, 14
Veniamin (Novitskii), Bishop of the Autonomous Ukrainian Church, proposed as a Bishop of Baranovichi-Novogrudok of the Belorussian Church, 118, 156
Viazma, 134
Vienna meeting of Orthodox émigré clergy (1943) and declaration, 91, 92, 93, 95, 97, 129
Vileika, 125
Vilno, 98, 103, 111, 118, 121
Vinnitsa, 159, 162, 163, 164, 170, 181
Vishniakov, Aleksandr, priest of the Autonomous Ukrainian Church, 176
Vissarion, Rumanian Archbishop, later Metropolitan in Transnistria, 189, 190
Vitebsk, 118, 122, 134, 137
Vlasov, General Andrew A. (d. 1945), 131 n.
Voronezh, 50
Vvedenskii monastery, 181
Vvedenskii, Aleksandr, Dean, later Metropolitan of the Living Church, 15, 17, 59, 55 n.
Volynia, eparchy, 157, 162, 174, 182, 183, 184

W

Warsaw, 109, 110, 179
World Council of Churches, 203

X

X . . ., priest, member of the Pskov Mission, 100, 101

Z

Zagajec Monastery, 180
Zaporozh'e, 177
Zaslavl, 138
Zhirovetskii Monastery, 114, 116, 117, 119
Zhitomir, 159, 163, 164, 165, 176, 177, 181
Zhmerinka, 190

LIBRARY OF DAVIDSON COLLEGE

Books on regular loan may be checked out for **two weeks.** Books must be presented at the Circulation Desk in order to be renewed.

A fine is charged after date due.

Special books are subject to special regulations at the discretion of library staff.